AN INTRODUCTION TO AUCTION THEORY

An Introduction to Auction Theory

FLAVIO M. MENEZES
University of Queensland

PAULO K. MONTEIRO
EPGE/FGV

OXFORD
UNIVERSITY PRESS

OXFORD
UNIVERSITY PRESS

Great Clarendon Street, Oxford OX2 6DP

Oxford University Press is a department of the University of Oxford.
It furthers the University's objective of excellence in research, scholarship,
and education by publishing worldwide in

Oxford New York

Auckland Bangkok Buenos Aires Cape Town Chennai
Dar es Salaam Delhi Hong Kong Istanbul Karachi Kolkata
Kuala Lumpur Madrid Melbourne Mexico City Mumbai Nairobi
São Paulo Shanghai Taipei Tokyo Toronto

Oxford is a registered trade mark of Oxford University Press
in the UK and in certain other countries

Published in the United States
by Oxford University Press Inc., New York

British Library Cataloguing in Publication Data

Data available

Library of Congress Cataloging in Publication Data

Data available

ISBN 978–0–19–927598–4 (Hbk.)
978–0–19–927599–1 (Pbk.)

1 3 5 7 9 10 8 6 4 2

Typeset by SPI Publisher Services, Pondicherry, India
Printed in Great Britain
on acid-free paper by
Biddles Ltd., King's Lynn, Norfolk

To Our Wives, Laura and Nair

Preface

Hugo Sonnenschein, in his 1983 inaugural Nancy Schwartz Memorial Lecture,[1] argued that one of the most important contributions of economics has been to the understanding of how incentives work—in particular, of how to design institutional arrangements that might induce individuals to behave in a way so that a certain outcome (e.g., an ex-post efficient outcome) prevails.

About twenty years later economists have been recognized for their contribution to the design of several auction-like mechanisms such as the U.S. Federal Communications Commission spectrum auctions, the 3G auctions in Europe and beyond, the auction markets for electricity in Australia and elsewhere in the world, the allocation of the rights to land at airports, regulations governing access pricing in natural gas pipelines, and the sale of former government-owned companies around the globe. Perhaps it is significant that "Market Architecture" was the title chosen by Robert Wilson for his 1999 Econometric Society Presidential Address (Wilson 2002). Similarly, Alvin Roth's Fischer-Schultz Lecture at 1999 European Econometric Society Meeting was entitled "The Economist as an Engineer" (Roth 2002).

The concept of market architecture or engineering relies on insights from game theory (in particular, games of incomplete information) and mechanism design. It also relies on our understanding of how to tackle informational issues but perhaps some of the most important insights come from auction theory. The practical and theoretical importance of auction theory is widely recognized. Indeed, some of the more celebrated results from the single-object auction theory (e.g., the revenue equivalence theorem or the characterization of the optimal auction) are now usually taught in advanced undergraduate courses on the economics of information.

However, a step-by-step self-contained treatment of the theory of auctions does not exist to the best of our knowledge. Thus, our aim is to provide an introductory textbook that will allow students and readers with a calculus background, and armed with some degree of persistence, to work through all the basic results. For example, the reader will be able to derive by himself or

---

[1] *Frontiers of Research in Economic Theory; The Nancy L. Schwartz Memorial Lectures* (1983–1997), eds. D. Jacobs, E. Kalai and M. Kamien, Cambridge University Press, 1998.

herself the celebrated Revenue Equivalence Theorem and to evaluate the effects of introducing affiliation into the standard auction theory model.

Graduate microeconomics textbooks (such as Mas-Colell et al. 1995) typically approach auctions as applications of mechanism design techniques. Game theory textbooks (such as Fudenberg and Tirole 1991) examine auctions as an application of Bayesian games. Thus, their focus is on techniques rather than on results. On the other hand, there are several excellent surveys focusing on the results of auction theory rather than on techniques. In contrast we will focus both on results and techniques. The main idea is that although reading some of the original papers can be quite a daunting task for an advanced undergraduate student or for a first-year graduate student, it is possible to present this material in a more friendly way. Paul Klemperer (1999), when referring to some of the earlier literature on auctions, argues that with the exception of Vickrey's first 1961 paper, the other papers "are no longer for the beginner." Our aim is to make this material available to the "beginner."

Acknowledgements

This book was born from the lecture notes used to teach courses at the Australian National University and at EPGE-FGV. Its completion was facilitated by an Australian Research Council Grant (no. A0000000055) that allowed Flavio Menezes to visit EPGE-FGV and Paulo Monteiro to visit the ANU. Paulo Monteiro acknowledges the support of CNPq-Brazil. Several students (current and former) have contributed to the improvement of this text. In particular, we would like to thank Joisa Dutra, Craig Malam, Guilherme Norman and Louise Sutherland for very detailed comments. Many colleagues have been very supportive of this project but special thanks go to Simon Grant and Steve Dowrick for their advice and encouragement. Menezes acknowledges the financial support from the Australian Research Council (ARC Grants DP 0557885 and 0663768) for the revisions and additions in this new edition.

Contents

1

Introduction

The theory of auctions is one of the most successful modern economic theories. Its success is reflected in a coherent body of theory but also in its ability to provide insights into many practical policy issues. Indeed, we claim that the label "auction theory" is somewhat misleading—although we will use it for the remainder of this book—as the economics behind auction theory are actually common to many other applications. We will not elaborate here on the indirect connection between auction theory and economics in general. Instead, we refer the reader to Klemperer (2004) for a detailed discussion. What we do below is to provide three examples to illustrate the importance of auction theory to modern economics.

First, consider the problem faced by a regulator who wants to regulate a monopolist with unknown costs: a regulator wants to choose instruments (a price or a quantity, a subsidy or a tax, issuing a license to operate) so that the regulated monopolist chooses the action (how much to produce or how much to charge) to promote efficiency (second-best efficiency as in the presence of asymmetric information: first-best efficiency is not possible). It turns out that this is analogous to the problem faced by a seller who wants to extract the most expected revenue possible when selling an object without knowing the valuation of the buyers. (Indeed Roger Myerson wrote both one of the seminal papers on the optimal auction (Myerson 1981) and together with David Baron, the paper on how to regulate a monopolist with unknown costs (Baron and Myerson 1982).) When regulating a monopolist, the regulator fixes a price menu (and a subsidy to cover fixed costs) that rewards low marginal cost types for choosing the "right quantity or price"—this is the informational rent kept by the monopolist. In an auction, you allocate the object to the individual with the highest valuation at a price equal to the largest of the second highest valuation and the optimally chosen reserve price—the difference is the informational rent kept by the buyer.

Our second example also relates to regulation. When it is not possible to have competition in the market, we have to design a mechanism that will establish competition for the market. For example, when allocating spectrum (for mobile telephony) or cable-TV licenses or the license to build a transmission line, we want to design an auction that will allocate the licenses to those who value them the most highly. Some of these auctions raised several billion dollars for governments around the globe.

Finally, our third example is the design of the spot market for electricity: one wants to design a market (a rule that will determine who is going to sell and the price at which they will sell) that reflects the cost of the marginal generator—the highest cost generator that has to supply to meet system demand. This will guarantee dynamic efficiency. Electricity restructuring involving the establishment of a spot market is pervasive in developed and developing countries alike.

Comparison with recent contributions

There are several excellent surveys of the auction theory literature available, including Engelbrecht-Wiggans (1980), Maskin and Riley (1985), Milgrom (1985, 1987, 1989), McAfee and McMillan (1987), Riley (1989), Wilson (1992), Wolfstetter (1996), and Klemperer (1999). These surveys provide a guide to the auction theory literature that covers papers that are not realistically accessible to a wider audience. Although these surveys are excellent and do provide some help in reading the original papers, our aim here is to provide considerably more detail so that readers can work their way through the most important results. We also include exercises.

As was noted above, current treatment of auctions in existing graduate microeconomics textbooks is limited to applications either of Bayesian games or mechanism design. Two exceptions are Laffont and Tirole (1993) and Wolfstetter (1999). Laffont and Tirole devote a chapter to auctions covering the optimal auction and the revelation principle in auctions. Wolfstetter also devotes a chapter (60 pages) to auction theory. The main topics covered include some of the basic theory, auction rings, optimal auctions and common value auctions. It is also worth mentioning Vijay Krishna's *Auction Theory*. Krishna's book is well-written and provides a very comprehensive overview of auction theory. Our aim is different; our objective is to start, whenever possible, from basic principles (calculus and introductory probability is the only assumed knowledge) and to equip students with the techniques that are necessary to master the theory of auctions. As a result, our coverage has to be less comprehensive than Krishna's. Our hope is that by having worked through the book, the reader will have the confidence and technical ability to derive all the results in the book and to construct and solve simple and sensible auction models. In addition, the reader will have a "working knowledge" of mechanism design—as applied to auctions.

Finally, there is a high degree of complementarity between this textbook and Klemperer (2004). Klemperer's approach is to introduce the basic auction theory in a non technical fashion, relegating to appendices some of the more technical material. Thus, the reader, for example, can read Klemperer's excellent book to obtain an overview of basic theory. However, to master the techniques and to develop a working knowledge of the subject, the reader can then work through this book. Once this is done, the reader can then return to Klemperer for applications of auction theory.

Intended audience

This book is intended for first-year graduate students and advanced honours undergraduates in economics and related disciplines. This text can also be used to teach a special topics course on auction theory or, more likely, it could be used as a supplementary textbook for an advanced microeconomics course focusing on the economics of information. In our experience, teaching auction theory prior to introducing mechanism design is helpful to students as they can relate these more abstract techniques to the more concrete auction context.

In addition, this book could be used as a supplementary textbook for courses on game theory or for a stand-alone graduate or advanced undergraduate course on auction theory, perhaps in conjunction with Klemperer (2004). Of course, this book can also be used by independent readers who want to understand auction theory.

Organization

Chapter 2 introduces the equilibrium concept used throughout the book, namely, that of a Bayesian Nash equilibrium. It also introduces the idea of studying auctions as games and defines some notation. Chapters 3, 4, and 5 cover the private, common and affiliated values models, respectively. Chapter 6 relates the field of mechanism design to auction theory by deriving a general version of the Revenue Equivalence Theorem and by characterizing the optimal auction, that is, the auction that maximizes the seller's expected revenue. In Chapter 7, we opted for covering some existing multi-object auction models in order to complement the analysis in Vijay Krishna's book. Chapter 8 provides some guidance on how the reader can extend his or her knowledge of auctions beyond what is covered in this book. Finally, there are four appendices covering probability theory, differential equations and affiliation.

Using this book as a textbook

A graduate or advanced undergraduate course in auction theory should cover Chapters 2–6. Chapter 7 is optional and includes material that is substantially more difficult than the rest of the book. If used as a supplement to a graduate or advanced undergraduate course on the economics of information, the instructor can concentrate on the case of independent private values and cover Chapters 2, 3, and 6. Chapter 6 can be read on its own as an introduction to mechanism design and Chapter 5 can be read on its own as an introduction to affiliation.

2

Preliminaries

In this chapter, we introduce the equilibrium notion to be used in the book, namely that of a Bayesian Nash equilibrium. We then formally define an auction as a game of incomplete information. We first introduce some notation that will be used throughout the book.

2.1 Notation

In this book, we try to follow as closely as possible the standard notation of auction theory papers. Some notation is standard in other fields, other is peculiar to auction theory.

We denote by $\mathbb{N} = \{1, 2, \ldots\}$ the set of natural numbers. The set of real numbers is denoted by $\mathbb{R}$ and the set of non-negative real numbers is denoted by $\mathbb{R}_+$ or $\mathbb{R}^+$. If X_i is a set for $i = 1, 2, \ldots, n$, $n \in \mathbb{N}$ then $X = X_1 \times X_2 \times \cdots \times X_n$ is the Cartesian product of $X_1, X_2, \ldots, X_n$. If the sets X_i are the same, say $X_i = C$ for all i then we write C^n for $C \times \cdots \times C$ (n times). Thus $[0, 1]^2 = [0, 1] \times [0, 1]$. And if $X_i = \{\text{high}, \text{low}\}$, $i = 1, 2$ then

$$\{\text{high}, \text{low}\}^2 = \{(\text{high}, \text{high}), (\text{high}, \text{low}), (\text{low}, \text{high}), (\text{low}, \text{low})\}.$$

The following convention will be used throughout the book. If $x = (x_1, x_2, \ldots, x_n)$ is a vector of n coordinates we denote by x_{-i} the vector obtained from x by the removal of the ith coordinate. Thus,

$$x_{-i} = (x_1, x_2, \ldots, x_{i-1}, x_{i+1}, \ldots, x_n)$$

is a vector with $n - 1$ coordinates. For example, if $s = (s_1, s_2, s_3)$ then $s_{-1} = (s_2, s_3)$.

The maximum of a finite sequence of real numbers, $x_1, x_2, \ldots, x_n$ is denoted either by $\max\{x_1, x_2, \ldots, x_n\}$ or by $x_1 \vee x_2 \vee \cdots \vee x_n$. The maximum between x and 0 is denoted by x^+. Thus $x^+ = \max\{x, 0\} = x \vee 0$. If $Z_1, \ldots, Z_n$ are random variables, we will frequently consider the maximum of $Z_1, \ldots, Z_n$

denoted by $\max\{Z_1, \ldots, Z_n\}$ or $Z_1 \vee Z_2 \vee \ldots \vee Z_n$. Similarly we denote by $Z_1 \wedge Z_2 \wedge \ldots \wedge Z_n$ the minimum of $Z_1, Z_2, \ldots, Z_n$. We will denote by Y the random variable that represents the highest number amongst $Z_2, \ldots, Z_n$. Thus $Y = \max\{Z_2, \ldots, Z_n\}$.

A function $f \colon \mathbb{R} \to \mathbb{R}$ is increasing if $x < y$ implies that $f(x) \leq f(y)$. It is strictly increasing if $x < y$ implies $f(x) < f(y)$. Thus, an increasing function may be flat for parts of the domain. A strictly increasing function will have no flat part in the domain.

We say that a function $f \colon \mathbb{R} \to \mathbb{R}$ is continuously differentiable if for every $x \in \mathbb{R}$ it has a derivative $f'(x) := \lim_{y \to x} (f(y) - f(x))/(y - x)$ and $x \to f'(x)$ is a continuous function. The inverse of a (injective and onto) function $f \colon A \to B$ is denoted by $f^{-1} \colon B \to A$. The composition of the function $g \colon B \to C$ and $f \colon A \to B$ is denoted $g \circ f$. That is $g \circ f(a) = g(f(a))$.

If a set X is finite we denote by $\#X$ the number of elements of X. Occasionally we use the notation $\forall x$ which translates to "for all x".

2.2   Bayesian Nash Equilibrium

Throughout the book, we will use the notion of a Bayesian Nash equilibrium as defined by Harsanyi (1967). His approach is to transform a game of incomplete information into one of imperfect information; any buyer who has incomplete information about other buyers' values is treated as if he were uncertain about their types. It is like introducing an extra player—nature—that chooses the type for each player.

We can think of games of incomplete information as a two-stage game. Prior to the beginning of the game, before players make a decision, nature chooses a type for each player. At this stage, each player knows his own type but not the types of other players. In the second stage, each players chooses a strategy knowing his own type and the initial distribution of all types.

To introduce formally the equilibrium notion we will need some notation. This notation will also be used in the remaining chapters. The set of players will be denoted by $I = \{1, 2, \ldots, n\}$. The set of possible types for each player $i \in I$ is denoted by X_i. This set will be an interval, $[0, \bar{v}]$, in most of the book. We denote by $F(\cdot)$ the probability distribution over $X = X_1 \times X_2 \times \cdots \times X_n$, which reflects the probabilities attached to each combination of types occurring.

We denote by S_i the set of strategies for player $i \in I$ and by $s_i \colon X_i \to S_i$ the decision function of player i. It is a mapping from the set of possible types to the set of possible strategies. (In a particular case below we will set $S_i = \mathbb{R}_+$ and $X_i = X_j$, for all i, j). We denote by $\hat{F}_i(x_{-i} \mid x_i)$ the probability distribution of types x_{-i} of the players $j \neq i$ given that i knows his type is x_i. That is, player i updates his prior information about the distribution of the other types using Bayes rule upon learning that his type is x_i.

We let $\pi_i(s_i, s_{-i}, x_i, x_{-i})$ denote i's profits given that his type is x_i, that he chooses $s_i \in S_i$ and that the other players follow strategies $s_{-i}(x_{-i}) = (s_j(x_j))_{j \neq i}$ (the function $s_j \colon X_j \to S_j$ being j's decision function) and their types are x_{-i}. For each vector $(x_1, x_2, \ldots, x_n)$ chosen by nature, there are updated beliefs given by $\hat{F}_1(x_{-1} \,|\, x_1), \ldots, \hat{F}_n(x_{-n} \,|\, x_n)$.

A *Bayesian Game* is defined as a five-tuple

$$G = [I, \{S_i\}_{i \in I}, \{\pi_i(\cdot)\}_{i \in I}, X_1 \times \cdots \times X_n, F(\cdot)].$$

That is, it is a set of players, a strategy set for each player, a payoff (or utility) function for each player, a set of possible types and a distribution over the set of types.

A *Bayesian Nash equilibrium* is a list of decision functions $(s_1^*(\cdot), \ldots, s_n^*(\cdot))$ such that $\forall i \in I, \forall x_i \in X_i$ and $\forall s_i \in S_i$:

$$\int_{x_{-i} \in X_{-i}} \pi_i(s_i^*, s_{-i}^*, x_i, x_{-i}) \, \mathrm{d}\hat{F}_i(x_{-i} \,|\, x_i)$$

$$\geq \int_{x_{-i} \in X_{-i}} \pi_i(s_i, s_{-i}^*, x_i, x_{-i}) \, \mathrm{d}\hat{F}_i(x_{-i} \,|\, x_i).$$

In words, each player chooses a strategy contingent on his type—that is, he uses a Bayesian decision function. We can then apply the Nash equilibrium notion to these decision functions: each player forms a best response strategy of choosing the best Bayesian decision functions, based on the best response strategies of other players (who are choosing their Bayesian decision functions).

In part of the book, the distribution of players types is independent. That is,

$$F(x) = F_1(x_1)F_2(x_2) \cdots F_n(x_n).$$

In this case,

$$\hat{F}_i(x_{-i}) = F_1(x_1) \cdots F_{i-1}(x_{i-1})F_{i+1}(x_{i+1}) \cdots F_n(x_n).$$

Remark 1 *A symmetric Bayesian Nash equilibrium is such that all players choose the same decision function.*

In the next few chapters, the reader will have ample opportunity to check his or her understanding of the symmetric Bayesian Nash equilibrium notion in the context of auctions. For the remainder of this section we work through an example to apply this equilibrium notion when the set of types is discrete and in a context that will be familiar to many readers.

Example 1 *Consider a Cournot model where two firms, 1 and 2, produce a homogeneous good and compete in quantities. The inverse market demand is given by $p = 1 - Q$, where Q is the sum of quantities produced by each firm. Unit* *costs of both firms are constant. However, the unit cost may be either high, c_h, or low, c_l. We assume that $4 - 5c_h + c_l \geq 0$. The joint probability distribution is given by*

$$F(c_h, c_h) = F(c_h, c_l) = F(c_l, c_l) = F(c_l, c_h) = \frac{1}{4}.$$

Let us compute the symmetric Bayesian Nash equilibrium.
First, note that we can apply Bayes rule to compute $\hat{F}(c_h \mid c_h)$, $\hat{F}(c_l \mid c_h)$, $\hat{F}(c_l \mid c_l)$, and $\hat{F}(c_h \mid c_l)$. Since the distribution determining the types is the same for both players, $\hat{F}(c_h \mid c_h)$, for example, denotes the probability that Player 1 who is of type c_h faces a Player 2 of type c_h but also the probability that a type c_h Player 2 faces a type c_h Player 1. Thus,

$$\hat{F}(c_h \mid c_h) = \frac{F(c_h, c_h)}{F(c_h, c_h) + F(c_l, c_h)} = \frac{1}{2}.$$

Similar calculations yield:

$$\hat{F}(c_l \mid c_h) = \hat{F}(c_l \mid c_l) = \hat{F}(c_h \mid c_l) = \frac{1}{2}.$$

Note that the symmetric Bayesian Nash equilibrium is a pair of decision functions $(q^*(\cdot), q^*(\cdot))$, one for each player, indicating that player's action if his type is c_h and his action if his type is c_l. We will proceed along the following line of reasoning, which will be used in the entire book: We posit that Player 2 is following a strategy $q(\cdot) = (q(c_l), q(c_h))$, in this case one action for each possible type, and compute 1's best reply. In the symmetric equilibrium both players are using the same strategy.

Accordingly, suppose Player 2 is choosing $q(\cdot)$ and Player 1 is of type c_l and has to choose a "number" s_l determining how much he will produce. The expected profits of Player 1 are given by:

$$\pi_1(s_l, q(\cdot), c_l) = \tfrac{1}{2}(1 - q(c_l) - s_l - c_l)s_l + \tfrac{1}{2}(1 - q(c_h) - s_l - c_l)s_l.$$

Maximizing with respect to s_l we obtain:

$$\tfrac{1}{2}(1 - q(c_l) - 2s_l - c_l) + \tfrac{1}{2}(1 - q(c_h) - 2s_l - c_l) = 0.$$

Given that we are looking at symmetric equilibrium, we can set $s_l = q(c_l)$ to obtain

$$q(c_h) = 2 - 5q(c_l) - 2c_l. \tag{2.1}$$

Similarly we need to consider the case where Player 2 is choosing $q(\cdot)$ and Player 1 is of type c_h and has to choose a "number" s_h determining how much he will produce. His expected profits are given by:

$$\pi_1(s_h, q(\cdot), c_h) = \tfrac{1}{2}(1 - q(c_l) - s_h - c_h)s_h + \tfrac{1}{2}(1 - q(c_h) - s_h - c_h)s_h.$$

We then obtain

$$q(c_l) = 2 - 5q(c_h) - 2c_h. \tag{2.2}$$

By solving the "best-response functions" (2.1) and (2.2) simultaneously, we obtain the symmetric Bayesian Nash equilibrium:

$$q^*(c_h) = \frac{4 - 5c_h + c_l}{12}$$

and

$$q^*(c_l) = \frac{4 - 5c_l + c_h}{12}.$$

Note that a high cost producer in the symmetric equilibrium produces less than a low cost producer.

2.3 Auctions as Games

In this section we provide a brief introduction to auctions, explain how we view auctions as games of incomplete information and define some notation.

2.3.1 What is an Auction?

Cassady (1967) provides a very nice guide to the various practical uses of auctions. If such a guide were to be revised today, it would be many times thicker than the original version. The reason is that auctions have become an effective tool to implement public policy. Their use now ranges from the allocation of radio spectrum necessary for mobile communication, to spot markets trading electricity and pollution permits, as well as being widely used in government procurement.

We can define an auction by one of its central properties: as a market clearing mechanism, to equate demand and supply. Other market mechanisms include fixed price sales (as in a supermarket) or bargaining (as in the negotiated sale of a house or a used car). Within the class of market mechanisms which allocate scarce resources, one particular characteristic of the auction is that the price formation process is explicit. That is, the rules that determine the final price are usually well-understood by all parties involved.

Auctions are often used in the sale of goods for which there is no established market. Auctions were instrumental in the mass privatization in Eastern Europe given the absence of a price system that could guide the valuation process for firms being privatized. Rare or unique objects are typically sold in auctions as the markets for these objects are likely to be very thin. However, auctions are also used to sell Treasury bills and the markets for these assets are very thick. The reason is that only governments can legally produce such bonds and therefore the sale in an auction is an exercise in revenue maximization.

Auctions are more flexible than a fixed price sale and perhaps less time-consuming than negotiating a price. Auctions are used to sell hundreds of goods, such as bales of wool or used cars, in a few hours. One can imagine how many hours it would take to sell 100 used cars through negotiated sales. The reader should then ask the question why then car dealers do not switch to auctions as a sales mechanism. Although a complete answer to this question is beyond the scope of this book, we could expect that under certain conditions a negotiated sale or even a fixed price might result in higher expected revenue for the seller. We will touch on this in Chapter 6.

2.3.2   Auction Types

Auctions can be classified according to several distinct criteria. For example, we distinguish between open auctions and sealed-bid auctions. In the former type of auction, all bids are publicly observable whereas in the latter they are not. We can also differentiate between ascending and descending price auctions. In both types of auctions bids are public, but the ascending auction starts at a low price and bids have to be increasing, whereas in the latter bidding starts at a high price that continuously declines until one of the bidders stops the process by acquiring the object.

Auctions for single objects are also distinct from auctions for multiple objects. There are several possible designs available when selling multiple objects which are not available when selling a single indivisible good. For example, a multiple object auction format might allow for bids on combinations of items (combinatorial auctions) or objects might be sold sequentially. Chapter 7 describes some multiple object auction types (simultaneous versus sequential, discriminatory versus uniform price). However, most of this book (Chapters 3–6) deals with single-object auctions. We will examine four basic formats: English, Dutch, First-Price, and Vickrey auctions. Although most readers are familiar with at least some of these auction formats, for completeness we describe them below.

The English or ascending-price auction is the best-known format. It is an open auction where an auctioneer (there are also electronic implementations) starts requesting bids at a low price and bidders bid by meeting the increments proposed by the auctioneer. The auction stops when no bidder is willing to increase his bid above the highest standing bid. The bidder with the highest standing bid wins the auction and pays the highest bid. This auction is commonly used in the sales of rare paintings, used cars, houses and many other objects. There can be several aspects such as secret reserve prices, dummy bids (bids made by the seller or the auctioneer, perhaps without the knowledge of the bidders) and sometimes even the possibility of negotiation between the winner of the auction and the seller. While auction theory can be used to accommodate these possibilities, we ignore such issues in the theory expounded in this book. We will model English auctions in the tradition of Milgrom and

Weber (1982) and model English auctions as "button auctions".[1] Later we discuss the implications of such a modeling assumption.

In both first- and second-price (or Vickrey) sealed-bid auctions, each bidder submits his or her bid without the knowledge of the bids made by others. The winner in both cases is the bidder with the highest bid. He or she will pay his or her bid in a first-price auction and the second highest bid in a second-price auction. Whereas first-price auctions are typically used in the procurement of goods and services,[2] second-price auctions have remained relatively rare until more recently when they have been adopted by business to business platforms.

Finally, the Dutch auction is an open descending price auction. It is widely known for its use in selling flowers in the Netherlands. Bidding starts at a high price that continuously decreases on an automated clock. The auction ends when one of the participants stops the clock. This bidder wins the object and pays the price at which the clock stopped.

2.3.3 Auction as Bayesian Games

To define an auction as a Bayesian game G, we will keep the notation defined above for the set of potential bidders $I = \{1, 2, \ldots, n\}$, $X_i = [0, \bar{v}]$ will denote the set of possible types of player $i, i = 1, \ldots, n$, and v_i the type received by player i. $F(\cdot) : [0, \bar{v}]^n \to [0, 1]$ is the joint distribution of types and the associated density is denoted by $f(\cdot) : [0, \bar{v}]^n \to \mathbb{R}_+$. The set of possible bids or strategies for player $i, i = 1, \ldots, n$, is $S_i = \mathbb{R}_+$.

It should be noted here that for simplicity, we assume that the seller's valuation is zero (and the seller will therefore not accept any negative bids). Moreover, it is assumed throughout the book that there is no secondary market, and no other resale possibility. This is because our objective is to provide a thorough exposition of standard auction theory for the beginner, rather than covering all existing research in auctions.[3]

Finally, the payoff to player i will depend on his or her attitude towards risk, on a valuation or utility function $u_i(v_1, \ldots, v_n)$ and on the rules of the auction. The precise nature of this relationship will be made explicit in the

---

[1] Each bidder presses a button while the price increases continuously. A participant drops out when she takes her hand off the button. The auction ends when there is only one bidder left pressing the button. This bidder wins the auction and pays the price at which the next-to-last player stopped pressing the button.

[2] In a procurement auction, several sellers are competing to sell a good to the buyer. In a first-price procurement auction, the winner is the seller with the lowest bid and the buyer pays the equivalent to this bidder's bid. The analysis is completely analogous to that of a standard first-price auction. In this book we concentrate on the latter. Note that both governments and large private buyers are increasingly using alternative auction formats such as electronically descending auctions to buy goods and services.

[3] While this research currently includes numerous interesting and relevant examples for practitioners (see, e.g., Grant et al. 2006), our objective is instead to provide the building blocks that are necessary to understand this research.

chapters below. Here, we will offer a general view on the existing auction models. Auction models typically fall into three categories. In a private values model, each potential buyer knows his or her own value for the object, which is not influenced by how other potential buyers value it (see Chapter 3). If individuals' types are independent from each other—for example, one may think of types being determined by independent draws from a fixed distribution—then we have the independent private value (IPV) model. If valuations are dependent on one another, then we have the correlated private value model. More generally, a private values model might be more appropriate for non-durable goods with no resale value.

In the common value model (see Chapter 4), the object is worth the same to every potential bidder, but this value is unknown at the time of bidding. Typically, individuals have some information about the (unknown) true value of the object. If information is correlated across individuals, then we have a dependent common value model. If information is independent across individuals, then we have an independent common value model. The common value model is often more appropriate for analyzing the sale of mineral rights and offshore oil drilling leases.

Finally, Milgrom and Weber (1982) introduce the notion of affiliated values (see Chapter 5), which includes both private and common values as special cases. Roughly speaking, affiliated values capture the idea that individuals' valuations for an object have a private component but are influenced by how other people value it. In most sales we can imagine, a bidder's valuation for the object being sold does have a private component, but that valuation is also influenced by other individuals' valuations. For instance, when bidding for a house, one takes into account both the personal value of the house as well as how easily it would be to resell it in the future.[4] Affiliation, however, is a notion of global positive correlation and this has particular implications for the ranking of auction formats according to the expected revenue they generate, as will be discussed in Chapter 5.

---

[4] This relates to how individuals value objects. Of course, even in the IPV model, bidders' bidding behavior will depend on how they think others will bid.

3

Private Values

In this chapter, we examine the case where bidders' values for the object being auctioned off is a function only of their own types. As seen in Chapter 2, individuals' types can be either independent or correlated. In the case of independent types we have the IPV model. This is the benchmark model for auction theory and it provides several useful insights. This model will be covered in the next section. The correlated private values model will be covered in the subsequent section. The last section examines the effects of risk aversion on bidding behavior and on the seller's expected revenue for the private values model.

3.1 The Independent Private Values Model

A single object will be sold to one of n bidders. Each bidder i, $i = 1, \ldots, n$, receives a type v_i and his valuation is equal to $u_i(v_i) = v_i$. The implicit assumption here is that buyers are *risk-neutral*, that is, they are indifferent between a lottery that yields an expected value of x and receiving x for certain.

Each bidder knows his own valuation v_i and that his opponents' valuations are drawn independently from the distribution $F(\cdot)$ with density $f(\cdot) > 0$ in the interval $[0, \bar{v}]$. (Appendix A contains an introduction to probability theory.) That is, $F(x)$ denotes the probability that the random variable v is less than or equal to a certain number x.

This is the IPV model where the value of the object to a bidder depends only on his own type. Bidding behavior, however, depends on one's expectation about other bidders' valuations and about how they bid. Although the independent private value model is only appropriate to describe the case where the object does not have a resale value (or it is too costly to resell), it allows us to derive several important insights. For simplicity, we assume that the seller sets the reserve price at zero and that there are no entry fees.

In this chapter, we will compute the equilibrium bidding strategies and the seller's expected revenue in four distinct types of auctions: first- and second-price sealed-bid, English, and Dutch auctions. As we have seen in Chapter 2, each bidder submits his bid without observing the bids made by other players in a sealed-bid auction. In a first-price auction, the winner is the bidder with the highest bid and he pays his bid. In a second-price auction, the winner is still the bidder with the highest bid but he pays the second highest bid.

A naive commentator would argue that a first-price auction should generate more revenue than the second-price auction as the winner pays his bid in the former and the second highest bid in the latter. However, this argument fails because bidders behave strategically. We will show below that bidders bid less than their valuations in the unique symmetric equilibrium of a first-price auction and bid their valuations in the unique symmetric equilibrium of the second-price auction.

3.1.1   First-price Auctions

We start our search for a symmetric Bayesian Nash equilibrium by analyzing the game from the point of view of one of the players, say Player 1. Suppose this player has a valuation $v = v_1$ and believes that other players follow a bidding strategy $b(\cdot)$. Knowing only his value and the distribution of the valuations of players $2, \ldots, n$, Player 1 has to figure out what is his best reply. Suppose bidder $i = 2, \ldots, n$ has valuation v_i. Thus bidder $i \geq 2$ bids $b_i = b(v_i)$. Then if Player 1 bids b_1 the object is won if $b_1 > b_i$ for $i \geq 2$. That is if $b_1 > \max\{b_2, \ldots, b_n\}$. If $b_1 < \max\{b_2, \ldots, b_n\}$ Player 1 does not win the object. Let us suppose that in case of a draw, that is if $b_1 = \max\{b_2, \ldots, b_n\}$, the object is not sold. Thus Player 1's payoff is

$$\begin{cases} v - b_1 & \text{if } b_1 > \max\{b(v_2), \ldots, b(v_n)\} \\ 0 & \text{if } b_1 \leq \max\{b(v_2), \ldots, b(v_n)\}. \end{cases}$$

The expected profits from bidding b_1 are given by

$$\pi(b_1) = \pi(v, b_1, b(\cdot)) = (v - b_1) \Pr(b_1 > \max\{b(v_2), \ldots, b(v_n)\}).$$

We can rewrite the expression above as

$$\pi(b_1) = (v - b_1) \Pr(b_1 > b(v_2), \ldots, b_1 > b(v_n)).$$

For the moment assume that the function $b(\cdot)$ is strictly increasing and differentiable. (We will later verify that our equilibrium strategy is indeed increasing and differentiable in the domain and thus our analysis is justified.) Thus, the range of $b(\cdot)$ is an interval: $b([0, \bar{v}]) = [\underline{b}, \bar{b}]$. The bidder will never bid higher than $\bar{b}$ since the payment will be higher and the object will be won as well. Any bid lower than $\underline{b}$ is a losing bid. Thus we may suppose, without loss of generality that $b_1 \in [\underline{b}, \bar{b}]$. Therefore there exists $x \in [0, \bar{v}]$ such that

$b_1 = b(x)$. The problem of bidder 1 is therefore equivalent to choose $x \in [0, \bar{v}]$ to maximize expected utility

$$\bar{\pi}(x) = \pi(b(x)) = (v - b(x)) \Pr(b(x) > b(v_2), \ldots, b(x) > b(v_n))$$
$$= (v - b(x)) \Pr(x > v_2, \ldots, x > v_n). \tag{3.1}$$

In the second line of the above equation, we used the fact that $b(\cdot)$ is strictly increasing and that all players follow the same strategy in equilibrium since all of them are faced with the same maximization problem. Since the v_js are independent and identically distributed random variables, we can rewrite (3.1) as follows:

$$\bar{\pi}(x) = (v - b(x)) \Pr(x > v_2) \cdots \Pr(x > v_n) = (v - b(x)) F(x)^{n-1}. \tag{3.2}$$

The derivative of $\bar{\pi}$ is now easy to calculate:

$$\bar{\pi}'(x) = (v - b(x))(n - 1) f(x) F(x)^{n-2} - b'(x) F(x)^{n-1}. \tag{3.3}$$

In a symmetric equilibrium, the expected profit is maximized at $x = v$.[1] Thus the first-order condition is $\bar{\pi}'(v) = 0$. Using (3.3) we obtain

$$b'(v) F(v)^{n-1} = (v - b(v))(n - 1) f(v) F(v)^{n-2}. \tag{3.4}$$

This differential equation can be easily solved. Note that using (3.4), we can write

$$(b(v) F(v)^{n-1})' = b'(v) F(v)^{n-1} + b(v)(n - 1) f(v) F(v)^{n-2}$$
$$= v(n - 1) f(v) F(v)^{n-2}. \tag{3.5}$$

The Fundamental Theorem of Calculus yields:

$$b(v) F(v)^{n-1} = \int_0^v x(n - 1) f(x) F(x)^{n-2} \, dx + k,$$

where k is the constant of integration. If $v \to 0$ the left-hand side tends to zero since $b(\cdot)$ is bounded. Thus, we conclude that $k = 0$. That is, the candidate equilibrium bidding strategy is given by

$$b^*(v) = \begin{cases} \dfrac{(n-1) \displaystyle\int_0^v x f(x) F(x)^{n-2} \, dx}{F(v)^{n-1}} & \text{if } 0 < v \leq \bar{v}; \\ 0 & \text{if } v = 0. \end{cases} \tag{3.6}$$

---

[1] It is convenient to pause and think through the approach taken: we posited the existence of an increasing, symmetric equilibrium function $b(\cdot)$. We then consider a "direct revelation" game where bidders are asked to announce a signal and their bids are then defined using the function $b(\cdot)$. Further, we assume that bidders $2, \ldots, n$ announce their true signals and ask what is Bidder 1's best response. This approach is pursued throughout the remainder of the book and it is formally expounded in Chapter 6.

We need to check that $b(v)$ is continuous. It suffices to show this only for $v = 0$. Note that when $v > 0$,

$$b^*(v) = \frac{(n-1)\int_0^v x f(x) F(x)^{n-2}\,\mathrm{d}x}{F(v)^{n-1}} \tag{3.7}$$

$$< \frac{(n-1)\int_0^v v f(x) F(x)^{n-2}\,\mathrm{d}x}{F(v)^{n-1}} = v. \tag{3.8}$$

Thus $b(v)$ is continuous at zero and hence everywhere. Now let us check that b^* is indeed an equilibrium. From (3.3) and (3.4) we see that

$$\bar{\pi}'(x) = (v - b(x))(n-1)f(x)F(x)^{n-2} - b'(x)F(x)^{n-1}$$
$$= (v - x)(n-1)f(x)F(x)^{n-2}.$$

Therefore if $x < v, \bar{\pi}'(x) > 0$. And if $x > v, \bar{\pi}'(x) < 0$. It is clear then that $x = v$ maximizes the expected utility. Note that (3.6) has a revealing interpretation. The equilibrium bid of a player with value v is equal to the expected value of the individual with the second highest valuation conditional on v being the highest valuation (see Appendix (A.20)). If my value v is the highest among all players, then in a symmetric equilibrium where strategies are increasing, it suffices for me to bid just to outbid the opponent with the second highest valuation.

It is a simple task to check that the equilibrium bidding strategy in (3.6) is strictly increasing in v (simply differentiate 3.6).

From (3.7) we conclude that $b^*(v) < v$. Now from (3.4) we get that $(b^*)'(v) > 0$. Thus, the amount $v - b^*(v)$ indicates by how much a bidder shades his bid in equilibrium. In particular it says how much the bidder reduces his bid compared to his valuation. To calculate the shading we integrate expression (3.6) by parts. The rule for integration by parts is as follows:

$$\int_a^b u\,\mathrm{d}z = uz\,|_a^b - \int_a^b z\,\mathrm{d}u.$$

Letting $z = F(x)^{n-1}$ implies that $\mathrm{d}z = (n-1)F(x)^{n-2}f(x)\,\mathrm{d}x$. Similarly, letting $\mathrm{d}u = \mathrm{d}x$ implies (by integration) that $u = x$. Therefore,

$$(n-1)\int_0^v x f(x) F(x)^{n-2}\,\mathrm{d}x = \int_0^v u\,\mathrm{d}z$$

$$= xF(x)^{n-1}\,|_0^v - \int_0^v F(x)^{n-1}\,\mathrm{d}x$$

$$= vF(v)^{n-1} - \int_0^v F(x)^{n-1}\,\mathrm{d}x. \tag{3.9}$$

Replacing (3.9) into (3.6), we obtain

$$b^*(v) = v - \frac{\int_0^v F(x)^{n-1}\,\mathrm{d}x}{F(v)^{n-1}}. \qquad (3.10)$$

The amount of shading is therefore $\int_0^v (F(x)/F(v))^{n-1}\,\mathrm{d}x$. It decreases with the number of bidders. The larger is the number of my opponents, the closer to my valuation I will bid.

Now that we have a prediction for how bidders will behave in a first-price auction, it is possible to ask what is the expected revenue for the seller from a first-price auction, denoted by R^1. The expected revenue is simply the expected value of the highest bid, that is,

$$R^1 = E[\max\{b^*(v_1),\ldots,b^*(v_n)\}] = E[b^*(\max\{v_1,\ldots,v_n\})]$$

From the viewpoint of the seller, buyers are ex-ante identical. Thus, the probability that all valuations are below a given value v is simply $F(v)^n$ and its density is $nF(v)^{n-1}f(v)$ (see Appendix A). As a result, the expected revenue can be written as:

$$R^1 = \int_0^{\bar{v}} nb^*(v)F(v)^{n-1}f(v)\,\mathrm{d}v. \qquad (3.11)$$

In the remainder of this section we investigate individual behavior and compute the seller's expected revenue from a Dutch auction. We will need the following definition.

Definition 1   *Two games with the same set of players and the same strategy space are said to be* strategically equivalent *if each player's expected profits under one of the games are identical to his expected profits in the other game.*

We show that the Dutch auction is strategically equivalent to the first-price auction. A bidding strategy in a Dutch auction is a function $b(\cdot) : [0, \bar{v}] \to \mathbb{R}_+$. For example, consider the strategy profile $(b_1^*, \ldots, b_n^*)$. Suppose b_1^* is the highest bid. In a first-price auction, player 1 wins the object and his profits are $v_1 - b_1^*$, while the profits of all other players are equal to zero. In a Dutch auction, if player 1 is the one stopping the clock at price b_1^*, his profits are equal to $v_1 - b_1^*$, while the profits of all other players are equal to zero. Player 1, however, was chosen arbitrarily. The conclusion is that for any player with the highest bid, if the same profile of strategies is used in both auctions, this profile yields the same profits for all players. That is, the first-price auction and the Dutch auction are strategically equivalent. Thus, these two auction formats yield the same expected revenue given by (3.11).

3.1.2   Second-price Auctions

In a second-price sealed-bid auction, players submit their bids simultaneously without observing the bids made by other players. We now explain Vickrey's (1961) original insight that in such auctions it is in a bidder's best interest to always bid his own valuation. We will need the following definitions.

Definition 2   *A strategy $b_i \in [0, \bar{v}]$ is a* dominant strategy *for player i if*

$$\pi_i(v_i, b_i, b_{-i}) \geq \pi_i(v_i, \hat{b}_i, b_{-i})$$

for all $\hat{b}_i \in [0, \bar{v}]$ and for all $b_{-i} \in [0, \bar{v}]^{n-1}$.

In words, b_i is a dominant strategy for player i if it maximizes i's expected profits for any strategies of the other players. An equilibrium in dominant strategies is one where every bidder plays his dominant strategy. Formally,

Definition 3   *An outcome $(b_1^*, \ldots, b_n^*)$ is said to be an* equilibrium in dominant strategies *if b_i^* is a dominant strategy for each player $i, i = 1, \ldots, n$.*

The reader can immediately show an equilibrium in dominant strategies is a Bayesian Nash equilibrium. The converse is not always true. Also it is easy to see that bidding one's true valuation is a dominant strategy in a second-price auction. This is a remarkable property of the Vickrey auction. We explain intuitively why truth telling is a dominant strategy in a second-price auction.

Let us look at bidder 1 who has valuation equal to v_1. Denote by $\hat{b}$ the highest bid among players $2, \ldots, n$. Assume first that bidder 1 bids $b_1 < v_1$. If $b_1 > \hat{b}$ then bidder 1 wins the object as he would have won with a bid equal to v_1. However, if $b_1 < \hat{b} < v_1$ then bidder 1 loses the auction. By bidding his valuation he would have won the auction and earned expected profits equal to $v_1 - \hat{b}$. Therefore, bidder 1 does not gain by bidding less than his valuation and could possibly lose. That is, his expected profits decrease with a bid $b_1 < v_1$.

Now suppose that bidder 1 bids $b_1 > v_1$. If $b_1 < \hat{b}$, then bidder 1 loses the auction as he would have lost if he had bid his valuation. However, if $v_1 < \hat{b} < b_1$, then Player 1 wins the object and pays more than his valuation. That is, he loses $\hat{b} - v_1$. Therefore, bidder 1 does not gain by bidding more than his valuation but could possibly lose. Thus, his expected profits decrease with a bid $b_1 > v_1$.

We now show formally that telling the truth is a Bayesian Nash equilibrium bidding strategy. We examine the auction from the viewpoint of bidder 1, who has a value equal to v_1, and chooses a bid b_1 to maximize his expected profits given that players $2, \ldots, n$ follow some strategy $b(\cdot)$. Bidder 1's expected profits can be written as

$$\pi_1(v_1, b_1, b(\cdot)) = E[(v_1 - Y)\, I_{b_1 > Y}], \tag{3.12}$$

where $I_{b_1 > Y}$ denotes an indicator variable that is equal to 1 when $b_1 > Y$ and takes the value 0 otherwise. Moreover, we suppose that bidder 1 assumes that he receives the object in case of a draw[2] and we let Y denote the highest valuation among players $2, \ldots, n$. That is, bidder 1's expected profits are equal to the expected value of the difference between 1's valuation and the second highest bid for the case when 1's bid is greater than Y. The distribution function of the highest among $n - 1$ samples is simply $F(x)^{n-1}$ (see Appendix A). Therefore, we can take the expected value in (3.12) to obtain

$$\pi_1(v_1, b_1, b(\cdot)) = \int_0^{b_1} (n - 1)(v_1 - x) \, f(x) \, F(x)^{n-2} \, dx. \qquad (3.13)$$

Bidder 1's problem is to choose a b_1 to maximize (3.13). Suppose first that $b_1 < v_1$. Then if b_1 is increased to v_1 the integral in (3.13) increases by the amount

$$\int_{b_1}^{v_1} (n - 1)(v_1 - x) f(x) \, F(x)^{n-2} \, dx.$$

This is true since if $b_1 < x < v_1$, we have that $v_1 - x > 0$. The reverse happens if $b_1 > v_1$ since in the region $b_1 > x > v_1$ and the integrand is negative. Thus, the expected profit maximizing bid is $b_1 = v_1$.

What is the expected revenue generated by the second-price auction? Given that each bidder bids his true valuation, the expected revenue is the expected value of the second highest valuation. From Appendix A, the probability that the second largest of n draws from a fixed distribution is less than a certain value v is equal to $F(v)^n + nF(v)^{n-1}[1 - F(v)]$. The first term of the sum denotes the probability that all draws are less than v and the second term of the sum presents the probability that v is the second highest value. (Considering that there are n ways to choose the highest valuation, $F(v)^{n-1}$ represents the probability of $n - 1$ valuations being smaller than v, and $1 - F(v)$ denotes the probability of exactly one valuation being higher than v.) Therefore, the density of the second highest is $n(n-1)F(v)^{n-2}[1 - F(v)]f(v)$ and the seller's expected revenue is given by

$$R_2 = \int_0^{\bar{v}} n(n - 1)vF(v)^{n-2}[1 - F(v)]f(v) \, dv. \qquad (3.14)$$

As noted in the previous chapter, oral or English auctions are perhaps the most popular amongst auction mechanisms. Is it possible to analyze bidding behavior in such complex auction format? Of course, these auctions are very difficult to formalize. What should be the strategy space? For example, it is not uncommon for bidders to make their bids by raising a hand or nodding to the auctioneer instead of calling out their bids. It is also common for bidders

---

[2] It is left as an exercise for the reader to prove that the following reasoning holds whatever is the tie-breaking method used.

to wait until the very last minute to make a bid after being silent for most of the auction. We will ignore many of these complications and will refer to the following version (sometimes referred to as Japanese auctions and introduced by Milgrom and Weber (1982)): each bidder presses a button while the price increases continuously. A participant drops out when he takes his hand off the button. The auction ends when there is only one bidder left pressing the button. This bidder wins the auction and pays the price at which the next-to-last player stopped pressing the button. A strategy in this auction is a function from $[0, \bar{v}]$ into the non-negative real numbers. The strategy says that price at which the bidder releases the button.

Consider a strategy profile $(b(\cdot), \ldots, b(\cdot)) = (v_1, \ldots, v_n)$. Suppose that $b(v_1)$ is the highest bid and that $b(v_2)$ is the second highest bid. In a second-price auction, bidder 1 wins the auction and has profits equal to $v_1 - v_2$. Player $2, \ldots, n$ receive zero profits. In the oral auction—represented by the button auction—bidder 1 is the last pressing the button, while bidder 2 takes his hand off the button when the price reaches v_2. Bidder 1's profits are equal to $v_1 - v_2$, while bidders $2, \ldots, n$ earn zero profits. Note that the choice of players 1 and 2 was completely arbitrary. Thus, the same profile of strategies in both auctions yields the same profits for all players. That is, oral auctions and second-price auctions are strategically equivalent. The expected revenue generated by both types of auction is given by (3.14).

3.1.3   Revenue Equivalence

Among the four types of auctions considered above, first- and second-price, Dutch, and English auctions, which one generates the highest expected revenue for the seller? It turns out that with independent private values, these four auction formats generate the same expected revenue! This result is actually quite general as we will see in Chapter 6 and it is a by-product of the Envelope Theorem. A direct proof of the result below can be provided by just comparing expressions (3.11) and (3.14).

Theorem 1 (revenue equivalence)   *With private independent values, the four auction formats analyzed, first- and second-price, Dutch and Oral, yield the same expected revenue.*

Proof:
$$R^1 = \int_0^{\bar{v}} b^*(x) n F^{n-1}(x) f(x)\, dx = \int_0^{\bar{v}} n f(x) [b^*(x) F^{n-1}(x)] dx.$$

We can then use integration by parts to rewrite the above expression as:
$$= n F(x) b^*(x) F^{n-1}(x)\big|_0^{\bar{v}} - \int_0^{\bar{v}} n f(x) [b^*(x) F^{n-1}(x)]' dx.$$

$$= n b^*(\bar{v}) - \int_0^{\bar{v}} n(n-1) f(x) x F^{n-1}(x)\, dx$$

We can use (3.6) to rewrite this expression as:

$$= n \int_0^{\bar{v}} x(n-1)F^{n-2}(x)f(x)dx - \int_0^{\bar{v}} n(n-1)xf(x)F^{n-1}(x)]dx$$

$$= \int_0^{\bar{v}} n(n-1)xF^{n-2}(x)f(x)[1-F(x)]dx = R^2. \qquad \blacksquare$$

What happens to the seller's expected revenue if the number of participants increases? Since the addition of one bidder valuation does not decrease the second highest valuation and might increase it, expected profits should increase with the number of bidders. The proof is not difficult. Rewrite $R^2 = R^2(n)$,

$$R^2 = \int_0^{\bar{v}} n(n-1)v[F(v)^{n-2} - F(v)^{n-1}]f(v)\,dv$$

$$= \int_0^{\bar{v}} v[nF(v)^{n-1} - (n-1)F(v)^n]'\,dv$$

$$= v[nF(v)^{n-1} - (n-1)F(v)^n]|_0^{\bar{v}} - \int_0^{\bar{v}} [nF(v)^{n-1} - (n-1)F(v)^n]\,dv$$

$$= \bar{v} - \int_0^{\bar{v}} [nF(v)^{n-1} - (n-1)F(v)^n]\,dv.$$

Now if $h(n) = -[nF(v)^{n-1} - (n-1)F(v)^n]$ we have that $h(n+1) - h(n)$

$$= -((n+1)F(v)^n - nF(v)^{n+1}) + (nF(v)^{n-1} - (n-1)F(v)^n)$$
$$= nF(v)^{n+1} - 2nF(v)^n + nF(v)^{n-1}$$
$$= nF(v)^{n-1}[F(v)^2 - 2F(v) + 1]$$
$$= nF(v)^{n-1}(F(v) - 1)^2 \geq 0.$$

Thus it follows that $R^2 = \int h(n)\,dv$ is strictly increasing with n. Thus we have proved the following.

Corollary 1   *The seller's expected revenue in any of the four auction formats increases with the number of participants.*

The Revenue Equivalence Theorem is really quite remarkable. In its general form it establishes that any auction that allocates the object to the bidder with the highest valuation (and satisfies a technical condition on assigning zero expected profits to the player with the lowest possible valuation) yields the same expected revenue. The astute reader, however, will point out that in the introduction we gave several examples of objects that are sold exclusively by oral auctions (e.g., houses, paintings, wool, etc.), objects that are sold by first-price auctions (e.g., government purchases), objects that are sold exclusively by Dutch auctions (e.g., flowers) and that second-price auctions are rare. The Revenue Equivalence Theorem would predict that the auction mechanism does not matter so we would expect to see flowers, for example, being sold by different auction formats.

One could argue that tradition plays an important role in the establishment of the auction format. This argument is difficult to justify, however, as in some cases these are new markets (such as auctions of used cars). Although we do observe changes in auction formats (e.g., wool in Australia is now sold by electronic auctions whereas it used to be sold through oral English auctions) in some markets, there are several examples of little experimentation with other auction formats. This leads us to conclude that there may be other factors at work that are not captured by the IPV model.

Indeed later we will examine several extensions of the Independent Private Values model where revenue equivalence breaks down; for example, when bidders are risk averse or when their valuations are correlated.

Although the revenue equivalence result is not robust, some of the insights developed above are robust and have been applied successfully to the design of several new markets. In a later chapter we will pursue a more abstract approach and analyze the private independent values model under the realm of the revelation principle. In the remainder of this section we examine the effect of the seller setting a reserve price (above his valuation, which is equal to zero by assumption) or an entry fee or both to try to raise his expected revenue.

3.1.4   Reserve Prices and Entry Fees

We denote the reserve price by r and the entry fee by δ. The reserve price is assumed to be known to all bidders and the seller is assumed to have committed to not selling below the reserve. In essence, the reserve price is the minimum bid.

Note that these two instruments, the reserve price and the entry fee, generate two opposing effects: they reduce bidder's incentives to participate in the auction but they might increase revenue as the seller collects extra revenue either via the entry fee—those bidders who enter have to pay the entry fee to the seller—or via the effect of a reserve price on bidding behavior—those bidders who enter bid more aggressively. We allow the seller to set both a reserve price and an entry fee concurrently.

We will only examine the effects of a reserve price and entry fees on equilibrium behavior and on the seller's expected revenue in a first-price auction. The analysis of their effects in second-price auctions is left as an exercise for the reader. The objective here is to illustrate that these two instruments can be used to increase the seller's expected revenue. This theme will be discussed again in Section 6.3 when we use the mechanism design approach to identify the optimal auction—the auction that maximizes the seller's expected revenue.

Below we will find a cut-off value ρ for player i such that if $v_i < \rho$, i does not participate in the auction. If $v_i \geq \rho$ then i does participate. We will assume that players $2, \ldots, n$ follow this participation rule and bid according to a strictly increasing differentiable function $b(\cdot)$. Then we compute 1's best reply. We find an equilibrium such that $b(\rho) = r$. Suppose Player 1's valuation is $v_1 = v$. His problem is to choose a participation rule and a bid b_1 so as to maximize his expected profits:

$$\pi_1 = E[(v - b_1)I_{b_1} \geq \max\{b(Z), r\}] - \delta,$$

where $Z = \max\{v_j; v_j \geq \rho, j = 2, \ldots, n\}$ if the set is non-empty and $Z = 0$ otherwise. In order to bid, bidder 1's bid must be greater than or equal to r. Thus, 1's expected profits can be rewritten as

$$\pi_1 = -\delta + (v - b_1) \Pr[b_1 \geq \max\{b(Z), r\}]$$
$$= -\delta + (v - b_1) \Pr[b_1 \geq \max\{b(Z), b(\rho)\}].$$

If $b_1 = r$ then $\pi_1 = -\delta + (v - r)F^{n-1}(\rho)$. If $b_1 = b(s) > r$ then

$$\pi_1 = -\delta + (v - b(s)) \Pr[s > Z] = -\delta + (v - b(s))F^{n-1}(s). \qquad (3.15)$$

Note that $s > \rho$. We can now compare (3.15) with (3.2) and conclude that the first-order condition is the same as in the case where both the reserve price and the entry fee were equal to zero. The only distinction is that the boundary condition has to reflect the fact that a bidder with value equal to ρ has to be indifferent between entering or not and therefore $b(\rho) = r$. Thus, the equilibrium bidding function is given by:

$$b^*(v) = \begin{cases} v - \dfrac{\delta + \int_\rho^v F(x)^{n-1}dx}{F(v)^{n-1}}, & \text{if } v \geq \rho. \\ \text{not bid, otherwise} \end{cases} \qquad (3.16)$$

We leave as an exercise to the reader to analyze the case $b(\rho) > r$ and show that this cannot arise as a symmetric equilibrium.

We can now compare (3.16) with the equilibrium bidding strategy (3.10) under zero entry fees and zero reserve price. Note that while entry fees will only affect a bidder's decision whether or not to enter, a non-zero reserve price will affect both the decision to enter and the bidding strategies—those bidders who do enter bid more aggressively in the symmetric equilibrium. Nevertheless, entry fees and reserve prices affect the seller's expected revenue in a similar fashion as we will explain below.

To fully characterize equilibrium behavior we still need to compute the cut-off value ρ. Recall that a player with value ρ is indifferent between participating or not:

$$-\delta + (\rho - r)F^{n-1}(\rho) = 0.$$

That is, when the indifferent player participates, he pays the entry fee δ. Since he only wins if he is the only participant, the price paid in the auction is the reserve price r. $F^{n-1}(\rho)$ denotes the probability that the indifferent bidder is the only participating bidder. We can rewrite this expression as:

$$(p - r)F^{n-1}(\rho) = \delta. \tag{3.17}$$

Clearly we have $\rho > r$ and $\delta < \bar{v} - r$. This last inequality follows from the fact that the maximum value of $\rho - r$ is equal to $\bar{v} - r$ and that $F^{n-1}(\rho) < 1$. Thus, we can conclude that $\delta + r < \bar{v}$. If this inequality were not true, then no bidder would ever participate in this auction.

From (3.16) and (3.17) we note that there are two effects on equilibrium behavior from imposing an entry fee and a reserve price. Firstly, lower valuation bidders will not participate in the auction. Secondly, those who do participate bid more aggressively—the reason is that to win the auction now a player has to bid the expected value of the highest among his opponents with values between ρ and $\bar{v}$, and not between 0 and $\bar{v}$ as before. Lower participation reduces the seller's expected revenue but more aggressive bidding increases it. Thus, we can now ask what is the combination of reserve price and entry fee that maximizes the seller's expected revenue. Firstly, let us write the seller's expected revenue:

$$R^1 = \int_\rho^{\bar{v}} b^*(v) n F^{n-1}(v) f(v) dv + n\delta(1 - F(\rho)),$$

where the second term in the RHS (right hand side) represents the expected revenue from the entry fee when players follow $b^*(\cdot)$, that is

$$\delta \sum_{k=0}^n \binom{n}{k} (n - k) F(\rho)^k (1 - F(\rho))^{n-k} = n\delta(1 - F(\rho)).$$

Note that the entry fee δ and the reserve price r are linked via equation (3.17). For example, we can set $\delta = 0$ and $r = \rho$. Alternatively, we can set $r = 0$ and $\delta = \rho F^{n-1}(\rho)$ or any pair satisfying (3.17). Let us assume that $\delta = 0$ and $r = \rho$ and so we can rewrite R^1 as

$$R^1 = \int_\rho^{\bar{v}} \left(v - \frac{\int_\rho^v F(x)^{n-1} \, \mathrm{d}x}{F(v)^{n-1}} \right) n F^{n-1}(v) f(v) \, \mathrm{d}v$$

$$= \int_\rho^{\bar{v}} v n F(v)^{n-1} f(v) \, \mathrm{d}v - \int_\rho^{\bar{v}} \left(\int_\rho^v F(x)^{n-1} \, \mathrm{d}x \right) n f(v) \, \mathrm{d}v.$$

Changing the order of integration in the double integral yields (as $\rho < x < v$ and $\rho < v < \bar{v}$, we have that when integrating over v, first we obtain

$\int_x^{\bar{v}} f(v)\, \mathrm{d}v = 1 - F(x))$:

$$R^1 = \int_\rho^{\bar{v}} vnF(v)^{n-1}f(v)\, \mathrm{d}v - \int_\rho^{\bar{v}} n(1 - F(v))F(v)^{n-1}\, \mathrm{d}v.$$

Since we are trying to find the value of ρ that maximizes R^1, we use Leibnitz's rule to differentiate the above expression and obtain:

$$\frac{\partial R^1}{\partial \rho} = -\rho nF(\rho)^{n-1}f(\rho) + n(1 - F(\rho))F(\rho)^{n-1}$$

$$= nF(\rho)^{n-1}\{-\rho f(\rho) + 1 - F(\rho)\}.$$

At an interior maximum:

$$nF(\rho)^{n-1}f(\rho)\left(-\rho + \frac{1 - F(\rho)}{f(\rho)}\right) = 0 \tag{3.18}$$

or

$$\rho = \frac{1 - F(\rho)}{f(\rho)}. \tag{3.19}$$

That is, condition (3.19) tells us the level of the reserve price that maximizes the expected revenue of a seller using a first-price auction when the seller does not charge any entry fees. It turns out that setting a positive reserve price (i.e., a reserve price above the seller's valuation) maximizes the seller's expected revenue. We will discuss this in more detail in Chapter 6 but the economics behind it is very simple. It relates to the standard monopoly pricing: just as a standard monopolist charges a price higher than the marginal cost to extract surplus from higher valuation buyers at the sacrifice of lower valuations buyers who do not consume the good, a seller sets a reserve price to extract more expected surplus from the highest valuation bidder but it excludes the participation of lower valuation buyers.

Of course, this is not (ex-post) efficient as the seller will not sell the object in some events whereas efficiency dictates that it should be sold given that the seller's value is assumed to be zero. This is analogous to the deadweight loss resulting from a standard monopolist not serving lower valuation costumers.

3.2 The Correlated Private Values Model

In this section, we relax one of the main hypotheses of the IPV model of auctions. More specifically, we assume that individuals' types are correlated. The set of types is $[0, \bar{v}]^n$. Bidder i knows his type but does not know the other bidders' types. The distribution of types is common knowledge but it is no longer independent. When a bidder receives his type, he updates his beliefs about other bidders' types. More specifically, we assume that $f : [0, \bar{v}]^n \to [0, \infty)$ is the density of the vector of types $(X_1, X_2, \ldots, X_n)$. As mentioned in Chapter 2, our viewpoint when comparing auctions is that of the seller or from an analyst that does not have information about individuals' types. Moreover, we focus on settings where the identity of an individual bidder is not particularly relevant. That is, we assume that bidders are ex-ante symmetric. In order to introduce the notion of symmetry we need the following definition.

Definition 4   *A permutation of the set S is a bijection $\sigma : S \to S$.*

We can now define the notion of a symmetric function.

Definition 5   *A function $u : [0, \bar{v}]^n \to \mathbb{R}$ is symmetric if for every permutation σ of the set $\{1, \ldots, n\}$ and for every $x \in [0, \bar{v}]^n$, $u(x_1, x_2, \ldots, x_n) = u(x_{\sigma(1)}, x_{\sigma(2)}, \ldots, x_{\sigma(n)})$.*

For example, if $n = 3$, $u(a, b, c)$ is symmetric if

$$u(a, b, c) = u(a, c, b) = u(b, a, c) = u(b, c, a)$$
$$= u(c, a, b) = u(c, b, a)$$

for every $(a, b, c) \in [0, \bar{v}]^3$.

We will apply this concept to the distribution of types. For example, exchanging the types of bidders 1 and 2 in a vector $(x_1, x_2, x_3, \ldots, x_n)$ is of no consequence, that is, $f(x_1, x_2, x_3, \ldots, x_n) = f(x_2, x_1, x_3, \ldots, x_n)$. This assumption is stated below along with some regularity restrictions.

Symmetry   The density f is symmetric, strictly positive and continuous.

We now investigate equilibrium bidding behavior in second- and first-price auctions. We should note that with private values, the English button auction and the second-price auction are strategically equivalent. There is no information being revealed in an English (button) auction that changes an individual's valuation. As we mentioned in the previous section, Dutch and first-price auctions are always strategically equivalent no matter what the structure of values is.

3.2.1   Second-price Auction

Let us show that in the second-price auction the equilibrium is still to bid one's value which is given by one's type in our model. Recall that $Y = \max_{j \geq 2} X_j$. Thus, suppose bidder j bids x_j, $j = 2, \ldots, n$ and let us find the best reply of bidder 1. If he bids $t \geq 0$, then his expected utility is given by

$$h(t) = E[(x - Y)I_{t>Y} \mid X_1 = x].$$

That is, when bidders $2, \ldots, n$ bid their true values, then bidder 1 wins the difference between his value and the second highest value if he bids more than Y. Note that the expectation is taken with respect to the highest value amongst 1's opponents conditional on 1's type being x. Otherwise, his profits are zero.

Suppose that $t > x$. Then we have that $x - Y < 0$ whenever $t > Y > x$. Thus, bidder 1's expected profits can be written as:

$$h(t) = E[(x - Y)I_{t>Y \geq x} + (x - Y)I_{t>x>Y} \mid X_1 = x]$$
$$\leq E[(x - Y)I_{x>Y} \mid X_1 = x] = h(x).$$

That is, bidder 1 can increase his expected profits by decreasing his bid t when $t > x$. Now suppose that $t < x$. Then $x - Y > 0$ whenever $x > t > Y$. Thus by a similar reasoning we can conclude that

$$h(t) \leq E[(x - Y)I_{x>Y} \mid X_1 = x] = h(x).$$

That is, bidder 1 can increase his expected profits by increasing his bid t when $t < x$. Therefore, the best reply of bidder 1 is to bid $t = x$, his type. If we denote by f_X the marginal density of X_1 the expected payment of bidder 1 when his type is x is given by

$$P_s(x) := E[Y I_{x \geq Y} \mid X_1 = x]$$
$$= \int_{x_j \leq x, j \geq 2} \max_{2 \leq j \leq n} x_j \frac{f(x, x_2, \ldots, x_n)}{f_X(x)} \, dx_2 \cdots dx_n.$$

That is, bidder 1's expected payment in a second-price auction is simply equal to the expected value of the highest type amongst his opponents, Y, conditional on bidder 1's having received a type $x > Y$. Note that the seller's revenue is equal to expected payment of the highest valuation bidder.

3.2.2 First-price Auction

To find the equilibrium equation for the first-price sealed-bid auction with correlated types is a harder task. Denote by $f_{Y|X}$ the conditional density of Y given X and by $F_{Y|X}$ the conditional distribution. That is,

$$f_{Y|X}(y \mid x) = \frac{f(x, y)}{\int f(x, y) \, dy} \quad \text{and} \quad F_{Y|X}(y \mid x) = \int_0^y f_{Y|X}(z \mid x) \, dz.$$

Suppose bidders $j = 2, \ldots, n$ bid accordingly to $b(\cdot)$. Suppose bidder 1 bids $t = b(s)$. Then his expected utility is

$$h(s) = (x - b(s))E[I_{s>Y} \mid X = x] = (x - b(s))\, F_{Y|X}\,(s \mid x).$$

Differentiating, we obtain

$$h'(s) = -b'(s)\, F_{Y|X}\,(s \mid x) + (x - b(s))\, f_{Y|X}\,(s \mid x). \qquad (3.20)$$

If $s = x$ is to be optimum then

$$-b'(x)\, F_{Y|X}(x \mid x) + (x - b(x))\, f_{Y|X}\,(x \mid x) = 0.$$

Solving for b' we obtain the differential equation

$$b'(x) = (x - b(x))\frac{f_{Y|X}\,(x \mid x)}{F_{Y|X}\,(x \mid x)}. \qquad (3.21)$$

To solve this equation we use the integrating factor method which is explained in Appendix B. Define $\gamma(x) = f_{Y|X}(x \mid x)/F_{Y|X}(x \mid x)$. We may rewrite the equation as

$$b'(x) + \gamma(x)b(x) = x\gamma(x).$$

It is now clear that an integrating factor must solve $P' = P\gamma$. Therefore $P(x) = \exp[-\int_x^{\bar{v}} \gamma(u)du]$ is an integrating factor. Thus,

$$\begin{aligned}(Pb)'(x) &= P(x)b'(x) + P'(x)b(x) \\ &= P(x)(b'(x) + \gamma(x)b(x)) \\ &= P(x)x\gamma(x).\end{aligned}$$

Now since $b(0) = 0$ and $P(0) \leq 1$ we obtain integrating between 0 and x that:

$$P(x)b(x) = \int_0^x P(u)\gamma(u)u\,\mathrm{d}u = \int_0^x P'(u)\,u\,\mathrm{d}u. \qquad (3.22)$$

Thus, we get from the first equality

$$b(x) = \int_0^x \exp\left[-\int_u^x \gamma(v)\,\mathrm{d}v\right]\gamma(u)\,u\,\mathrm{d}u.$$

If we integrate by parts the last term of equation (3.22) we obtain that

$$b(x) = \frac{\int_0^x P'(u)\,u\,\mathrm{d}u}{P(x)} = x - \frac{\int_0^x P(u)\,\mathrm{d}u}{P(x)}.$$

To show that this is an equilibrium, we go back to (3.20):

$$\begin{aligned}h'(s) &= -b'(s)F_{Y|X}(s \mid x) + (x - b(s))f_{Y|X}(s \mid x) \\ &= -b'(s)F_{Y|X}(s \mid x) + (x - s)f_{Y|X}(s \mid x) + (s - b(s))f_{Y|X}(s \mid x).\end{aligned}$$

Using (3.21) we may write

$$h'(s) = -b'(s)F_{Y|X}(s\,|\,x) + (x-s)f_{Y|X}(s\,|\,x) + b'(s)\frac{f_{Y|X}(s\,|\,x)}{\gamma(s)}$$

$$= f_{Y|X}(s\,|\,x)\left(x - s + b'(s)\left(\frac{1}{\gamma(s)} - \frac{F_{Y|X}(s\,|\,x)}{f_{Y|X}(s\,|\,x)}\right)\right).$$

Suppose that $x \to f_{Y|X}(s\,|\,x)/F_{Y|X}(s\,|\,x)$ is increasing. Then $h'(s) > 0$ if and only if $x > s$. Thus we proved the following:

Theorem 2   *If the ratio $f_{Y|X}(s|x)/F_{Y|X}(s|x)$ is increasing in x then a symmetric equilibrium of the first-price sealed-bid auction is given by the function $b_{\mathrm{f}}(\cdot)$ defined by*

$$b_{\mathrm{f}}(x) = \int_0^x \exp\left[-\int_u^x \gamma(v)\,\mathrm{d}v\right]\gamma(u)\,u\,\mathrm{d}u$$

$$= x - \int_0^x \exp\left[-\int_u^x \gamma(v)\,\mathrm{d}v\right]\mathrm{d}u. \qquad (3.23)$$

where $\gamma(u) = f_{Y|X}(u\,|\,u)/F_{Y|X}(u\,|\,u)$. Moreover, $b_{\mathrm{f}}(x)$ solves the differential equation

$$b'(x) = (x - b(x))\,\gamma(x)$$

with initial condition $b(0) = 0$.

Remark 1   *The condition that $f_{Y|X}(s\,|\,x)/F_{Y|X}(s\,|\,x)$ is increasing in x is satisfied if $f_{(X,Y)}$ has the monotone likelihood ratio property (see Definition 6 on page 47). This property will be studied in detail in Chapter 4.*

3.2.3   Comparison of Expected Payment

We may easily compare the expected payment of the bidders in the first- and second-price auctions. The expected payment of a bidder with valuation x in the first-price auction is given by $b_{\mathrm{f}}(x)F_{Y|X}(x\,|\,x)$, that is, his bid times the conditional probability of winning. Thus

$$P_{\mathrm{f}}(x) := b_{\mathrm{f}}(x)F_{Y|X}(x\,|\,x)$$

$$= F_{Y|X}(x\,|\,x)\int_0^x \exp\left[-\int_u^x \gamma(v)\,\mathrm{d}v\right]\gamma(u)\,u\,\mathrm{d}u.$$

We can also write the expected payment of a bidder with valuation x in a second-price auction as:

$$P_s(x) = E[Y \mid X = x] = \int_0^x y f_{Y|X}(y \mid x) \, dy$$

$$= \int_0^x (y - b_f(y)) \, f_{Y|X}(y \mid x) \, dy + \int_0^x b_f(y) \, f_{Y|X}(y \mid x) \, dy$$

$$= \int_0^x b_f'(y) \frac{f_{Y|X}(y \mid x)}{\gamma(y)} \, dy + \int_0^x b_f(y) f_{Y|X}(y \mid x) \, dy.$$

Now note that since $y < x$, $1/\gamma(y) = F_{Y|X}(y \mid y)/f_{Y|X}(y \mid y) \geq F_{Y|X}(y \mid x)/f_{Y|X}(y \mid x)$. Therefore, the inequality $f_{Y|X}(y \mid x)/\gamma(y) \geq F_{Y|X}(y \mid x)$ is true. Thus

$$P_s(x) \geq \int_0^x b_f'(y) F_{Y|X}(y \mid x) \, dy + \int_0^x b_f(y) \, f_{Y|X}(y \mid x) \, dy$$

$$= \int_0^x [b_f'(y) F_{Y|X}(y \mid x) + b_f(y) f_{Y|X}(y \mid x)] \, dy$$

$$= \int_0^x [b_f(y) F_{Y|X}(y \mid x)]' \, dy = b_f(x) F_{Y|X}(x \mid x) = P_f(x).$$

That is, with correlated types, the second-price auction yields more expected revenue than a first-price auction.

Example 2 *Suppose $f(x, y) = (1 + f(x)f(y))/2$ where $f(x)$ is an increasing density on $[0, 1]$. Then*

$$\frac{f_{Y|X}(s \mid x)}{F_{Y|X}(s \mid x)} = \frac{1 + f(x)f(s)}{s + f(x)F(s)}$$

is increasing. To see this note that the marginal density is

$$f_X(x) = \int f(x, y) \, dy = \frac{1 + f(x)}{2} = f_Y(x).$$

The conditional density

$$f_{Y|X}(y \mid x) = \frac{f(x, y)}{f_X(x)} = \frac{1 + f(x)f(y)}{1 + f(x)}$$

and the conditional distribution is

$$F_{Y|X}(y \mid x) = \frac{y + f(x)F(y)}{1 + f(x)}.$$

Thus, the likelihood ratio is given by:

$$\gamma(y, x) = \frac{f_{Y|X}(y \mid x)}{F_{Y|X}(y \mid x)} = \frac{1 + f(x)f(y)}{y + f(x)F(y)}. \tag{3.24}$$

Then

$$\frac{\partial \gamma(y,x)}{\partial x} = \frac{\partial}{\partial x}\left(\frac{1+f(x)f(y)}{y+f(x)F(y)}\right)$$

$$= \frac{f'(x)f(y)}{y+f(x)F(y)} - \frac{(1+f(x)f(y))f'(x)F(y)}{(y+f(x)F(y))^2}$$

$$= f'(x)\frac{f(y)(y+f(x)F(y)) - (1+f(x)f(y))F(y)}{(y+f(x)F(y))^2}$$

$$= f'(x)\frac{yf(y)-F(y)}{(y+f(x)F(y))^2} \geq 0,$$

since $F(y) = \int_0^y f(z)\,\mathrm{d}z \leq \int_0^y f(y)\,\mathrm{d}z = f(y)y.$

Let us particularize further with an example to explicitly compute the equilibrium strategies.

Example 3 *Suppose $F(x) = x^2$. Then*

$$\gamma(x) = \frac{1+4x^2}{x(1+2x^2)} \quad and \quad P(x) = x\sqrt{\frac{1+2x^2}{3}}.$$

The first-price auction equilibrium bidding function is given by:

$$b(x) = x - \frac{\int_0^x u\sqrt{(1+2u^2)/3}\,\mathrm{d}u}{x\sqrt{(1+2x^2)/3}}.$$

This function is plotted below, for comparison, together with the function $x \to x/2$.

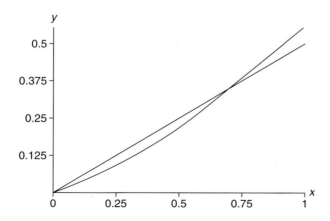

3.3   The Effect of Risk Aversion

We start with the second-price auction. We are now assuming that bidders are risk averse and calculate their utility with the concave von Neumann-Morgenstern utility $u(\cdot)$. We suppose $u' > 0 \geq u''$. We normalize $u(0) = 0$. We want to prove that to bid this type is still an equilibrium bidding function. Thus suppose bidders $j = 2, \ldots, n$ bid x_j. If bidder 1 bids $t \geq 0$ his expected utility is

$$h(t) = E[u(x - Y)I_{t>Y}|X = x] = \int_0^t u(x - y)f_{Y|X}(y \mid x)\, dy.$$

Differentiating we have that

$$h'(t) = u(x - t)f_{Y|X}(t \mid x).$$

Thus, $h'(t) > 0$ if and only if $u(x - t) > 0$. That is, $h'(t) > 0$ if and only if $t < x$. Hence, $t = x$ maximizes the expected utility.

We now consider the first-price auction. Suppose $b(\cdot)$ is a strictly increasing continuous bidding strategy played by bidders $i \neq 1$. Let us find bidder 1's best reply. If he bids $t = b(s)$ the expected utility is

$$h(s) = u(x - b(s)) \Pr(s > Y \mid X = x) = u(x - b(s))F_{Y|X}(s \mid x).$$

Differentiating, we obtain

$$h'(s) = -b'(s)u'(x - b(s))F_{Y|X}(s \mid x) + u(x - b(s))f_{Y|X}(s \mid x).$$

If $s = x$ is to be the optimal then $h'(x) = 0$ and therefore,

$$b'(x) = \frac{u(x - b(x))}{u'(x - b(x))}\frac{f_{Y|X}(x \mid x)}{F_{Y|X}(x \mid x)}. \tag{3.25}$$

Suppose now that $b(\cdot)$ solves this differential equation. Then

$$\frac{h'(s)}{F_{Y|X}(s \mid x)} = -b'(s)u'(x - b(s)) + u(x - b(s))\frac{f_{Y|X}(s \mid x)}{F_{Y|X}(s \mid x)}$$

$$= -\frac{u(s - b(s))}{u'(s - b(s))}\frac{f_{Y|X}(s \mid s)}{F_{Y|X}(s \mid s)}u'(x - b(s)) + u(x - b(s))\frac{f_{Y|X}(s \mid x)}{F_{Y|X}(s \mid x)}.$$

If $s > x$ then $f_{Y|X}(s\,|\,x)/F_{Y|X}(s\,|\,x) \le f_{Y|X}(s\,|\,s)/F_{Y|X}(s\,|\,s)$ and $x - b(s) < s - b(s)$. Thus,

$$-\frac{u(s-b(s))}{u'(s-b(s))}\frac{f_{Y|X}(s\,|\,s)}{F_{Y|X}(s\,|\,s)}u'(x-b(s)) + u(x-b(s))\frac{f_{Y|X}(s\,|\,x)}{F_{Y|X}(s\,|\,x)}$$

$$\le \left(-\frac{u(s-b(s))}{u'(s-b(s))}u'(x-b(s)) + u(x-b(s))\right)\frac{f_{Y|X}(s\,|\,s)}{F_{Y|X}(s\,|\,s)}$$

$$= \left(-\frac{u(s-b(s))}{u'(s-b(s))} + \frac{u(x-b(s))}{u'(x-b(s))}\right)\frac{f_{Y|X}(s\,|\,s)u'(x-b(s))}{F_{Y|X}(s\,|\,s)}$$

$$\le \left(-\frac{u(s-b(s))}{u'(s-b(s))} + \frac{u(s-b(s))}{u'(s-b(s))}\right)\frac{f_{Y|X}(s\,|\,s)u'(x-b(s))}{F_{Y|X}(s\,|\,s)} = 0.$$

The first inequality follows $f_{Y|X}(s\,|\,x)/F_{Y|X}(s\,|\,x) \le f_{Y|X}(s\,|\,s)/F_{Y|X}(s\,|\,s)$ and the second inequality follows from $u(x)/u'(x)$ being increased. Analogously we can show that if $s < x$, $h'(s) > 0$. Thus $b(\cdot)$ defined by the differential equation above is the equilibrium.

For example suppose $u(x) = x^t, t \in (0,1)$. Then

$$\frac{u(x-b(x))}{u'(x-b(x))} = \frac{(x-b(x))^t}{t(x-b(x))^{t-1}} = \frac{x-b(x)}{t}.$$

In this case, the differential equation becomes:

$$b'(x) = \frac{u(x-b(x))}{u'(x-b(x))}\gamma(x) = (x-b(x))\frac{\gamma(x)}{t}.$$

3.3.1   Revenue Comparison

Define $b_1(\cdot)$ as the equilibrium bidding function in a first-price auction when there is indifference to risk. Suppose $b_2(\cdot)$ is the equilibrium bidding function in a first-price auction when risk aversion is captured by the utility function u. Since u is concave, $u(z) \ge u'(z)z$. Thus,

$$b_2'(x) = \frac{u(x-b_2(x))}{u'(x-b_2(x))}\gamma(x) \ge (x-b_2(x))\gamma(x).$$

The following inequality is immediate from this:

$$(b_2(x) - b_1(x))' = b_2'(x) - b_1'(x)$$

$$\ge (x-b_2(x))\gamma(x) - (x-b_1(x))\gamma(x)$$

$$= (b_1(x) - b_2(x))\gamma(x).$$

Thus if $P(x) = e^{-\int_x^{\bar{v}} \gamma(s) ds}$ then $P' = P\gamma(x)$ and therefore (we omit the argument x for conciseness)

$$\frac{d}{dx}(P(b_2 - b_1)) = P\gamma(b_2 - b_1) + P(b_2 - b_1)'$$

$$\geq P\gamma(b_2 - b_1) + P(b_1 - b_2)\gamma = 0.$$

Finally, we have that $P(x)(b_2(x) - b_1(x)) \geq 0$. Thus, a risk-averse bidder bids uniformly more aggressively than a risk-neutral bidder. Hence, we have just proved the following result.

Theorem 3 *If there are risk aversion and private values the first-price auction generates more revenue than the second-price auction or the English auction.*

3.4   The Discrete Valuation Case

In this section, we relax another assumption from the standard IPV model. We allow valuations to be drawn from a discrete distribution. We will use an example to illustrate that with discrete types we will have to look for a Bayesian Nash equilibrium in mixed strategies as a pure strategy equilibrium will not exist.

Example 4 *Suppose we have two bidders with valuations $x \in \{0, 1\}$ with equal probabilities. Then, there is no equilibrium of the first-price auction in pure strategies. To see this, suppose bidder 2 bids 0 if his valuation is 0 (a bidder with zero valuation will never bid higher than zero). And if his valuation is 1 his bid is $b \geq 0$. Similarly, bidder 1 bids zero if his valuation is zero. What is his bid if his valuation is 1? The expected utility of bidder 1 is*

$$\pi_1 = \tfrac{1}{2}(1 - 0) + \tfrac{1}{2}(1 - b_1) \quad \text{if } b_1 > b.$$

Thus if $b \geq 1$, bidder 1 bids $b_1 = 0$. If $b < 1$ and $b_1 > b$, $\pi_1 = \tfrac{1}{2} + \tfrac{1}{2}(1 - b_1)$. Thus, if $b \geq 1$ the best reply of bidder 1 is to bid 0 and if $b < 1$ there is no best reply since the expected utility increases as $b_1 > b$ decreases. That is, there is no pure strategy Bayesian Nash equilibrium.

Let us find a mixed strategy equilibrium. First, note that if bidder 2 has a zero valuation, then he bids zero for sure. If bidder 2 has valuation 1, suppose that his bid belongs to $[0, x]$ with probability $G(x)$. For G to define an equilibrium strategy, we need that $\Pr(\{x\}) = 0$ whenever $x > 0$—given that if $\Pr(\{x\}) > 0$ whenever bidder 1 intends to bid x, he may slightly increase his bid increasing his probability of winning by $\Pr(\{x\})$. What is the best reply for bidder 1? His expected utility is

$$\pi_1 = \tfrac{1}{2}(1 - b) + \tfrac{1}{2}(1 - b)G(b).$$

Thus, bidder 1 will bid b such that b maximizes $(1 - b)(1 + G(b))$. *Thus if F is the distribution of bidder's 1 bids we have that*

$$F(\{b; b \text{ does not maximize } (1 - b)(1 + G(b))\}) = 0;$$
$$G(\{b; b \text{ does not maximize } (1 - b)(1 + F(b))\}) = 0.$$

Suppose $k = \max_{b \geq 0}(1 - b)(1 + G(b))$. *Then if x, x' are such that $F(x)F(x') > 0$,*

$$(1 - x)(1 + G(x)) = k = (1 - x')(1 + G(x')).$$

The infimum of such x must satisfy $(1 - x) = k$ or $x = 1 - k$. The supremum of $x' : (1 - x')2 = k$. Thus the support of the distribution is $[1 - k, 1 - \frac{k}{2}]$. If $k = 1$,

$$F(x) = G(x) = \frac{1}{1 - x} - 1 = \frac{x}{1 - x};$$
$$x \in \left[0, \tfrac{1}{2}\right].$$

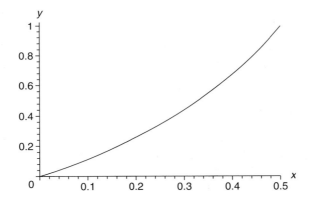

These probability distributions represent the mixed strategy equilibrium for this example. They are depicted in the diagram above. The interpretation is that a bidder who receives a type 1 will submit a bid in $[0, \alpha]$ with probability $\alpha/(1 - \alpha)$ if $\alpha \leq \frac{1}{2}$ and will never submit a bid higher than $\frac{1}{2}$.

3.5 Exercises

1. Compute the equilibrium bidding strategy in both first- and second-price auctions when the seller sets a reserve price equal to v_0. That is, the seller only accepts bids that are greater or equal to v_0. What is the seller's expected revenue in both auctions? Does revenue equivalence still hold?

2. (Riley and Samuelson 1981): Consider an auction with two buyers with valuations drawn independently from the uniform $[0, 1]$ distribution. The seller sets a reserve price equal to $\frac{1}{2}$ and she employs the following auction rules:

   (a) There is a single round of bidding. Buyer 1 is given the opportunity to make a bid a price $b_1 \geq \frac{1}{2}$.

   (b) If buyer 1 bids $b_1 \geq \frac{1}{2}$, buyer 2 can match b_1 and win the object. If buyer 1 makes no bid, buyer 2 can obtain the good at price $\frac{1}{2}$ if he so chooses.

      (i) Does this auction resemble any selling mechanism that you know of?

      (ii) Can you compute the buyers' equilibrium bidding strategies and the seller's expected revenue?

      (iii) Is the object in equilibrium always allocated to the individual with the highest valuation?

      (iv) Compare the expected revenue generated by this auction with the expected revenue generated by a second-price auction with reserve price equal to $\frac{1}{2}$.

3. The deduction leading to equation (3.1) is incomplete as b_1 may not be in the range of $b(\cdot)$. Reduce the general case to the case $b_1 \in b([0, 1])$.

4. Compute the seller's expected revenue if the number of bidders goes to infinity.

5. In the text we assumed that in case of a tie the object is not delivered to any bidder. Show that the equilibrium strategies obtained above (for both first- and second-price auctions) still hold under any tie-breaking rule.

6. Show formally that to bid one's own value is a dominant strategy in the Vickrey auction.

7. Suppose we have an auction in which every bidder pays his bid whether or not he wins the object. Find the equilibrium strategies in this case if there are n bidders and the distribution is uniform. (This auction format is called an all-pay auction for obvious reasons.)

8. Suppose there are two bidders and the distribution is uniform. Suppose if you win or not you pay the second highest bid. Find the equilibrium strategies. What is peculiar about them? (This auction format is referred to as the war of attrition.)

9. Characterize equilibrium behavior and the seller's expected revenue in a second-price auction with independent private values, a reserve price r and an entry fee δ. Show that the expected revenue is the same as the one generated by a first-price auction with reserve price r and entry fee δ as derived in Section 3.1.4.

10. Suppose there are two bidders. Calculate the expected revenue from a first-price auction as a function of the reserve price r for the following

distributions defined for $x \in [0, 1]$:

(a) $F(x) = x$

(b) $F(x) = x^2$

(c) $F(x) = \sqrt{x}$.

11. Find the optimal reserve price for each distribution of the previous exercise.

12. Now suppose the two bidders of exercise (3.5) collude to bid together and that the auctioneer knows this. Find the new optimal reserve prices for each of the distributions above. If the numbers are different from those calculated in (a), (b) and (c) above, explain why this does not contradict the fact that the optimal reserve price is independent of the number of bidders.

13. In Example 2, suppose that $F(X) = x^\theta$ and therefore $f(x) = \theta x^{\theta - 1}$. Show that

$$P(x) = \exp \left[- \int_x^1 \gamma(x) \, dx \right] = \frac{x \sqrt{a + \theta x^{2\theta - 2}}}{\sqrt{a + \theta}}.$$

And that

$$b_{\mathrm{f}}(x) = x - \frac{1}{x\sqrt{a + \theta x^{2\theta - 2}}} \int_0^x u \sqrt{a + \theta u^{2\theta - 2}} \, du.$$

14. Show that $k = 1$ is necessary for an equilibrium in the reasoning underlying Example 4.

15. Find the equilibrium distribution if the set of valuations is $\{0, 1, 2\}$ and there are two bidders.

16. Is the equilibrium in the discrete case efficient?

17. Show that setting the reserve price $\rho = 0$ is never optimal for the seller.

18. Find the equilibrium bidding functions of the first-price auction for distribution $F(x) = x^\theta, \theta > 0$ and $n > 1$ bidders.

19. Show that $\gamma(y, x)$ in (3.24) is increasing in x if $f(x)$ is decreasing.

20. Show that (3.10) is increasing in n and that the limit of the seller's expected revenue when $n \to \infty$ is equal to $\bar{v}$.

4

Common Value

In this chapter, we consider a situation where the value of the object being sold is the same for all players but this value is not known at the time that bidding takes place. A typical example includes bidding for the rights of exploration of some natural resource. For given international prices, the amount of oil available in a particular area is fixed but it is only really known after the auction and when the successful bidder starts drilling.

Most auctions will have a common value component associated with the object being sold. For example, in a house auction the common value component might be the expected market value of the house.

Common value auctions are usually associated with a phenomenon known as the "winner's curse". Capen et al. (1971) claim that "the winner tends to be the player who most overestimates the true tract value" and that resulted in low profits earned by oil companies on offshore tracts in the 1960s. Our reader will have to ask himself or herself how a fully rational bidder, indeed like the bidders we consider in this book, can overestimate the true value of the object. Given that equilibrium behavior requires maximization of ex-ante payoffs, there cannot be a winner's curse in our setting. That is, bidders will take into account the possibility that they might overestimate the value and will bid more cautiously. How cautiously they bid will vary with the auction format and this will have implications for auction design and the seller's expected revenue. A full account of this relationship is given in the next chapter. Here we work our way through some examples to illustrate the effects of the common value assumption in bidding behavior and on the seller's expected revenue. In this process, we will touch on several topics that will be dealt with in greater detail in the next chapter.

In common value auction models we usually refer to the bidders' types as bidders' signals. We do this because we prefer to think of types as completely determining the bidders preferences whereas in common values models the bidders' preferences might be a function of the other bidders types/signals as well. In our first example we assume that the individual signals about the true value of the object are independently determined. In the second example, we allow for types to be correlated.

4.1   An Example with Independent Signals

4.1.1   First-price Auction

Let us consider the case where the true value of the object is $V = v_1 + v_2$, where the v_i's are independent and uniformly distributed on $[0, 1]$. For example, it might be the case that the true value of the object has two components, bidder 1 receives a signal about the first component, bidder 2 about the second, and the true value of the object is the sum of both components. For example if V is the amount of oil on a particular tract, v_1 might indicate the amount of oil on part of the tract and v_2 the amount of oil in the complementary area.

We will now look at bidding behavior in a first-price auction and compare with that developed in Chapter 3. Suppose bidder 2 follows some strictly increasing strategy $b(\cdot)$. Bidder 1, who has received signal $v_1 = v$, will choose $b_1 = b(\omega)$ to maximize expected profits:

$$\pi_1 = \int_0^\omega (v + y - b(\omega)) \, \mathrm{d}y = v\omega + \frac{\omega^2}{2} - b(\omega)\omega,$$

where we are integrating over all cases where Player 1 wins the auction, that is, when $b(\omega) > b(y)$ or $\omega > y$. Thus differentiating with respect to ω and setting the derivative equal to zero yields

$$v + \omega - b(\omega) - \omega b'(\omega) = 0.$$

We can now set $\omega = v$ as we are looking for the symmetric equilibrium:

$$2v - b(v) - vb'(v) = 0.$$

Thus,

$$2v = (vb(v))'.$$

If a bidder with signal $v = 0$ bids $b_0 \geq 0$ (why we cannot dismiss $b_0 > 0$?), integrating both sides yields:

$$vb(v) = vb(v) - 0 \cdot b_0 = \int_0^v 2y \, \mathrm{d}y = v^2.$$

Thus $b(v) = v$ if $v > 0$. Since we are supposing $b(\cdot)$ continuous, $b_0 = b(0) = \lim_{v \to 0} v = 0$. Therefore,

$$b^{\mathrm{F}}(v) = v.$$

This is the equilibrium bidding strategy in this first-price auction. Note that in a symmetric increasing equilibrium it suffices to outbid one's opponent.

By bidding one's signal, in a symmetric equilibrium, one is guaranteed to win the auction if one has the highest signal. Note that by following such bidding strategy a bidder will never pay more than the true value of the object! Is this the rule in common values models? To analyze further this possibility let us consider a more general distribution. Suppose each bidder valuation $v \in [0, 1]$ is drawn from the distribution $F(\cdot)$. Suppose also that it has a density $f = F'$ which is continuous and strictly positive. We look again for a symmetric equilibrium $b(\cdot)$. Suppose bidder 1 has a signal v. If bidder 2 bids according to $b(\cdot)$, bidder 1's expected profit by bidding $b = b(\omega)$ is given by

$$\pi = \int_0^\omega (v + y - b(\omega))f(y)\,\mathrm{d}y = \int_0^\omega (v + y)f(y)\,\mathrm{d}y - b(\omega)F(\omega). \tag{4.1}$$

Thus, the first-order condition is

$$\pi' = (v + \omega)f(\omega) - (b(\omega)F(\omega))' = 0. \tag{4.2}$$

In an equilibrium $\omega = v$ and thus we obtain the differential equation

$$(b(v)F(v))' = 2vf(v). \tag{4.3}$$

If $b(0) = b_0$, the solution of this differential equation is given by:

$$b(v)F(v) = b(v)F(v) - b_0 F(0) = \int_0^v 2yf(y)\,\mathrm{d}y.$$

Therefore,

$$b(v) = \frac{\int_0^v 2yf(y)\,\mathrm{d}y}{F(v)}. \tag{4.4}$$

The reader can verify that the continuity of $b(\cdot)$ implies that $b_0 = 0$. It is a simple matter to check that this is really a symmetric equilibrium bidding strategy. Just use (4.3) to substitute $(b(\omega)F(\omega))'$ by $2\omega f(\omega)$ in (4.2). Let us particularize further and assume that $F(v) = v^\theta, \theta > 0$. Then by following the steps above we obtain

$$b(v) = \frac{2\theta}{\theta + 1} v.$$

Thus, a bidder will bid higher than his signal v if $\theta > 1$, and he will bid less than his signal if $\theta < 1$. If $\theta > 1$ it might happen that after the auction the bidder discovers (i.e., if the losing bid is announced as well) that his bid is higher than the true value of the object. That is the bidder regrets bidding as he bid. However, this does not mean that the bidder has suffered the winner's curse—this bidder has fully taken into account that he might pay more than the true value of the object. In comparison, if $\theta < 1$ winning the auction is quite a pleasurable experience.

4.1.2   Second-price Auction Example

Now let us examine the bidding behavior in a second-price auction. Suppose first the distribution is uniform on $[0,1]$. Assume again that bidder 2 follows some strictly increasing strategy $b(\cdot)$. Player 1, who has received signal $v_1 = v$, will choose $b_1 = b(\omega)$ to maximize expected profits:

$$\pi_1 = \int_0^\omega (v + y - b(y))\, dy.$$

Differentiating with respect to ω and setting the derivative equal to zero yields:

$$v + \omega - b(\omega) = 0.$$

Therefore, the equilibrium bidding strategy in this second-price auction is

$$b^S(v) = 2v.$$

That is, a bidder bids more than the expected value of the object conditional on having the highest signal. (This expected value is $3v/2$.) Does this mean that this player is suffering from a winner's curse? The answer again is no. The winning bidder does not pay his bid but rather the second highest bid. Conditional on having the highest signal, this bidder expected to pay $p^S = 2(v/2) = v$—this is the bid submitted by his opponent. Note that the seller's expected revenue is again the expected payment of the highest bidder: $\frac{2}{3}$. But this is the same expected revenue from the first-price auction above! Is this a coincidence?

The fact that the two auctions formats generate the same expected revenue in this example is no coincidence. In Chapter 6, we will prove a general version of the Revenue Equivalence Theorem that will cover this example.

4.2   An Example with Correlated Types

We will now consider a simple example where signals are correlated. We will maintain the assumption that the true value of the object is $V = v_1 + v_2$. However, the joint distribution of the v_i's is now given by:

$$f(v_1, v_2) = \tfrac{4}{5}(1 + v_1 v_2), \quad \text{for } v_1, v_2 \in [0,1].$$

To be able to obtain the density $f(v_1)$ we integrate the above expression with respect to v_2:

$$f(v_1) = \int_0^1 \tfrac{4}{5}(1 + v_1 v_2)\, dv_2 = \tfrac{4}{5}\left(1 + \frac{v_1}{2}\right).$$

Similarly,

$$f(v_2) = \int_0^1 \tfrac{4}{5}(1 + v_1 v_2)\,dv_1 = \tfrac{4}{5}\left(1 + \frac{v_2}{2}\right).$$

We also need the conditional densities. For example,

$$f(v_2 \mid v_1) = \frac{f(v_1, v_2)}{f(v_1)} = \frac{2(1 + v_1 v_2)}{2 + v_1}.$$

Similarly,

$$f(v_1 \mid v_2) = \frac{f(v_1, v_2)}{f(v_2)} = \frac{2(1 + v_1 v_2)}{2 + v_2}.$$

4.2.1 First-price Auction

Now we are ready to compute equilibrium bidding behavior in a first-price auction. We consider that both bidders are using the same strategy $b(\cdot)$, bidder 2 bids $b(v_2)$ when he receives signal v_2. Bidder 1, who receives signal v_1, will choose to "announce" a value s so as to maximize his expected profits:

$$\pi_1(s) = E[(v - b(s))I_{s > v_2} \mid v_1]$$
$$= E[(v_1 + v_2 - b(s))I_{s > v_2} \mid v_1].$$

Taking the expected value yields:

$$\pi_1(s) = \int_0^s (v_1 + v_2 - b(s))\frac{2(1 + v_1 v_2)}{2 + v_1}\,dv_2$$
$$= \int_0^s \frac{2(v_1 + v_2)(1 + v_1 v_2)}{2 + v_1}\,dv_2 - b(s)\int_0^s \frac{2(1 + v_1 v_2)}{2 + v_1}\,dv_2.$$

Differentiating with respect to s yields:

$$(2 + v_1)\pi_1'(s)$$
$$= 2(v_1 + s)(1 + v_1 s) - b'(s)\int_0^s 2(1 + v_1 v_2)\,dv_2 - b(s)2(1 + v_1 s).$$

This derivative is equal to zero when $s = v_1$. That is, in equilibrium our bidder chooses $b(s) = b(v_1)$. Thus,

$$4v_1(1 + v_1^2) = b'(v_1)\int_0^{v_1} 2(1 + v_1 v_2)\,dv_2 + b(v_1)2(1 + v_1^2).$$

Integrating this expression we obtain the following differential equation:

$$b'(v) + 2b(v)\frac{(1 + v^2)}{2v + v^3} = \frac{4(1 + v^2)}{2 + v^2}.$$

We solve this differential equation by using the integrating factor method (see Appendix B). Define $P = v\sqrt{2 + v^2}$. Then

$$(v\sqrt{2 + v^2}\, b(v))' = v\sqrt{2 + v^2}\, b'(v) + 2\frac{1 + v^2}{\sqrt{(2 + v^2)}} b(v)$$

$$= v\sqrt{2 + v^2}\left(b'(v) + 2\frac{1 + v^2}{v(2 + v^2)} b(v)\right)$$

$$= \frac{4(1 + v^2)}{2 + v^2} v\sqrt{2 + v^2} = \frac{4v(1 + v^2)}{\sqrt{2 + v^2}}.$$

Integrating both sides of our differential equation and using the boundary condition $b(0) = 0$ to obtain the value of the constant, we obtain our symmetric equilibrium

$$b^{\mathrm{F}}(v) = \frac{4}{3}\frac{\sqrt{2 + v^2}(v^2 - 1) + \sqrt{2}}{v\sqrt{2 + v^2}}.$$

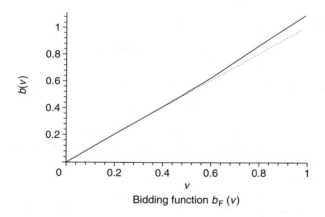

Bidding function $b_{\mathrm{F}}(v)$

The dotted line is the graph of x, it is included just for comparison. To compute the seller's expected revenue we have to consider the distribution of the maximum between v_1 and v_2:

$$\Pr[\max\{v_1, v_2 \leq \lambda\}] = \Pr[v_1 \leq \lambda, v_2 \leq \lambda]$$

$$= \int_0^\lambda \int_0^\lambda \tfrac{4}{5}(1 + v_1 v_2)\, dv_1\, dv_2 = \frac{4}{5}\left(\lambda^2 + \frac{\lambda^4}{4}\right).$$

Thus, the density of the maximum $V_1 \vee V_2$ is

$$f_{V_1 \vee V_2}(x) = \frac{4}{5}(2x + x^3).$$

The seller's expected revenue then can be written as:

$$R^{\mathrm{F}} = \int_0^1 b^F(x)\tfrac{4}{5}(2x + x^3)\,\mathrm{d}x.$$

The reader can check that $R^{\mathrm{F}} = 0.735$.

4.2.2   Second-price Auction

We can now compute equilibrium behavior in a second-price auction. Let us follow the same approach and write bidder 1's expected profits given that both players are using strategy $b(\cdot)$, bidder 1 has received signal v_1 but chooses to announce a value s to maximize his expected value:

$$E[(v_1 + v_2 - b(v_2))I_{s>v_2} \mid v_1].$$

Taking the expected value yields:

$$\pi_1(s) = \int_0^s (v_1 + v_2 - b(v_2))\frac{2(1 + v_1 v_2)}{2 + v_1}\,\mathrm{d}v_2.$$

Differentiating with respect to s yields:

$$\pi_1'(s) = (v_1 + s - b(s))\frac{2(1 + v_1 s)}{2 + v_1}.$$

In equilibrium the derivative equals to zero when $s = v_1$. Thus,

$$b^S(v_1) = 2v_1.$$

That is, in the symmetric equilibrium of the second-price auction bidders bid more than their expected value for the object conditional on having the highest signal. However, as in the example with independent signals, this does not mean that they expect to pay more than the true value of the object. Recall that in this auction format they pay the second highest bid!

We can now compute the seller's expected revenue. First, we need to determine the distribution of the minimum of the two signals:

$$\Pr[\min\{v_1, v_2\} \le \lambda] = 1 - \Pr(\min\{v_1, v_2\} > \lambda)$$

$$= 1 - \int_\lambda^1 \int_\lambda^1 \tfrac{4}{5}(1 + v_1 v_2)\,\mathrm{d}v_1\,\mathrm{d}v_2$$

$$= 1 - \frac{4}{5}\left[(1 - \lambda)^2 + \left(\frac{1 - \lambda^2}{2}\right)^2\right].$$

Thus, the density of the minimum of v_1 and v_2 ($V_1 \wedge V_2$) is given by

$$f_{V_1 \wedge V_2}(x) = \frac{8}{5}(1 - x) + \frac{4}{5}x(1 - x^2).$$

Therefore, the seller's expected revenue is equal to:

$$R^S = \int_0^1 2x \left(\tfrac{8}{5}(1-x) + \tfrac{4}{5}x(1-x^2) \right) \, \mathrm{d}x = 0.746.$$

Unlike the example with independent signals, the expected revenue generated by the second-price auction is higher than that generated by the first-price
auction. The reason is related to the so-called linkage principle. In a second-
price auction, the price paid by the winner is based on the signal received by
the runner up whereas in a first-price auction it is based on his own signal
only and signals are positively correlated. This means that rational bidders bid
more cautiously in first-price auctions than in second-price auctions resulting
in lower expected revenue for the seller. This will be explained in detail in the
next chapter in the context of affiliation.

4.3   The Symmetric Model with Two Bidders

To prepare the terrain for the next chapter, we consider a model which is a
generalization of both the private values model and the common values model.
However, in this section we limit ourselves to the simple case of two symmetric
bidders as defined below.

Valuation symmetry   The valuation of bidder i is given by
$u_i \colon [0, \bar{v}]^2 \to \mathbb{R}$ satisfying $u_2(x_1, x_2) = u_1(x_2, x_1)$.

Example 5   *Suppose $u_1(x_1, x_2) = x_1 + x_2/2$ and $u_2(x_1, x_2) = x_2 + x_1/2$. Then
the bidders' valuations are symmetric.*

Thus, if bidder 1 were in the same situation as bidder 2, bidder 1 will have
the same valuation as bidder 2. Thus this example is neither a pure common
values model (since in general $u_1(x_1, x_2) \neq u_2(x_1, x_2)$) nor a private values
model (since $u_1(x_1, x_2) \neq x_1$).
    Define $u(a, b) = u_1(a, b)$. Then $u_2(x_1, x_2) = u(x_2, x_1)$. Define also $D = [0, \bar{v}]^2$. We now introduce a regularity assumption:

Regularity $u \colon D \to \mathbb{R}$, is non-negative, continuously differentiable and
strictly increasing in the first variable and increasing in the second variable.

Regularity is a purely technical assumption. Its role will be clearer below.
    We suppose the distribution of the random vector (X, Y) has a density
$f(\cdot, \cdot)$. Although not strictly necessary we impose the following additional
assumption:

Symmetric density   The density $f \colon D \to \mathbb{R}$ is continuous, strictly positive
and symmetric. That is, for every $(x, y) \in D$, $f(x, y) = f(y, x)$.

Example 6 *The density $f(v_1, v_2) = (1 + v_1 v_2)/2$ defined for $v_1, v_2 \in [0, 1]$ is a symmetric density. If $g(v_1, v_2)$ is a continuous strictly positive density then $f(v_1, v_2) = (g(v_1, v_2) + (g(v_2, v_1)))/2$ is a symmetric density.*

The next property plays an important part in the definition of affiliation for two random variables.

Definition 6 *The positive function f satisfies the* monotone likelihood ratio property *if for every $(a, c), (b, d) \in D$, whenever $a > b$ and $c > d$, then*

$$\frac{f(a, c)}{f(a, d)} \geq \frac{f(b, c)}{f(b, d)}.$$

Alternatively, we could say that the ratio $f(x, c)/f(x, d)$ increases in x if $c > d$.

Example 7 *If X and Y are independent then the joint density satisfies the monotone likelihood ratio property. This is not difficult to see. Suppose $f(x, y) = f_1(x) f_2(y)$. Then*

$$\frac{f(a, c)}{f(a, d)} = \frac{f_1(a) f_2(c)}{f_1(a) f_2(d)} = \frac{f_2(c)}{f_2(d)} = \frac{f(b, c)}{f(b, d)}.$$

Example 8 *Suppose $f(\omega, x) = \beta(\omega) e^{x\omega} g(x)$, $(\omega, x) \in [0, 1]^2$ where $g(x) > 0$ and $\beta(\omega) > 0$. Then f satisfies the monotone likelihood ratio property. To prove this consider $a > b$ and $c > d$. Then*

$$\frac{f(a, c)}{f(a, d)} = \frac{\beta(a) e^{ac} g(c)}{\beta(a) e^{ad} g(d)} = e^{a(c-d)} \frac{g(c)}{g(d)}$$

$$\geq e^{b(c-d)} \frac{g(c)}{g(d)} = \frac{\beta(b) e^{bc} g(c)}{\beta(b) e^{bd} g(d)} = \frac{f(b, c)}{f(b, d)}.$$

An immediate consequence of the definition is as follows.

Lemma 1 *If the density of (X, Y) satisfies the monotone likelihood ratio property then for every $y \in [0, \bar{v}]$, $F_{Y|X}(y \mid x)/f_{Y|X}(y \mid x)$ decreases with x.*

Proof: The conditional density of Y given $X = x$ is $f_{Y|X}(y \mid x) = f(x, y)/\int_0^{\bar{v}} f(x, z) \, \mathrm{d}z$. The conditional distribution is therefore given by:

$$F_{Y|X}(y \mid x) = \int_0^y f_{Y|X}(z \mid x) \, \mathrm{d}z = \frac{\int_0^y f(x, z') \, \mathrm{d}z'}{\int_0^{\bar{v}} f(x, z) \, \mathrm{d}z}.$$

Thus,

$$\frac{F_{Y|X}(y\,|\,x)}{f_{Y|X}(y\,|\,x)} = \frac{\int_0^y f(x,z')\,\mathrm{d}z'}{\int_0^{\bar{v}} f(x,z)\,\mathrm{d}z} \Big/ \frac{f(x,y)}{\int_0^{\bar{v}} f(x,z)\,\mathrm{d}z} = \frac{\int_0^y f(x,z')\,\mathrm{d}z'}{f(x,y)}.$$

Suppose $x' > x$. Then for every $z' < y$, the monotone likelihood ratio property implies that $f(x',y)/f(x',z') \geq f(x,y)/f(x,z')$. Taking the reciprocal: $f(x,z')/f(x,y) \geq f(x',z')/f(x',y)$ and integrating we obtain

$$\frac{F_{Y|X}(y\,|\,x)}{f_{Y|X}(y\,|\,x)} = \frac{\int_0^y f(x,z')\,\mathrm{d}z'}{f(x,y)} \geq \frac{\int_0^y f(x',z')\,\mathrm{d}z'}{f(x',y)} = \frac{F_{Y|X}(y\,|\,x')}{f_{Y|X}(y\,|\,x')}. \qquad \square$$

Definition 7 *The random variables (X,Y) are affiliated if the joint density satisfies the monotone likelihood ratio property.*

When f is twice differentiable it turns out that we can characterize affiliation in the following way.

Proposition 1 *If the density $f\colon D \rightarrow \mathbb{R}_{++}$ is twice differentiable, then it satisfies the monotone likelihood ratio property if and only if $\partial^2/\partial x \partial y (\log f(x,y)) \geq 0$.*

Proof: First note that the following equivalences are true:

$$\frac{f(x,c)}{f(x,d)} \text{ is increasing in } x$$

$$\Updownarrow \qquad\qquad (4.5)$$

$$\log\left(\frac{f(x,c)}{f(x,d)}\right) \text{ is increasing in } x$$

$$\Updownarrow$$

$$\text{For every } x, \frac{\partial}{\partial x}(\log f(x,c) - \log f(x,d)) = \frac{\partial}{\partial x}\log\left(\frac{f(x,c)}{f(x,d)}\right) \geq 0.$$

Suppose first that f satisfies the monotone likelihood ratio property. Then whenever $c > d$, $f(x,c)/f(x,d)$ is increasing and therefore for every x, $\frac{\partial}{\partial x}\log f(x,c) - \frac{\partial}{\partial x}\log f(x,d) \geq 0$. Hence dividing by $c - d$ and making c converges to d we conclude that $\frac{\partial^2}{\partial x \partial y}(\log f(x,y)) \geq 0$. Reciprocally, if for every x, $\frac{\partial^2}{\partial x \partial y}(\log f(x,y)) \geq 0$ then if $c > d$ the last line of (4.5) is true. Hence, the first line is true and the monotone likelihood property as well. $\square$

Remark 3 *The proof above is from Karlin (1957). This proposition is easy to apply. For example, if $f(x,\omega) = \beta(\omega)\,\mathrm{e}^{x\omega}g(x)$ then*

$\log f(x, \omega) = \log(\beta(\omega)) + x\omega + \log g(x)$. _Therefore_, $\frac{\partial}{\partial x}(\log f(x, \omega)) = \omega + g'(x)/g(x)$ _and hence_ $\frac{\partial^2}{\partial \omega \partial x} \log f(x, \omega) = 1 > 0$.

The next theorem will not be used in this chapter but illustrates quite nicely a property of the densities with the monotone likelihood ratio property. This property is important in establishing the results in Chapter 5, specifically (5.10).

Theorem 4 *If $u(x, y)$ is increasing in both variables then $E[u(X, Y) | Y = y]$ is increasing in y.*

Proof: Suppose $y' < y''$. We suppose first that u does not depend on y. Then since $E[u(X)|Y = y] = \int u(x)f(x, y)\, dx / \int f(a, y)\, da$ we have to prove that

$$\frac{\int u(x)f(x, y')\, dx}{\int f(a, y')\, da} \leq \frac{\int u(x)f(x, y'')\, dx}{\int f(a, y'')\, da}.$$

This is equivalent to prove that

$$\int f(a, y'')f(b, y')u(b)\, da\, db = \int f(a, y'')\, da \cdot \int u(x)f(x, y')\, dx$$

$$\leq \int u(x)f(x, y'')\, dx \cdot \int f(a, y')\, da$$

$$= \int f(a, y')f(b, y'')u(b)\, da\, db.$$

We now rewrite the first integral as

$$\int f(a, y'')u(b)f(b, y')\, da\, db =$$

$$\int_{a<b} f(a, y'')u(b)f(b, y')\, da\, db + \int_{b\leq a} f(a, y'')u(b)f(b, y')\, da\, db =$$

$$\int_{a<b} f(a, y'')u(b)f(b, y')\, da\, db + \int_{a\leq b} f(b, y'')u(a)f(a, y')\, da\, db =$$

$$\int_{a<b} f(a, y'')u(b)f(b, y')\, da\, db + \int_{a<b} f(b, y'')u(a)f(a, y')\, da\, db =$$

$$\int_{a<b} (f(a, y'')f(b, y')u(b) + f(b, y'')f(a, y')u(a))\, da\, db.$$

Analogously we write

$$\int f(a, y')u(b)f(b, y'') \, \mathrm{d}a \, \mathrm{d}b$$

$$= \int_{a<b} (f(a, y')f(b, y'')u(b) + f(b, y')f(a, y'')u(a)) \, \mathrm{d}a \, \mathrm{d}b.$$

Finally, since $a < b$ we have that

$$f(a, y')f(b, y'')u(b) + f(b, y')f(a, y'')u(a) - f(a, y'')f(b, y')u(b)$$
$$- f(b, y'')f(a, y')u(a)$$
$$= f(a, y')f(b, y'')(u(b) - u(a)) + f(b, y')f(a, y'')(u(a) - u(b))$$
$$= (f(a, y')f(b, y'') - f(b, y')f(a, y''))(u(b) - u(a)) \geq 0.$$

This ends the proof if u does not depend on y. Let us consider now the general case. Suppose again that $y' < y''$. Define $\bar{u}(x) = u(x, y')$. Then by the previous case we have that

$$E[u(X, Y) \,|\, Y = y'] = E[u(X, y') \,|\, Y = y'] = E[\bar{u}(X) \,|\, Y = y']$$
$$\leq E[\bar{u}(X) \,|\, Y = y''] = E[u(X, y') \,|\, Y = y'']$$
$$\leq E[u(X, y'') \,|\, Y = y''] = E[u(X, Y) \,|\, Y = y'']. \qquad \square$$

4.3.1   Second-price Auctions

We now find equilibrium strategies for the second-price auction. We look for a symmetric equilibrium. We will first find a candidate equilibrium. Then we shall prove that our candidate is indeed an equilibrium. Thus suppose bidder 2 plays $b(y)$, a strictly increasing continuous bidding strategy. Let us find the best reply of bidder 1. If he bids $t \geq 0$ then he wins the object if $t > b(y)$ and the payment is $b(y)$. The expected utility is

$$E[(u(x, y) - b(y))I_{t>b(y)} \,|\, X = x].$$

However, since $b(\cdot)$ is continuous, the range of $b(\cdot)$ is a closed interval, say $[\alpha, \beta]$. If $t < \alpha$ the bidder never wins the object. If $t > \beta$ the bidder wins the object but also wins with $t = \beta$. Thus, to maximize the expected utility we may assume that $t \in [\alpha, \beta]$. That is, we assume that $t = b(s), s \in [0, \bar{v}]$. Bidder 1's expected profits, as a function of the announced type s (that implicitly defines the bid t), can be written as:

$$\pi(s) := E[(u(x, y) - b(y))I_{s>y} \,|\, X = x]$$
$$= \int_0^s (u(x, y) - b(y))f_{Y|X}(y \,|\, x) \, \mathrm{d}y.$$

Differentiating with respect to s we obtain

$$\pi'(s) = (u(x,s) - b(s))f_{Y|X}(s \mid x).$$

Thus if $s = x$ is to be optimal we need that $u(x,x) = b(x)$. We found the candidate equilibrium. We proceed to show that it is an equilibrium. First, note that $b(x) = u(x,x)$ is strictly increasing since $u(\cdot,\cdot)$ is non-decreasing in the second variable and strictly increasing in the first variable. Moreover, $b(x)$ is continuous as $u(\cdot,\cdot)$ is continuous by assumption. Thus,

$$\pi'(s) = (u(x,s) - u(s,s))f_{Y|X}(s \mid x).$$

If $s > x$ then $u(s,s) > u(x,s)$ and then $\pi'(s) < 0$. Analogously if $s < x$, $\pi'(s) > 0$. Therefore it is optimum to set $s = x$. We have proved the following result.

Theorem 5 (second-price auction equilibrium) *A symmetric equilibrium bidding strategy for the second-price auction with two bidders with affiliated values is $b_s(x) = u(x,x)$.*

Our reader will ask himself or herself whether affiliation was used at all in the above reasoning. It was not! This result is quite general. Note, however, that the interpretation of the symmetric equilibrium here is quite different from the interpretation under the IPV model. In the latter, a bidder bids his true valuation, whereas under affiliation a bidder bids:

$$b(x) = u(x,x) = E[u(x,y) \mid X = x, Y = x],$$

that is, the expected value of the object to this player conditional on the other player having received the same type. Recall that Theorem 4 implies that when $u(x,y)$ is increasing in both variables, $E[u(x,y) \mid Y = y]$ is also increasing in y.

4.3.2 First-price Auctions

In this section, we find a symmetric equilibrium of the first-price auction with affiliation. To be more precise, we want to prove the following.

Theorem 6 *The first-price auction has a symmetric equilibrium under affiliation described by a bid function $b_f \colon [0, \bar{v}] \to \mathbb{R}$ such that*

$$b_f(x) = u(x,x) - \int_0^x \exp\left[-\int_t^x \frac{f_{Y|X}(u \mid u)}{F_{Y|X}(u|u)}\,du\right]\left(\frac{d}{dt}(u(t,t))\right)\,dt. \quad (4.6)$$

Moreover, b_f solves

$$b_f'(x) = (u(x,x) - b_f(x))\frac{f_{Y|X}(x \mid x)}{F_{Y|X}(x \mid x)}; \quad (4.7)$$

$$b_f(0) = u(0,0).$$

Before proving the theorem, we first show where the differential equation (4.7) comes from. Suppose $b(\cdot)$ is continuous and strictly increasing. We assume that bidder 2 bids according to the function $b(\cdot)$ and we will find the best reply of bidder 1. The expected utility of bidder 1 when he bids $t = b(s)$ is given by:

$$\pi(s) = E[(u(x, y) - t)I_{t > b(y)} \mid X = x]$$
$$= E[(u(x, y) - b(s))I_{s > y} \mid X = x]$$
$$= \int_0^s (u(x, y) - b(s))f_{Y|X}(y \mid x)\, dy$$
$$= \int_0^s u(x, y)f_{Y|X}(y \mid x)dy - b(s)F_{Y|X}(s \mid x).$$

Note that once more we transformed bidder 1's problem from one where he was choosing a bid t, to one where he is choosing to announce a type s and then the bid is set at $b(s)$.

Differentiating $\pi(s)$ with respect to s we obtain

$$\pi'(s) = -b'(s)F_{Y|X}(s \mid x) + (u(x, s) - b(s))f_{Y|X}(s \mid x).$$

Thus if $s = x$ is to be optimal:

$$\pi'(x) = -b'(x)F_{Y|X}(x \mid x) + (u(x, x) - b(x))f_{Y|X}(x \mid x) = 0.$$

This yields the differential equation

$$b'(x) = (u(x, x) - b(x))\frac{f_{Y|X}(x \mid x)}{F_{Y|X}(x \mid x)}. \tag{4.8}$$

Note that if we set $u(x, x) = x$ in the expression above and the random variables X and Y are independent, we get

$$b'(x) = (x - b(x))\frac{f_Y(x)}{F_Y(x)}.$$

This is the same differential equation as in the IPV case.

We now solve differential equation (4.8). We will use the integrating factor method. Define

$$\gamma(s, x) = \frac{f_{Y|X}(s \mid x)}{F_{Y|X}(s \mid x)} \quad \text{and} \quad \gamma(s) = \frac{f_{Y|X}(s \mid s)}{F_{Y|X}(s \mid s)}.$$

We can rewrite (4.8) as

$$b'(x) + b(x)\gamma(x) = u(x, x)\gamma(x).$$

Define our integrating factor as $P(x) = \exp\left[-\int_x^{\bar{v}} \gamma(u)\,\mathrm{d}u\right]$. Thus

$$(Pb)'(x) = P(x)b'(x) + P'(x)b(x)$$
$$= P(x)b'(x) + \gamma(x)P(x)b(x)$$
$$= P(x)u(x,x)\gamma(x).$$

If $b(0) = u(0,0) = 0$ then integrating between 0 and x:

$$P(x)b(x) = \int_0^x P(t)u(t,t)\gamma(t)\,\mathrm{d}t.$$

Thus

$$b(x) = (P(x))^{-1}\int_0^x P(t)u(t,t)\gamma(t)\,\mathrm{d}t$$
$$= (P(x))^{-1}\int_0^x u(t,t)P'(t)\,\mathrm{d}t.$$

Integrating by parts the last integral we obtain:

$$b(x) = u(x,x) - (P(x))^{-1}\int_0^x P(t)\left(\frac{\mathrm{d}}{\mathrm{d}t}(u(t,t))\right)\,\mathrm{d}t.$$

Substituting $P(x)$ in the expression we obtain (4.6). Note that so far we have not used the affiliation assumption. Thus the solution above is potentially an equilibrium for any distribution function. However, we still need to check that $b(\cdot)$ is indeed an equilibrium. To do this will require affiliation.

From the reasoning above, since $b(\cdot)$ is strictly increasing and differentiable then

$$\pi'(s) = -b'(s)F_{Y|X}(s\,|\,x) + (u(x,s) - b(s))f_{Y|X}(s\,|\,x)$$
$$= F_{Y|X}(s\,|\,x)[-b'(s) + (u(x,s) - b(s))\gamma(s,x)]$$
$$= F_{Y|X}(s\,|\,x)[-b'(s) + (u(x,s) - u(s,s))\gamma(s,x) + (u(s,s) - b(s))\gamma(s,x)]$$
$$= F_{Y|X}(s\,|\,x)\left[-b'(s) + (u(x,s) - u(s,s))\gamma(s,x) + b'(s)\frac{\gamma(s,x)}{\gamma(s)}\right]$$
$$= F_{Y|X}(s\,|\,x)\left[(u(x,s) - u(s,s))\gamma(s,x) + b'(s)\left(\frac{\gamma(s,x)}{\gamma(s)} - 1\right)\right].$$

Thus if $s > x$,

$$\gamma(s,x) - \gamma(s) = \frac{F_{Y|X}(s\,|\,x)}{f_{Y|X}(s\,|\,x)} - \frac{F_{Y|X}(s\,|\,s)}{f_{Y|X}(s\,|\,s)} \geq 0$$

and $\pi'(s) < 0$. Also if $s < x$ then $\pi'(s) > 0$. Thus $s = x$ maximizes $\pi(s)$ ending the proof of the theorem.

4.3.3 Revenue Comparison

First note that bidder 1's expected payment in the second-price auction conditional on having received x is given by

$$P_{\text{sp}}(x) = \int_0^x u(y, y) f_{Y|X}(y \mid x) \, dy.$$

Thus, from the seller's point of view, her expected revenue is simply twice the expected value of $P_{\text{sp}}(x)$—the seller does not know bidder 1's (and bidder 2's) type and therefore she has to compute this expected value; her expected revenue.

Bidder 1's expected payment in the first-price auction is simply his bid times the probability that he wins with this bid:

$$P_{\text{fp}}(x) = b_{\text{f}}(x) F_{Y|X}(x \mid x).$$

Note that we can rewrite $P_{\text{sp}}(x)$ as:

$$P_{\text{sp}} = \int_0^x (u(y, y) - b_{\text{f}}(y)) f_{Y|X}(y \mid x) \, dy + \int_0^x b_{\text{f}}(y) f_{Y|X}(y \mid x) \, dy.$$

By using (4.8) we can write:

$$P_{\text{sp}} = \int_0^x b_{\text{f}}'(y) \frac{F_{Y|X}(y \mid y)}{f_{Y|X}(y \mid y)} f_{Y|X}(y \mid x) \, dy + \int_0^x b_{\text{f}}(y) f_{Y|X}(y \mid x) \, dy$$

$$\geq \int_0^x b_{\text{f}}'(y) F_{Y|X}(y \mid x) \, dy + \int_0^x b_{\text{f}}(y) f_{Y|X}(y \mid x) \, dy$$

$$= \int_0^x (b_{\text{f}}(y) F_{Y|X}(y \mid x))' \, dy = b_{\text{f}}(x) F_{Y|X}(x \mid x) = P_{\text{fp}}.$$

The last inequality follows from Lemma 1 which implies that:

$$\frac{F_{Y|X}(y \mid y)}{f_{Y|X}(y \mid y)} \geq \frac{F_{Y|X}(y \mid x)}{f_{Y|X}(y \mid x)} \quad \text{for } y \leq x.$$

Therefore, the expected revenue of the second-price sealed-bid auction is not less than the expected revenue of the first-price sealed-bid auction: $2E[P_{\text{sp}}] \geq 2E[P_{\text{fp}}]$.

Example 9 *Suppose the joint density of (X, Y) is*

$$f(x, y) = \frac{4(1 + xy)}{5}, \quad (x, y) \in [0, 1]^2.$$

It is easy to check that f has a monotone likelihood ratio. The marginal density of X is $f_X(x) = \int_0^1 f(x, y) \, dy = (4 + 2x)/5$ the conditional density is $f_{Y|X}(y \mid x) = f(x, y)/f_X(x) = 2(1 + xy)/2 + x$ and the conditional distribution is $F_{Y|X}(y|x) = \int_0^y (2(1+xz)/(2+x)) \, dz = (2y + xy^2)/(2+x)$. We suppose *that $u(x, y) = x + by, b \geq 0$. Thus the second-price auction equilibrium bidding function is $b_s(x) = u(x, x) = (1+b)x$. To find the first-price auction equilibrium bidding function define $\gamma(x) = f_{Y|X}(x \mid x)/F_{Y|X}(x \mid x) = 2(1 + x^2)/x(2 + x^2)$. Thus, from equation (4.6), the first-price auction equilibrium bidding function is*

$$b_f(x) = (1 + b)x - (1 + b) \int_0^x \exp\left[-\int_t^x 2\frac{1 + u^2}{u(2 + u^2)}du\right] dt$$

$$= (1 + b)\left(x - \frac{(2 + x^2)^{3/2} - 2}{3x\sqrt{2 + x^2}}\right).$$

Bidder 1's expected payment in a second-price auction is

$$2(1 + b)\int_0^x y\frac{1 + xy}{2 + x}dy = \frac{1 + b}{3}x^2\frac{2x^2 + 3}{2 + x}.$$

Bidder 1's expected payment in a first-price auction is

$$b_f(x)F_{Y|X}(x \mid x) = (1 + b)\left(x^2 - \frac{(2 + x^2)^{3/2} - 2}{3\sqrt{2 + x^2}}\right)\frac{2 + x^2}{2 + x}.$$

Thus, we can write:

$$\frac{P_{sp} - P_{fp}}{1 + b} = \frac{x^2(2x^2 + 3)}{3(2 + x)} - \left(x^2 - \frac{(2 + x^2)^{3/2} - 2}{3\sqrt{2 + x^2}}\right)\frac{2 + x^2}{2 + x}.$$

See the plot of $(P_{sp} - P_{fp})/(1 + b)$ below. Note that $P_{sp} - P_{fp}$ is bounded away from zero.

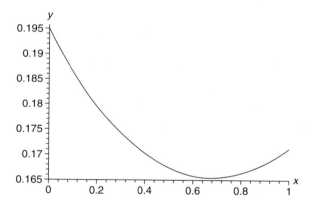

4.4   Exercises

1. Suppose there are two bidders with types distributed uniformly on the interval $[0, 1]$ and that the common value is given by $u(x_1, x_2) = 2x_1 - x_2$.

Find the equilibrium bidding strategies for the first- and second-price auctions. Compute the expected revenue associated with each auction format.

2. Suppose we have two bidders and that the common value is given by $u(x_1, x_2)$. Assume that types are independent. Give general conditions on $u(\cdot, \cdot)$ so that $b(x) = u(x, x)$ is a symmetric equilibrium bidding strategy of the second-price auction.

3. Check if the functions below satisfies the monotone likelihood ratio property:

    (a) $p(x, y) = \frac{nx^{n-1}}{y^n}, 0 < x < y$, and n a natural number;

    (b) $p(x, y) = n(n - 1)\frac{x^{n-2}(y-x)}{y^n}, 0 < x < y$ and $n \geq 2$ an integer;

    (c) $p(x, y) = \frac{1}{\pi} \frac{1}{1+(x-y)^2}, x, y \in \mathbb{R}$.

4. Calculate the seller's expected revenue for the second- and first-price auctions if the joint density is $f(x, y) = \frac{4(1+xy)}{5}$, $(x, y) \in [0, 1]^2$ and the common utility is $x + y$.

5. Discuss if the regret mentioned in (4.1.1) is an important concept?

6. Show that in the derivation of the second-price auction equilibrium it suffices that $u(x, y)$ is strictly increasing in the first variable and that $u(x, x)$ is increasing. Thus $u(x, y) = x - y/2$ is allowed?

7. Show that

$$F(x) = 1 - k \left(\frac{\sqrt{ax^2 + bx + c}}{1 - x} \right)^{-1/a+b+c} \exp\left[-\gamma \arctan\left(\frac{2xa + b}{\sqrt{4ac - b^2}} \right) \right]$$

defined on $x \in [0, 1]$ is a distribution function if $c > 0$, $4ac > b^2$, $\gamma = (2a + b)/(b + a + c)\sqrt{4ac - b^2}$ and k is chosen so that $F(0) = 0$. Show that you may chose a, b, c so that

$$\rho = \frac{1 - F(\rho)}{f(\rho)}$$

has three roots. Find the optimal reserve price for your choice of parameters.

8. Show that the bidding function (4.4) is continuous at zero if $b_0 = 0$.

9. Suppose $F(v) = v^2$ in the first-price auction example. Calculate the expected profit of the bidders and determine the "regret" region, that is,

$$\{(v, v_2); \text{bidder 1 regrets winning the auction}\}.$$

10. Generalize Theorem 4 to prove that $E[u(X, Y)|Y = y]$ is strictly increasing if $u(x, y)$ is strictly increasing in y.

5

Affiliated Values

As in the previous chapters, a single object will be sold to one of n bidders. Throughout this chapter, we assume once more that the seller's valuation for the object is equal to zero and she is risk neutral. Each bidder $j, j = 1, \ldots, n$, receives a type x_j and if $x = (x_1, x_2, \ldots, x_n)$ bidder i valuation is equal to $V_i = u_i(x)$—note that the value of the object for player i *does* depend on variables not observable by him, $x_{-i} = (x_1, \ldots, x_{i-1}, x_{i+1}, \ldots, x_n)$. Buyers' valuations are expressed in dollars and bidders are *risk-neutral*. The main distinction now vis-à-vis the previous chapters is that we will consider an auction model that will have the private and common value models seen before as special cases. In this chapter, we will explain in detail the notion of affiliation and analyze its implications in terms of equilibrium bidding functions and revenue.

The notion of affiliation, to be formally defined below, captures a global positive correlation between individuals' types, and allows the generalization of the theory of auctions beyond the private independent values case. The nature of correlation, however, will imply that the main result from the IPV case, namely, the Revenue Equivalence Theorem, will no longer hold. In particular, second-price sealed-bid auctions will generate (weakly) more expected revenue than first-price auctions. The English auctions, modeled as button auctions—and this modeling assumption will be extremely important for the result as we will argue below—will dominate in expected revenue second-price sealed-bid auctions. The strategic equivalence between the English button auction and the second-price auction will vanish under affiliation.

The main reference for this chapter is Milgrom and Weber (1982). However, we concentrate on distributions with density and provide more details. The chapter being on the whole more demanding and longer than the other chapters we deliberately leave out the results concerning the effects on the seller's revenue of credibly revealing information. The reader who wants to pursue these topics will do well to read the Milgrom and Weber paper. We expect that her or his task will be much facilitated by the study of this chapter. We also omit Milgrom and Weber's results regarding reserve prices and entry fees.

This chapter is organized as follows. In Section 5.1, we introduce the notion of affiliation in a general multivariate context and demonstrate a few theorems that are essential to understanding how affiliation works. Sections 5.2, 5.3, and 5.4, respectively, characterize equilibrium behavior in second-, first-price, and English button auctions. Section 5.5 contains the expected revenue comparisons for these three auction formats and Section 5.6 examines the effects of risk aversion.

5.1   The General Model

We now consider the case of $n \geq 2$ bidders. The set of possible types is $D = [0, \bar{v}]^n$. We will also impose that bidders are ex ante identical. To be able to define what that means with n bidders, we need to cover some preliminary ground work. Recall (Definition 4) that a permutation of S is a bijection on S. The symmetry definition to follow is very similar to Definition 5.

Definition 8   *A function $u : D \to \mathbb{R}$ is symmetric in the last $n - 1$ variables if for every permutation σ of the set $\{2, \ldots, n\}$ and for every $x \in D$,*
$$u(x_1, x_2, \ldots, x_n) = u(x_1, x_{\sigma(2)}, \ldots, x_{\sigma(n)}).$$

For example, when $n = 3$, $u(a, b, c)$ is symmetric in the last two variables if $u(a, b, c) = u(a, c, b)$ for every $(a, b, c) \in [0, \bar{v}]^3$. With four variables, $u(a, b, c, d)$ is symmetric in the last three variables if
$$u(a, b, c, d) = u(a, b, d, c) = u(a, c, b, d)$$
$$= u(a, c, d, b) = u(a, d, b, c) = u(a, d, c, b).$$

For example, the reader can check directly that the function
$$u(a, b, c, d) = a^2 + \frac{b + c + d}{2} + (bcd)^3$$
is symmetric in the last three variables.

Valuation symmetry   There exists a function $u : D \to \mathbb{R}$ such that $u_i(x) = u(x_i, x_{-i}), i = 1, \ldots, n$. The function u is symmetric in the last $n - 1$ variables, strictly increasing in the first variable and non-decreasing in the remaining variables.

Regularity $u : D \to \mathbb{R}$ is non-negative, continuous and strictly increasing.

Example 10   *The valuation function $u_i(x) = ax_i + b \sum_{j \neq i} x_j$ where $a > 0$ and $b \geq 0$ satisfies valuation symmetry. If $b = 0$ we have private values as in Chapter 3. If $a = b$ we have pure common values as in Chapter 4.*

We denote by $f(x)$ the joint probability density of the random variables $X_1, \ldots, X_n$. The density $f(\cdot)$ satisfies the following assumption:

Symmetry $f(\cdot)$ is symmetric in its n arguments.

For example, if f is symmetric then $f(x_1, x_2, x_3, \ldots, x_n) = f(x_2, x_1, x_3, \ldots, x_n)$. Thus $f(x_1, x_2) = x_1 + x_2$ is symmetric but $g(x_1, x_2) = 2x_1 + 6x_2^2$ is not.

We will also assume that $f(\cdot)$ is strictly positive and continuous in its domain. To define affiliation we need to specify some notation.

For every $x, y \in \mathbb{R}^n$ we denote the coordinate-wise supremum by $x \vee y$ and the coordinate-wise minimum by $x \wedge y$. Thus

$$x \vee y = (\max\{x_1, y_1\}, \ldots, \max\{x_n, y_n\})$$

and

$$x \wedge y = (\min\{x_1, y_1\}, \ldots, \min\{x_n, y_n\}).$$

For example take two vectors $x, y \in \mathbb{R}^4$, $x = (1, 2, 3, 4)$ and $y = (0, 1, 5, 2)$. Then $x \vee y = (1, 2, 5, 4)$ and $x \wedge y = (0, 1, 3, 2)$.

A non-negative function $f : D \to \mathbb{R}$ has the multivariate monotone likelihood ratio property if for every $x, y \in D$,

$$f(x \vee y) f(x \wedge y) \geq f(x) f(y).$$

We now define affiliation.

Definition 9   *The random variables $(X_1, \ldots, X_n)$ are affiliated if the joint density $f : D \to \mathbb{R}$ has the multivariate monotone likelihood ratio property.*

For example, let us check that independent random variables are affiliated. Independence implies that the joint density can be written as $f(x) = f_1(x_1) f_2(x_2) \cdots f_n(x_n)$. Then

$$f(x \vee y) f(x \wedge y) = \prod_{i=1}^n f_i(\max\{x_i, y_i\}) \, f_i(\min\{x_i, y_i\})$$

$$= \prod_{i=1}^n f_i(x_i) \, f_i(y_i) = f(x) \, f(y).$$

Above we used that $\{\max\{x_i, y_i\}, \min\{x_i, y_i\}\} = \{x_i, y_i\}$. We now prove a series of theorems that will be needed to allow us to characterize equilibrium bidding strategies for different auction formats and to compare the expected revenue they generate. The next result allows us to check directly whether a symmetric density is affiliated.

Theorem 7 *A symmetric density function $f : D \to \mathbb{R}$ is affiliated if for every $z \in [0, \bar{v}]^{n-2}$, the function*

$$(x_1, x_2) \to f(x_1, x_2, z)$$

satisfies the monotone likelihood ratio property.

Proof: From Proposition (10) in Appendix C it is enough to show that the density has a monotone likelihood ratio for every pair of variables (x_i, x_j). From symmetry, however, it is enough to show the monotone likelihood ratio property for (x_1, x_2). $\qquad\qquad\square$

Corollary 2 *The multivariate monotone likelihood ratio property holds for a twice differentiable function f if and only if $\frac{\partial^2}{\partial x_i \partial x_j} \log(f(x)) \geq 0$ for any $i \neq j$.*

For example if the random variables $X_1, X_2, \ldots, X_n$ are independent then $f(x_1, x_2, \ldots, x_n) = f_1(x_1) f_2(x_2) \cdots f_n(x_n)$ has the monotone likelihood ratio property since $\frac{\partial^2}{\partial x_i \partial x_j} \log f(x) = 0$.

As in the private and common value cases, the properties of the distribution of the highest types play an important role in deriving equilibrium behavior. Following the notation of previous chapters, we consider the different auction games from bidder 1's perspective and we denote by y^1 the largest type among $\{x_2, \ldots, x_n\}$, by y^2 the second largest and so on until y^{n-1} the $n-1$ largest (that is, the smallest) types among $\{x_2, \ldots, x_n\}$. Our symmetry assumption allows us to write

$$u_1(x) = u(x_1, x_{-1}) = u(x_1, y), \quad \text{with } y = (y^1, y^2, \ldots, y^{n-1}).$$

If $(X_1, X_2, \ldots, X_n)$ is a vector of random variables the $(X_1, Y^1, Y^2, \ldots, Y^{n-1})$ is the vector of random variables where $Y^1(\omega)$ is the largest of the numbers $\{X_2(\omega), \ldots, X_n(\omega)\}$. Then $Y^2(\omega)$ is the second largest and so on. Let us find the density of $(X_1, Y^1, Y^2, \ldots, Y^{n-1})$, knowing the density $f(x_1, x_2, \ldots, x_n)$ of $(X_1, X_2, \ldots, X_n)$.

Lemma 2 *The density of $(X_1, Y^1, Y^2, \ldots, Y^{n-1})$ is*

$$\bar{f}(x_1, y) = \begin{cases} (n-1)! f(x_1, y_1, \ldots, y_{n-1}) & \text{if } y_1 \geq \cdots \geq y_{n-1}, \\ 0 & \text{otherwise.} \end{cases} \tag{5.1}$$

Proof: We first find the distribution of $(X_1, Y^1, Y^2, \ldots, Y^{n-1})$. This is, for a given $(\bar{x}_1, a_1, \ldots, a_{n-1})$ defined by

$$F_{X_1, Y}(\bar{x}_1, \bar{a}_1, \ldots, \bar{a}_{n-1}) = \Pr[(X_1, Y^1, Y^2, \ldots, Y^{n-1}) \leq (\bar{x}_1, \bar{a}_1, \bar{a}_2, \ldots, \bar{a}_{n-1})]$$

$$= \Pr[X_1 \leq \bar{x}_1, Y^1 \leq \bar{a}_1, \ldots, Y^{n-1} \leq \bar{a}_{n-1}].$$

Now define $\mathcal{P}_{n-1}$ as the set of all permutations of $\{2, \ldots, n\}$. That is, $\sigma : \{2, \ldots, n\} \to \{2, \ldots, n\}$ is a permutation if it is a bijection. If $\sigma \in \mathcal{P}_{n-1}$ we define the set

$$C_\sigma = \{(x_2, \ldots, x_n) : x_{\sigma(2)} > \cdots > x_{\sigma(n)}\}.$$

The sets $C_\sigma, \sigma \in \mathcal{P}_{n-1}$ are pairwise disjoint. The union of C_σ is $\mathbb{R}^{n-1}$ except for the subset $\cup_{i \neq j} \{x \in \mathbb{R}^{n-1} ; x_i = x_j\}$. Since $\Pr[X_i = X_j] = 0$ (see Lemma 11 on page 151.) Hence

$$\Pr[X_1 \leq x_1, Y^1 \leq \bar{a}_1, \ldots, Y^{n-1} \leq \bar{a}_{n-1}]$$

$$= \sum_{\sigma \in \mathcal{P}_{n-1}} \Pr[X_1 \leq x_1, (X_2, \ldots, X_n) \in C_\sigma, X_{\sigma(2)} \leq \bar{a}_1, \ldots, X_{\sigma(n)} \leq \bar{a}_{n-1}]$$

$$= \sum_{\sigma \in \mathcal{P}_{n-1}} \Pr[X_1 \leq x_1, X_{\sigma(2)} > \cdots > X_{\sigma(n)}, X_{\sigma(2)} \leq \bar{a}_1, \ldots, X_{\sigma(n)} \leq \bar{a}_{n-1}]$$

$$= (n-1)! \Pr[X_1 \leq x_1, X_2 > \cdots > X_n, X_2 \leq \bar{a}_1, \ldots, X_n \leq \bar{a}_{n-1}]$$

$$= (n-1)! \int_0^{x_1} \int_{x_2=0}^{\bar{a}_1} \cdots \int_{x_n=0}^{\bar{a}_{n-1}} I_{x_2 > x_3 > \ldots > x_n} f(x) \, dx_1 dx_2 \ldots dx_n.$$

In the third line to the fourth line above we used the symmetry of the density $f(x)$ and that there are $(n-1)! = (n-1)(n-2)\cdots 3 \cdot 2$ permutations of $n-1$ elements. Therefore the distribution has a density $(n-1)! I_{x_2 > x_3 > \ldots > x_n} f(x)$. $\square$

Theorem 8 *If f is affiliated in X and symmetric then the random variables $X_1, Y_1, \ldots, Y_{n-1}$ are affiliated.*

Proof: First note that joint density of $X_1, Y_1, \ldots, Y_{n-1}$ is $\bar{f}(x, y)$

We now show that $\bar{f}$ has the multivariate monotone likelihood ratio property. We must show that

$$\bar{f}(x_1 \vee x_1', y \vee y') \bar{f}(x_1 \wedge x_1', y \wedge y') \geq \bar{f}(x_1, y) \bar{f}(x_1', y').$$

The right-hand side is different from zero only when $y_1 \geq \cdots \geq y_{n-1}$ and $y_1' \geq \cdots \geq y_{n-1}'$. In this case $\bar{f}(x_1, y) \bar{f}(x_1', y') = ((n-1)!)^2 f(x_1, y) f(x_1', y)$. Since $y_j \vee y_j' \geq y_{j+1}$ and $y_j \vee y_j' \geq y_{j+1}'$ we have that $y_j \vee y_j' \geq y_{j+1} \vee y_{j+1}'$ and so on: $y_1 \vee y_1' \geq y_2 \vee y_2' \geq \cdots \geq y_n \vee y_n'$. Analogously for the infimum. Thus,

$$\bar{f}(x_1 \vee x_1', y \vee y') \bar{f}(x_1 \wedge x_1', y \wedge y')$$

$$= ((n-1)!)^2 f(x_1 \vee x_1', y \vee y') f(x_1 \wedge x_1', y \wedge y')$$

$$\geq ((n-1)!)^2 f(x_1, y) f(x_1', y') = \bar{f}(x_1, y) \bar{f}(x_1', y'). \quad \square$$

We will now show that the function $E[V_1 \mid X_1 = x, Y_1 = y, \ldots, Y_{m-1} = y_{m-1}]$ is strictly increasing in x. Of course, there is no significance attached to the subscript 1 in V_1, since by symmetry if this function is increasing, it will still be increasing when we exchange subscripts.

Consider now the conditional expectation

$$h(x_{m+1}, \ldots, x_n) = E[u(x) \mid x_{m+1}, \ldots, x_n]$$

$$= \int u(x) \frac{f(x)}{\hat{f}(x_1, \ldots, x_m)} \, \mathrm{d}x_1 \cdots \mathrm{d}x_m,$$

where $\hat{f}(x_1, \ldots, x_m) = \int f(x_1, \ldots, x_n) \, \mathrm{d}x_{m+1} \cdots \mathrm{d}x_n$. If we prove that h is strictly increasing we will obtain our result for the conditional expectation. To do this, the following theorem is necessary.

Theorem 9 *Let f_1, f_2, f_3, and f_4 be non-negative functions on $\mathbb{R}^n$ such that for all $x, y \in \mathbb{R}^n$, $f_1(x) f_2(y) \leq f_3(x \vee y) f_4(x \wedge y)$. Then*

$$\int f_1(x) \, \mathrm{d}x \int f_2(x) \, \mathrm{d}x \leq \int f_3(x) \, \mathrm{d}x \int f_4(x) \, \mathrm{d}x.$$

This theorem is proved in Appendix C. We can now prove that the conditional expectation is increasing.

Theorem 10 *Suppose $(X_1, \ldots, X_n)$ is a random vector with affiliated density. Then for any increasing function $u : X \to \mathbb{R}_+$ we have that*

$$E[u(X) \mid X_{k+1} = x_{k+1}, \ldots, X_n = x_n]$$

is increasing in $(x_{k+1}, \ldots, x_n)$.

Proof: Define $z = (x_{k+1}, \ldots, x_n)$, $z' = (x^*_{k+1}, \ldots, x^*_n)$ and suppose $x_{k+1} \leq x^*_{k+1}, \ldots, x_n \leq x^*_n$. Define

$$g(z) = \int f(x_1, \ldots, x_k, z) \, \mathrm{d}x_1 \cdots \mathrm{d}x_k$$

and

$$g(z') = \int f(x_1, \ldots, x_k, z') \, \mathrm{d}x_1 \cdots \mathrm{d}x_k.$$

We now choose

$$f_1(x) = u(x) f(x \mid z), \quad f_2(x) = f(x \mid z'), \quad f_3(x) = u(x) f(x \mid z')$$

and finally $f_4(x) = f(x \mid z)$. Since

$$E[u(X) \mid X_{k+1} = x_{k+1}, \ldots,_n = x_n]$$

$$= \int u(x) f(x \mid z) \, \mathrm{d}x_1 \cdots \mathrm{d}x_k = \int f_1(x) \, \mathrm{d}x_1 \cdots \mathrm{d}x_k \cdot \int f_2(x) \, \mathrm{d}x_1 \cdots \mathrm{d}x_k$$

and

$$E[u(X) \mid X_{k+1} = x^*_{k+1}, \ldots, X_n = x^*_n]$$

$$= \int u(x)f(x \mid z') \, \mathrm{d}x_1 \cdots \mathrm{d}x_k = \int f_3(x) \, \mathrm{d}x_1 \cdots \mathrm{d}x_k \cdot \int f_4(x) \, \mathrm{d}x_1 \cdots \mathrm{d}x_k$$

it suffices to show that $f_1(x)f_2(y) \le f_3(x \vee y)f_4(x \wedge y)$ to finish the proof:

$$\frac{f_1(x)f_2(y)}{f_3(x \vee y)f_4(x \wedge y)} = \frac{u(x)f(x \mid z)f(y \mid z')}{u(x \vee y)f(x \vee y \mid z')f(x \wedge y \mid z)}$$

$$= \frac{u(x)f(x, z)f(y, z')}{g(z)g(z')u(x \vee y)f(x \vee y \mid z')f(x \wedge y \mid z)}$$

$$= \frac{u(x)f(x, z)f(y, z')}{u(x \vee y)f(x \vee y, z')f(x \wedge y, z)} \le 1. \qquad \square$$

Corollary 3   *If $u(x)$ is strictly increasing in x_i then*

$$E[u(X) \mid X_{k+1} = x_{k+1}, \ldots, X_n = x_n], \quad k < i$$

is strictly increasing in x_i too.

Proof: Suppose $i = k + 1$ and $x'_{k+1} > x_{k+1}$. Define $v(x) = u(x'_i, x_{-i})$. Since v is increasing the last theorem implies that

$$E[v(X) \mid X_i = x_i, \ldots, X_n = x_n] \le E[v(X) \mid X_i = x'_i, \ldots, X_n = x_n].$$

On the other hand, $u(x) < u(x_{-i}, x'_i) = v(x)$ for every x_{-i}. Thus,

$$E[u(X) \mid X_i = x_i, \ldots, X_n = x_n] < E[v(X) \mid X_i = x_i, \ldots, X_n = x_n]$$

$$\le E[v(X) \mid X_i = x'_i, \ldots, X_n = x_n]. \qquad \square$$

5.2   Second-price Auctions

The theoretical results established in the previous section will be useful in characterizing bidders' equilibrium behavior and comparing the expected revenue generated by different auction formats. We start by computing equilibrium bidding strategies in a second-price sealed-bid auction. As before we will consider the auction game from the perspective of bidder 1. Thus, it is convenient to define

$$w = \max_{j \ne 1} b(x_j).$$

Define the following function

$$v(x,y) = E[V_1 \mid X_1 = x, Y^1 = y]$$

$$= \int u(x,y,y_2,\ldots,y_{n-1}) \frac{\bar{f}(x,y,y_2,\ldots,y_{n-1})}{f_{X,Y}(x,y)} \, \mathrm{d}y_2 \cdots \mathrm{d}y_{n-1}.$$

Here

$$f_{X,Y}(x,y) = \int \bar{f}(x,y,y_2,\ldots,y_{n-1}) \, \mathrm{d}y_2 \cdots \mathrm{d}y_{n-1},$$

is the joint density of (X, Y^1). By the Corollary 3, $v(x,y)$ is strictly increasing in x and increasing in y. We will show that the equilibrium bidding function is given by:

$$b_s(x) = v(x,x) = E[V_1 \mid X_1 = x, Y^1 = x]. \tag{5.2}$$

Suppose bidders $i = 2,\ldots,n$ bid accordingly to $b(\cdot)$ which is continuous and strictly increasing. Bidder 1's expected profits conditional on having received a type x, chosen a bid t and given that other players are following bidding strategy $b(\cdot)$, are given by:

$$\pi(x,t) = E[(V_1 - w)I_{t>w} \mid X_1 = x], \tag{5.3}$$

where I indicates a characteristic function determining the cases where player 1 wins the auction. Thus, bidder 1's problem is to choose a bid $t \geq 0$ to maximize his or her expected utility. We are after the symmetric equilibrium, so we will assume that bidders $2,\ldots,n$ are following the equilibrium bidding strategy $b(\cdot)$ given in (5.2) and we will find bidder 1's best response. From Theorem 5, we can conclude that $b(\cdot)$ is increasing in x and therefore we can write

$$w = \max b(x_j) = b(Y_1).$$

Thus we can rewrite (5.3) as:

$$\pi(x,t) = E[(V_1 - b(Y_1))I_{t>b(Y_1)} \mid X_1 = x]. \tag{5.4}$$

Since $b(\cdot)$ is continuous, the range of $b(\cdot)$ is an interval $[u,v]$. If $t < u$, bidder 1 will never win the object. If $t > v$ bidder 1 wins the object but he wins with $t = v$ as well. Thus we may suppose $t \in [u,v]$ and, therefore there exists $s \in [0,\bar{v}]$ such that $b(s) = t$. Hence, we can write bidder 1's expected profits as a function of s alone:

$$h(s) = \pi(x,t) = E[(V_1 - b(Y_1))I_{s>Y_1} \mid X_1 = x].$$

Let $f_{Y|X}$ denote the conditional density of Y_1 given X_1 and $f_{X,Y}$ the joint density of (X_1, Y^1). By using the theorem of iterated conditional expectations (see Lemma 12), we can write:

$$h(s) = E[E[(V_1 - b(Y_1)I_{s>Y_1} \mid X_1, Y_1)] \mid X_1 = x]$$
$$= E[(E[V_1 \mid X_1, Y_1] - b(Y_1))I_{s>Y_1} \mid X_1 = x]$$
$$= \int_0^s (v(x,y) - b(y))f_{Y|X}(y \mid x)\,\mathrm{d}y.$$

Thus, differentiating we obtain

$$h'(s) = (v(x,s) - b(s))f_{Y|X}(s \mid x).$$

If $s = x$ is the optimal solution, $b(x) = v(x,x)$.

Hence, we have shown that bidder 1, who has received a type x, will bid according to (5.2). At this stage we can compute bidder 1's expected payment conditional on receiving a type $X_1 = x$:

$$P^{\mathrm{SP}} = E[b(Y_1) \mid X_1 = x, x > Y_1]$$
$$= E[v(Y_1, Y_1) \mid X_1 = x, x > Y_1] = \int_0^x v(\omega, \omega)f_{Y|X}(\omega \mid x)\,\mathrm{d}\omega. \tag{5.5}$$

The seller's expected revenue from a second-price auction in a symmetric environment is simply n times this expected payment.

5.3 First-price Auctions

Our main task in this section is to characterize equilibrium behavior in a first-price auction game. We will use the same approach as above and show directly that the symmetric equilibrium bidding function is given by (see equation 4.6):

$$b_{\mathrm{f}}(x) = v(x,x) - \int_0^x e^{\int_x^t \gamma(s)\,\mathrm{d}s}\,\frac{\mathrm{d}}{\mathrm{d}t}\,(v(t,t))\,\mathrm{d}t. \tag{5.6}$$

Recall that $\gamma(s) = f_{Y|X}(s \mid s)/F_{Y|X}(s \mid s)$. To find an equilibrium bidding strategy we first find a candidate equilibrium. Then we will show that our candidate is indeed an equilibrium. So suppose $b(\cdot)$ is a strictly increasing bidding strategy played by bidders $i \geq 2$. Let us find bidder 1's best response. The range of $b(\cdot)$ is an interval $[u, v]$. If bidder 1 bids $t < u$, he will never win the object. If $t > v$, then the bidder always wins but pays more than necessary. Thus we may suppose $t \in [u, v]$. We may therefore look for $s \in [0, \bar{v}]$ to maximize

$$h(s) = E[(V_1 - b(s))I_{b(s)>b(Y_1)} \mid X_1 = x]$$
$$= E[(V_1 - b(s))I_{s>Y_1} \mid X_1 = x].$$

If $v(x,y) = E[V_1 \mid X_1 = x, Y_1 = y]$ then

$$h(s) = E[(v(x,Y_1) - b(s))I_{s>Y_1} \mid X_1 = x]$$
$$= \int_0^s (v(x,y) - b(s))f_{Y|X}(y \mid x)\,\mathrm{d}y$$
$$= \int_0^s v(x,y)f_{Y|X}(y \mid x)\,\mathrm{d}y - b(s)F_{Y|X}(s \mid x).$$

Differentiating, we obtain

$$h'(s) = v(x,s)f_{Y_1|X_1}(s \mid x) - b'(s)F_{Y_1|X_1}(s \mid x) - b(s)f_{Y_1|X_1}(s \mid x).$$

If $s = x$ is to be optimal then

$$v(x,x)f_{Y|X}(x \mid x) - b'(x)F_{Y|X}(x \mid x) - b(x)f_{Y|X}(x \mid x) = 0.$$

Or

$$b'(x) = (v(x,x) - b(x))\frac{f_{Y|X}(x \mid x)}{F_{Y|X}(x \mid x)}. \tag{5.7}$$

The initial condition is $b(0) = v(0,0) = 0$. This differential equation is an old companion (see equation (4.7, page 51)) and its solution is:

$$b_{\mathrm{f}}(x) = u(x,x) - \int_0^x \exp\left[-\int_t^x \gamma(u)\,\mathrm{d}u\right] \left(\frac{\mathrm{d}}{\mathrm{d}t}(u(t,t))\right)\,\mathrm{d}t. \tag{5.8}$$

We now show that $b_{\mathrm{f}}(\cdot)$ as defined in (5.8) is a symmetric equilibrium bidding function.

It is clear that b_{f} is differentiable. From the differential equation we see that $b_{\mathrm{f}}(\cdot)$ is strictly increasing. Thus, if bidders play b_{f} the expected utility of bidder 1 when he bids $t = b_{\mathrm{f}}(s)$ is

$$h(s) = \int_0^s v(x,y)f_{Y|X}(y \mid x)\,\mathrm{d}y - b_{\mathrm{f}}(s)F_{Y|X}(s \mid x).$$

Thus

$$h'(s) = (v(x,s) - b_{\mathrm{f}}(s))f_{Y|X}(s \mid x) - b_{\mathrm{f}}'(s)F_{Y|X}(s \mid x).$$

We now use equation (5.7) in the first summand above:

$$(v(x,s) - b_{\mathrm{f}}(s))f_{Y|X}(s \mid x)$$
$$= (v(x,s) - v(s,s))f_{Y|X}(s \mid x) + (v(s,s) - b_{\mathrm{f}}(s))f_{Y|X}(s \mid x)$$
$$= (v(x,s) - v(s,s))f_{Y|X}(s \mid x) + b_{\mathrm{f}}'(s)\frac{f_{Y|X}(s \mid x)}{\gamma(s)}.$$

Thus

$$
h'(s) = (v(x,s) - v(s,s))f_{Y|X}(s \mid x) + b'_{\mathrm{f}}(s)\left(\frac{f_{Y|X}(s \mid x)}{\gamma(s)} - F_{Y|X}(s \mid x)\right)
$$

$$
= (v(x,s) - v(s,s))f_{Y|X}(s \mid x) + b'_{\mathrm{f}}(s)f_{Y|X}(s \mid x)\left(\frac{1}{\gamma(s)} - \frac{1}{\gamma(s,x)}\right).
$$

If $s > x$ then $v(x,s) - v(s,s) < 0$ and $f_{Y|X}(s \mid x)/F_{Y|X}(s \mid x) - f_{Y|X}(s \mid s)/F_{Y|X}(s \mid s) \leq 0$. And reciprocally if $s < x$, $h'(s) > 0$. Thus $s = x$ maximizes $h(s)$. That is, the strategy described in (5.8) is a symmetric equilibrium for the first-price auction.

We can now compute bidder 1's expected payment in a first-price auction. It is simply his bid multiplied by the probability that he has the highest bid and therefore wins the auction. Note that the probability of winning is equal to the probability of having the highest type, given that the equilibrium bidding strategies are strictly increasing. Thus, bidder 1's expected payment is:

$$
P^{\mathrm{FP}} = b_{\mathrm{f}}(x)F_{Y|X}(x \mid x)
$$

$$
= \left(v(x,x) - \int_0^x e^{-\int_t^x \gamma(u)\,\mathrm{d}u}\left(\frac{\mathrm{d}}{\mathrm{d}t}(v(t,t))\right)\mathrm{d}t\right)F_{Y|X}(x \mid x). \qquad (5.9)
$$

The seller's expected revenue from a first-price auction is simply n times the expected payment from bidder 1. Recall that first-price auctions are still strategically equivalent to Dutch auctions under affiliation and therefore they generate the same expected payment.

5.4   English Auctions

We will model the English auction as in Milgrom and Weber (1982); bidders bid by pressing a button. The price rises continuously on an automatic clock. By releasing the button a bidder drops out of the auction. The auction ends when the next-to-last person releases the button. The winner is the bidder who is still pressing the button and he wins at a price equal to the amount at which the next-to-last person has dropped out.

Of course, actual ascending auctions might be quite different in many respects. For example, you might not know when a bidder has dropped out. In some sense, this particular formulation of the English auction as a button auction probably reveals the most amount of information; remaining bidders know how many bidders have dropped out and at what price. In particular, in this auction, it is a weakly dominant strategy to bid up to one's estimate of the value of the object. Instead of characterizing equilibrium behavior in general, we chose to consider the case of three bidders who have received actual private types $x_1 = a, x_2 = b, x_3 = c$, respectively, with $a < b < c$.

The implicit assumption is that the price starts at zero and rises continuously. The first player to drop out is player 1 at price p_1 such that:

$$E[V_1 \mid x_1 = a = X_2 = X_3] = p_1.$$

Prior to bidder 1 dropping out, the expected values of bidders 2 and 3 were given, respectively, by:

$$E[V_2 \mid x_2 = b = X_1 = X_3]$$

and

$$E[V_3 \mid x_3 = c = X_1 = X_2].$$

After bidder 1 dropping out, these expected values are revised in the following way:

$$E[V_2 \mid x_2 = b, E[V_2 \mid X_1 = X_2 = X_3 = a] = p_1]$$

and

$$E[V_3 \mid x_3 = c, E[V_3 \mid X_1 = X_2 = X_3 = a] = p_1].$$

The price keeps rising until the final price p_2 and the winner is determined as follows:

$$E[V_2 \mid x_2 = b = X_3, p_1] = p_2.$$

The value of the object to player 3 prior to knowing p_2 is

$$E[V_3 \mid x_3 = c = X_2, p_1].$$

Bidder 3 wins the auction at price p_2. The generalization to n players should be clear to the reader and the expected price in the English button auction (i.e., the expected payment from say bidder 1) is then

$$P^{\mathrm{E}} = E[E[V_1 \mid X_1 = y_1 = Y_2, Y_3, \cdots, Y_n] \mid X_1 = x > Y_1].$$

Note that the button English auction is not strategically equivalent to second-price auctions as in the case of independent private values. The reason is that now there is information being revealed that is used by players to update their valuations for the good. The implications of this information revelation for the ranking of auction formats according to the expected revenue they generate will be explored in the next section.

5.5 Expected Revenue Ranking

We will start by showing that the second-price auction generates (weakly) more revenue than the first-price auction. This generalizes the revenue comparison of Section 4.3.3. Recall that for the special case when types are independently and identically distributed, these different auctions formats yield the same expected revenue (see Chapter 3). Thus, given that IPV is a special case of affiliation, the ranking of auction formats according to the expected revenue they generate cannot be strict.

We will compare the expected payment by the winner in a second-price auction (5.5) with that in a first-price auction (5.9). Recall that

$$P^{\text{SP}} = \int_0^x v(y,y) f_{Y|X}(y \mid x)\, \mathrm{d}y.$$

Thus

$$
\begin{aligned}
P^{\text{SP}} &= \int_0^x (v(y,y) - b_{\text{f}}(y)) f_{Y|X}(y \mid x)\, \mathrm{d}y + \int_0^x b_{\text{f}}(y) f_{Y|X}(y \mid x)\, \mathrm{d}y \\
&= \int_0^x b_{\text{f}}'(y) \frac{F_{Y|X}(y \mid y)}{f_{Y|X}(y \mid y)} f_{Y|X}(y \mid x)\, \mathrm{d}y + \int_0^x b_{\text{f}}(y) f_{Y|X}(y \mid x)\, \mathrm{d}y \\
&\geq \int_0^x b_{\text{f}}'(y) F_{Y|X}(y \mid x)\, \mathrm{d}y + \int_0^x b_{\text{f}}(y) f_{Y|X}(y \mid x)\, \mathrm{d}y \\
&= b_{\text{f}}(x) F_{Y|X}(x \mid x) = P^{\text{FP}}.
\end{aligned}
$$

We now show that expected payment in an English button auction is (weakly) higher than that in a second-price auction. Recall that

$$v(y,y) = E[V \mid X_1 = y, Y_1 = y].$$

The theorem of iterated expectations allows us to write

$$
\begin{aligned}
v(y,y) &= E[E[V \mid X_1 = y, Y_1 = y, Y_{-1}] \mid X_1 = y, Y_1 = y] \\
&\leq E[E[V \mid X_1 = y, Y_1 = y, Y_{-1}] \mid X_1 = x, Y_1 = y]. \qquad (5.10)
\end{aligned}
$$

This last inequality follows from Theorem 7, which is implied by affiliation. The expected payment from bidder 1 in a second-price auction with $x > y$ is given by

$$P^{\text{SP}} = E[E[v(y,y) \mid X_1 = x, x > Y_1 = y]].$$

By applying the conditional expectation to both sides of (5.10) we obtain:

$$
\begin{aligned}
E[E[v(y,y) \mid X_1 = x, x > Y_1 = y]] & \\
\leq E[E[E[V \mid X_1 = Y_1, Y_{-1}] \mid X_1 = x > Y_1 \mid X_1 = x > Y_1] & \\
= E[E[V \mid X_1 = Y_1, Y_{-1}] \mid X_1 = x > Y_1] = P^{\text{E}}. &
\end{aligned}
$$

We will now refer to the linkage principle (Milgrom and Weber: 1110) to explain the ranking of auction formats when types are affiliated. Let's think of the auction games as direct revelation games—that is, instead of computing $b^*(\cdot)$ each bidder will take the equilibrium bidding function as given and instead will report a type t.

In these direct revelation games, prices (at equilibrium) depend on the winner's type and on other information (e.g., on other bidders' types). In a first-price auction, the equilibrium price is a function only of the winner's type. In a second-price auction, the expected price is a function of the highest and the second highest types. In an English button auction, the expected price is a function of all types. That is, in a first-price auction there is no linkage to other bidders' types whereas in the other auction formats the linkage is stronger in the English button auction. The linkage works to increase the expected value of the object to a bidder conditional on having received the highest type. The stronger the linkage the stronger is the increase (due to affiliation) and therefore the higher is the bid (at equilibrium) and, thus, the higher is the expected price.

5.6 Exercises

1. Prove that the product of functions with the monotone likelihood ratio property also has the multivariate monotone likelihood ratio property.
2. Justify the reasoning that lead to (4.1).
3. Suppose $g(x_1, \ldots, x_n)$ has the monotone likelihood ratio property. Suppose also that $\phi_i(x_i)$ is increasing for every i. Show that $g(\phi_1(x_1), \ldots, \phi_n(x_n))$ has the monotone likelihood ratio property. Apply this result to

$$g(x, y) = 1 + xy$$

   to conclude that

$$f(x, y) = \frac{1 + f(x)f(y)}{1 + \left(\int_0^1 f(x)\, \mathrm{d}x \right)^2}$$

   has a monotone likelihood ratio if $f(x)$ is increasing in $[0, 1]$. Is the same conclusion true if $f(x)$ is decreasing?

6

Mechanism Design

In this chapter, we will approach auctions from a more abstract perspective. We will use the approach of Myerson (1981) to show that much of auction theory under independent types can be cast as a mechanism design problem. In particular, we can use this approach to show that the revenue equivalence between first- and second-price, Dutch, and English auctions is in fact more general: under some hypotheses (that hold in the analysis of Chapter 3), any two mechanisms that allocate the object in the same way and that yield the same expected surplus to the individual with the lowest type will generate the same expected revenue for the seller. We will also use these tools to characterize the optimal auction—the one that maximizes the seller's expected revenue.

In Section 6.1, we set up the basic notation, explain the revelation principle and why we can restrict ourselves to direct mechanisms. In Section 6.2, we examine direct mechanisms. In Section 6.3, we demonstrate a general version of the Revenue Equivalence Theorem and characterize the optimal auction. Section 6.4 extends the analysis of the optimal auction to non-monotonic marginal valuations. In this section, we also discuss the optimal auction when types are correlated, revenue equivalence for common value auctions and when there are several identical objects for sale but demand is unitary.

6.1 The Revelation Principle

Although this chapter is more abstract than previous ones, the reader will be amply compensated by the generality of the results.

There are n bidders. Each player $i = 1, \ldots, n$ receives a type $x_i \in X_i = [0, \bar{v}]$ that is distributed accordingly to the distribution $F_i(x) = \int_0^x f_i(z) \, dz, x \in X_i$. The density $f_i : X_i \to \mathbb{R}$ is continuous and strictly positive. The set of individual types is denoted by $X = \Pi_{i=1}^n X_i = [0, \bar{v}]^n$.

   Each bidder knows his type and knows the distribution of the types of other bidders. That is, i knows that the other bidders' types, $x_{-i} \in X_{-i} = [0, \bar{v}]^{n-1}$, are distributed according to the density $f_{-i}(x_{-i}) = \Pi_{j \neq i} f_j(x_j)$. We assume that the types are independent random variables. Thus, the joint density is

$$f(x_1, \ldots, x_n) = f_1(x_1) \times \cdots \times f_n(x_n) \quad \text{for } x \in X. \qquad (6.1)$$

If $W(x)$ is a random variable we denote by $E_{-i}[W(x)]$ its expectation with respect to the variables x_{-i}. That is,

$$E_{-i}[W(x)] = \int W(x_i, x_{-i}) f_{-i}(x_{-i}) \, \mathrm{d}x_{-i}.$$

We also assume, as in previous chapters, that the seller values the object at zero and that bidder i's utility is $V_i = u_i(x) = x_i$. That is, we consider the Independent Private Values model, bidders are risk neutral and their utilities are expressed in dollars.

   We now must consider the mechanisms the seller may use when designing the revenue maximizing auction. The simplest procedure is to allow every bidder to announce a number (the bid) and by means of some auction rule decide who gets the object and how much each participating bidder pays. This setup would cover the first- and second-price auctions as particular cases. It would not, however, cover the English auction as it does not allow bidders to rebid. Therefore, the seller has to be allowed to use a more flexible mechanism. Thus, suppose that the seller designs, for each bidder i, a set S_i of the possible choices allowed for bidder i. Define $S = \Pi_{i=1}^n S_i$ as the set of joint choices of all bidders. The seller has to choose, for each $s \in S$, an allocation rule $q(s)$—that is, a probability vector $q(s) = (q_1(s), \ldots, q_n(s))$, where $q_i(s)$ is the probability that bidder i wins the object for sale—and a payment vector, $P(s) = (P_1(s), \ldots, P_n(s))$, where $P_i(s) \in \mathbb{R}$ is the expected payment for bidder i when he participates in the auction.

   Since participation in the auction is voluntary, we assume that for every i there exists $np \in S_i$, which is the non-participation strategy. Naturally, if $s \in S$ and $s_i = np$, then $P_i(s) = 0$ and $q_i(s) = 0$. Formally,

Definition 10 *An auction rule (or mechanism) is a triple (S, q, P) such that:*

   1. $S = \Pi_{i=1}^n S_i$;
   2. $q = (q_1, \ldots, q_n) : S \rightarrow [0,1]^n, \sum_{i=1}^n q_i(s) \leq 1$;
   3. $P = (P_1, \ldots, P_n) : S \rightarrow \mathbb{R}^n$;
   4. *If $s \in S$ and $s_i = np$ then $q_i(s) = 0$ and $P_i(s) = 0$.*

Example 12 (first-price auction) *We can write the first-price auction as an auction rule. Define $S_i = \mathbb{R}_+ \cup \{np\}, i = 1, \ldots, n$. If $s \in S \setminus \{(np, \ldots, np)\}$*

define

$$b^*(s) = \max\{s_i; s_i \neq np, 1 \leq i \leq n\} \quad and$$
$$J(s) = \{i \leq n; s_i = b^*(s)\}.$$

That is, $b^*(s)$ is the highest bid when s is chosen and at least one bidder participates and $J(s)$ denotes the set of bidders who have the highest bid. Then

$$q_i(s) = \begin{cases} \dfrac{1}{\#J(s)} & \text{if } i \in J(s) \\ 0 & \text{if } i \notin J(s) \end{cases} \quad and \quad P_i(s) = q_i(s)b^*(s).$$

define the auction rule where the object is allocated to the highest bidder and if there is more than one bidder with the highest bid, these bidders have an identical probability of winning.

The second-price auction is formalized in a similar fashion. The English auction, however, is more difficult to formalize.

Example 13 (English button auction) *First, recall that in the English button auction bidders keep pressing a button while the price rises continuously. For simplicity, we assume that $p_t = t$. If a bidder releases the button then he leaves the auction and cannot bid again. The object goes to the bidder who is last to release the button and the price paid is the price at which the last but one bidder left.*

To formalize the auction we define the strategy set of a bidder. It has an initial decision to participate (p) or not (np) in the auction. Then it has a departure rule for each time $t > 0$ as a function of:

(i) the set of bidders who are still active at time t;
(ii) the set of bidders who left the auction and the price at which they left the auction.

We assume that the auction ends at time $T > 0$ if there is more than one active bidder at this time. Define for each bidder i the sets

$$\Delta^i = \{p, np\}^{n-1} \cup \{(t, x_{-i}); t \in (0, T), x_j \in \{p, t\}\} \quad and$$
$$\Gamma^i = \{\phi; \phi : \Delta^i \to [0, T], \phi(t, x_{-i}) \geq t, \forall t \in (0, T)\}.$$

The interpretation is that if $x_j = p$ bidder j is still bidding. If $x_j \neq p$ then bidder j left at time x_j. For $\phi^i \in \Gamma^i$ and $z \in \{p, np\}^{n-1}$ we have that $\phi^i(z)$ is the time at which bidder i leaves the auction if the set of active bidders (i.e., $\{j; z_j = p\}$) do not change. If $t > 0, \phi^i(t, x_{-i})$ is the time at which i quits if all the bidders who are active at time t (i.e., $\{j; x_j = p\}$) remain active until time T. Note that i may quit immediately at time t. Finally, we specify the *strategy set:*

$$S^i = \Gamma^i \cup \{np\}.$$

Thus, $S = S_1 \times \cdots \times S_n$.

We must now define, for each $\phi \in S$, the allocation rule $q(\phi)$. That is, we need to specify who receives the object.

At time $t = 0$ we define $z_j^0 = np$ if $\phi^j = np$ and $z_j^0 = p$ if $\phi^j \neq np$. If $\phi^i(0, z_{-i}^0) = 0$ for every participating bidder i, then the auctioneer keeps the object and charges nothing. If there is only one i such that $\phi^i(0, z_{-i}^0) > 0$, this bidder i wins the object at price 0. Otherwise, define

$$\tau^1 = \min\{\phi^i(0, z_{-i}^0); \phi^i \neq np, \phi^i(0, z_{-i}^0) > 0\} \quad and$$
$$H^1 = \{i; \phi^i(0, z_{-i}^0) = \tau^1, \phi^i \neq np\}.$$

If there is no bidder i such that $\phi^i(0, z_{-i}^0) > \tau^1$, then the object is allocated to one of the members of H^1 with probability $1/\#H^1$ at price τ^1. Otherwise, the auction proceeds.

Define $z_i^1 = p$ for every participating bidder such that $\phi^i(0, z_{-i}^0) > \tau^1$. Define also $z_i^1 = \tau^1$ if $i \in H^1$. Finally $z_i^1 = np$ if $\phi^i = np$. We proceed inductively defining

$$\tau^2 = \min\{\phi^i(\tau^1, z_{-i}^1); \phi^i(\tau^1, z_{-i}^1) > \tau^1\},$$

$$z_j^2 = \begin{cases} np & if \ \phi^j = np \\ \tau^1 & if \ \phi^j(\tau^1, z_{-j}^1) = \tau^1 \\ p & if \ \phi^j(\tau^1, z_{-j}^1) > \tau^1 \end{cases}$$

and so on. The process stops eventually since at every step at least one bidder leaves. The object is allocated to the last bidder to leave and he pays the price at which the next to last bidder dropped out.

For the following definition, we consider a given auction mechanism (S, q, P).

Definition 11 *A Bayesian Nash equilibrium of the auction mechanism (S, q, P) is a vector of strategies, $(b_i^*(\cdot))_{i=1}^n$, where $b_i^* : X_i \to S_i$ is such that for every i,*

$$E_{-i}[q_i(b_i^*(x_i), b_{-i}^*(x_{-i}))x_i - P_i(b_i^*(x_i), b_{-i}^*(x_{-i}))]$$
$$= \max_{y \in S_i} E_{-i}[q_i(y, b_{-i}^*(x_{-i}))x_i - P_i(y, b_{-i}^*(x_{-i}))].$$

Thus, in a Bayesian Nash equilibrium, if bidders $j \neq i$ are using strategies $b_j^*(x_j)$, the best bidder i with signal x_i can do is to choose strategy $b_i^*(x_i)$. We also need the following definitions.

Definition 12 *An auction mechanism (S, q, P) is direct if for every i, $S_i = X_i$. The direct mechanism (X, q, P) is incentive compatible if*

$$E_{-i}[(q_i(x)x_i - P_i(x))] = \max_{y \in X_i} E_{-i}[q_i(y, x_{-i})x_i - P_i(y, x_{-i})].$$

Finally, the direct mechanism (X, q, P) is individually rational if

$$E_{-i}[(q_i(x)x_i - P_i(x))] \geq 0.$$

Thus, we will examine strategies of the type $b_i^*(x_i) = x_i$ as candidate for a Bayesian Nash equilibrium. The revelation principle says that we only need to consider direct mechanisms.

Theorem 12 (Revelation principle) *For any Bayesian Nash equilibrium $(b_1(\cdot), \ldots, b_n(\cdot))$ of an auction mechanism (S, q, P), there exists an incentive compatible, individually rational, direct mechanism that yields the seller and bidders the same expected utilities as in the original auction mechanism.*

Proof: Define for every $x \in X$ the mechanisms

$$\bar{q}(x) = q(b_1(x_1), \ldots, b_n(x_n)) \quad \text{and} \quad \bar{P}(x) = P(b_1(x_1), \ldots, b_n(x_n)).$$

Now from

$$E_{-i}[(\bar{q}_i(x)x_i - \bar{P}_i(x))] = E_{-i}[q_i(b(x))x_i - P_i(b(x))]$$

and

$$\sum_{i=1}^{n} \bar{P}_i(x) = \sum_{i=1}^{n} P_i(b(x)),$$

it is immediate that the direct mechanism $(\bar{q}, \bar{P})$ gives the same expected utilities to seller and bidders as the original mechanism. The mechanism is incentive compatible since $b(x)$ is a Bayesian Nash equilibrium. Moreover, it is individually rational since bidders always have the non-participation option in the original mechanism. $\square$

6.2 Direct Mechanisms

As a result of the revelation principle, we can without loss of generality concentrate our efforts into analyzing direct mechanisms. In what follows we make the assumption that the direct mechanisms are Riemann integrable. This assumption is necessary to make sense of the integrals and expected values that will be calculated. Thus, the direct mechanism (q, P) is individually rational if (it is Riemann integrable and)

$$E_{-i}[q_i(x)x_i - P_i(x)] \geq 0. \qquad (6.2)$$

Condition (6.2) says that player i's expected profits when his type is x_i and when all players announce their true types is non-negative.

Now we can turn our attention to the incentive compatibility constraint that for each player i, $i = 1, \ldots, n$, and for every $y \in X_i$, requires:

$$E_{-i}[q_i(x)x_i - P_i(x)] \geq E_{-i}[q_i(\tilde{x})x_i - P_i(\tilde{x})], \qquad (6.3)$$

where $\tilde{x} = (y, x_{-i})$. That is, the incentive compatibility condition (6.3) guarantees that when all players other than player i are revealing their true types, it is optimal for player i to reveal his true type. Now we can write player i's expected profits when his type is x_i and when he reveals x_i as

$$\pi_i(x_i) = Q_i(x_i)x_i - E_{-i}[P_i(x)], \qquad (6.4)$$

where $Q_i(x_i) = E_{-i}[q_i(x)]$. Condition (6.3) implies that

$$\begin{aligned}
\pi_i(x_i) &\geq Q_i(y)x_i - E_{-i}[P_i(y, x_{-i})] \\
&= Q_i(y)(x_i - y) + Q_i(y)y_i - E_{-i}[P_i(y, x_{-i})] \\
&= Q_i(y)(x_i - y) + \pi_i(y).
\end{aligned}$$

Thus, we can conclude that

$$\pi_i(x_i) - \pi_i(y) \geq (x_i - y)Q_i(y) \quad \text{for any } x_i, y \in X_i. \qquad (6.5)$$

It is immediate from (6.5) that $\pi_i(x_i)$ is non-decreasing. We now prove that Q_i is non-decreasing as well.

Proposition 3 $Q_i(\cdot)$ *is a non-decreasing function.*

Proof: Let us exchange x_i and y in (6.5) above to obtain

$$\pi_i(y) - \pi_i(x_i) \geq (y - x_i)Q_i(x_i). \qquad (6.6)$$

Adding equations (6.5) and (6.6) yields

$$0 \geq (x_i - y)[Q_i(y) - Q_i(x_i)] = -(x_i - y)[Q_i(x_i) - Q_i(y)]. \qquad \square$$

Our next task is to show that condition (6.3) also requires that $\pi_i(\cdot)$ takes a particular form. We need the following intermediate result.

Lemma 3 *Let* $x_i > y$. *Then*

$$Q_i(x_i) \geq \frac{\pi_i(x_i) - \pi_i(y)}{x_i - y} \geq Q_i(y).$$

The lemma follows in a direct fashion from equations (6.5) and (6.6). We now show that π_i is completely defined by $\pi_i(0)$ and q_i.

Theorem 13 *Player i's expected profits in any direct incentive compatible mechanism is given by*

$$\pi_i(x_i) = \pi_i(0) + \int_0^{x_i} Q_i(t)\,\mathrm{d}t$$

$$= \pi_i(0) + \int_0^{x_i} \int q_i(t, x_{-i}) f_{-i}(x_{-i})\,\mathrm{d}x_{-i}\,\mathrm{d}t. \qquad (6.7)$$

Proof: Partition the interval $[0, x_i]$ as follows:

$$\left[0, \frac{x_i}{n}, \frac{2x_i}{n}, \ldots, \frac{nx_i}{n} \right].$$

We can write

$$\pi_i(x_i) - \pi_i(0) = \sum_{j=1}^n \left[\pi_i\left(\frac{jx_i}{n}\right) - \pi_i\left(\frac{(j-1)x_i}{n}\right) \right]$$

$$= \pi_i\left(\frac{x_i}{n}\right) - \pi_i(0) + \pi_i\left(\frac{2x_i}{n}\right) - \pi_i\left(\frac{x_i}{n}\right) + \cdots$$

$$+ \pi_i\left(\frac{nx_i}{n}\right) - \pi_i\left(\frac{(n-1)x_i}{n}\right),$$

where the first equality comes from "telescoping" (that is, cancelling the terms with opposite signs). Lemma 3 then allows us to write

$$\pi_i(x_i) - \pi_i(0) \geq \sum_{j=1}^n Q_i\left(\frac{(j-1)x_i}{n}\right) \frac{x_i}{n}.$$

We have shown that $Q_i(\cdot)$ is monotone (therefore it has at most a countable number of discontinuities). Thus, $Q_i(\cdot)$ is Riemann integrable (in the expression above we have the lower sums) and as a result as we can take n to infinity (i.e., as our partition becomes finer and finer) to obtain

$$\pi_i(x_i) - \pi_i(0) \geq \int_0^{x_i} Q_i(t)\,\mathrm{d}t.$$

By following a similar process for the upper sums we can show that

$$\pi_i(x_i) - \pi_i(0) \leq \int_0^{x_i} Q_i(t)\,\mathrm{d}t. \qquad \square$$

An immediate consequence of this theorem is the determination of the payment mechanism.

Corollary 4 *If the direct mechanism (q, P) is incentive compatible and individually rational, then there exists an $a_i \geq 0$ such that*

$$E_{-i}[P_i(x)] = Q_i(x_i)x_i - a_i - \int_0^{x_i} Q_i(t)\, \mathrm{d}t.$$

Proof: From the definition of expected profits (6.4) we have that

$$E_{-i}[P_i(x)] = Q_i(x_i)x_i - \pi_i(x).$$

It follows from (6.7) that

$$E_{-i}[P_i(x)] = Q_i(x_i)x_i - \pi_i(0) - \int_0^{x_i} Q_i(t)\, \mathrm{d}t.$$

The individual rationality constraint implies that $\pi_i(0) \geq 0$ and, thus, by defining $a_i = \pi_i(0)$, we are done.   □

The following definition will be useful below.

Definition 13   *An allocation rule $(q_i(x))_{i=1}^n$ is feasible if*

$$Q_i(x_i) = E_{-i}[q_i(x)] = \int q_i(x) f_{-i}(x_{-i})\, \mathrm{d}x_{-i}$$

is increasing and there are payments $(P_i(x))_{i=1}^n$ such that

$$E_{-i}[P_i(x)] = Q_i(x_i)x_i - a_i - \int_0^{x_i} Q_i(t)\, \mathrm{d}t, \quad a_i \geq 0. \tag{6.8}$$

Thus, if (q, P) is incentive compatible and individually rational, the allocation rule q is feasible. Reciprocally, if q is feasible and $(P_i(x))_{i=1}^n$ are associated payments, then (q, P) is incentive compatible and individually rational.

Remark 5   *Note that there are many ways to choose payments such that (6.8) is true. One simple way is to choose*

$$P_i(x_i) = Q_i(x_i) - a_i - \int_0^{x_i} Q_i(t)\, \mathrm{d}t.$$

This corresponds to an auction in which every bidder pays whether winning the object or not. Another possible payment rule is given by

$$P_i(x) = q_i(x)x_i - \int_0^{x_i} q_i(s, x_{-i})\, \mathrm{d}s.$$

In this case the bidder only pays as long as $q_i(x) > 0$.

6.3 Revenue Equivalence and the Optimal Auction

We start this section by reminding the reader that we have just shown that any incentive compatible direct mechanism is such that condition (6.7) holds. The seller's expected revenue in any such mechanism is given by

$$R = \int_0^{\bar{v}} \sum_{i=1}^n P_i(t) f(t) \, dt.$$

That is, the seller's expected revenue is simply the sum of the expected payments from players $i = 1, \ldots, n$. Recall that from (6.4) we can write:

$$E_{-i}[P_i(x)] = Q_i(x_i)x_i - \pi_i(x_i) = Q_i(x_i)x_i - \pi_i(0) - \int_0^{x_i} Q_i(t) \, dt, \qquad (6.9)$$

where the last equality follows from (6.7). From $E[P_i(x)] = E_i[E_{-i}[P_i(x)]]$ we have that

$$E[P_i(x)] = E_i \left[Q_i(x_i)x_i - \pi_i(0) - \int_0^{x_i} Q_i(t) \, dt \right]$$

$$= -\pi_i(0) + E_i \left[Q_i(x_i)x_i - \int_0^{x_i} Q_i(t) \, dt \right].$$

Thus we have proved the following general form of the revenue equivalence theorem:

Theorem 14 (General Revenue Equivalence Theorem) *If (q, P) and $(\bar{q}, \bar{P})$ are direct mechanisms with the same allocation rule, i.e. $q = \bar{q}$, and such that if a bidder has the lowest type his expected utility is the same in both mechanisms, then the seller's expected revenue is the same.*

This theorem generalizes the revenue equivalence theorem obtained in Chapter 3. To see this, suppose we are in the symmetric IPV case. Assume further that the bidder with the highest type receives the object. That is, $q_i(x) = 1$ if $x_i > \max_{j \neq i} x_j$. This implies that

$$Q_i(x_i) = \int q_i(x_i, x_{-i}) f_{-i}(x_{-i}) \, dx_{-i}$$

$$= \int_{x_i > \max_{j \neq i} x_k} \prod_{j \neq i} f_j(x_j) \, dx_{-i} = F(x_i)^{n-1}.$$

bidder i's expected payment is therefore,

$$E_{-i}[P_i(x)] = Q_i(x_i)x_i - \pi_i(x_i) = F(x_i)^{n-1} x_i - \pi_i(0) - \int_0^{x_i} F(t)^{n-1} \, dt.$$

$$(6.10)$$

In the first-price, second-price, Dutch, and English auctions, the bidder with lowest type (i.e., $x_i = 0$) receives expected utility equal to zero. Thus $\pi_i(0) = 0$. Hence, it follows that they all have the same expected revenue. This is summarized by the following result.

Theorem 15 *Consider any two auction mechanisms that allocate the object to the bidder with the highest type. Suppose further that in these two mechanisms the expected profits from the bidder with the lowest possible type is zero. Then these two mechanisms yield the same expected payment for each bidder given his type and the same expected revenue for the seller.*

Theorem 15 and equation (6.10) can be quite useful in determining equilibrium bidding strategies for any auction format. For example, consider a first-price sealed-bid auction. If bidder i wins the auction, he pays his bid. Therefore, his expected payment in equilibrium is equal to his bid multiplied by the probability of winning:

$$F(x_i)^{n-1} b^F(x_i) = F(x_i)^{n-1} x_i - \int_0^{x_i} F(t)^{n-1}(t)\, \mathrm{d}t.$$

Thus, his equilibrium bid is equal to

$$b^F(x_i) = x_i - \frac{\int_0^{x_i} F(t)^{n-1}(t)\, \mathrm{d}t}{F(x_i)^{n-1}},$$

which coincides with the expression obtained in Chapter 3.

Consider now an all-pay auction, where the winner is the bidder with the highest type but all bidders pay their bids. In this case, i's expected payment coincides with his equilibrium bid as he will pay regardless of whether he wins or not:

$$b^A(x_i) = F(x_i)^{n-1} x_i - \int_0^{x_i} F(t)^{n-1}(t)\, \mathrm{d}t.$$

We can now turn our attention to the optimal auction—the auction that maximizes the seller's expected revenue. We can use expression (6.9) determining individual i's expected payment in any direct mechanism to determine the seller's revenue. An individual's expected payment can be written as:

$$\tilde{P}_i = \int P_i(x) f_{-i}(x_{-i}) f_i(x_i)\, \mathrm{d}x_{-i}\, \mathrm{d}x_i$$

$$= \int_{x_i} \left[\int_{x_{-i}} P_i(x) f_{-i}(x_{-i})\, \mathrm{d}x_{-i} \right] f_i(x_i)\, \mathrm{d}x_i$$

$$= \int_{x_i} \left[Q_i(x_i) x_i - \pi_i(0) - \int_0^{x_i} Q_i(t)\, \mathrm{d}t \right] f_i(x_i)\, \mathrm{d}x_i.$$

The last equality follows from (6.9). Since $\pi_i(0) \geq 0$ we set $\pi_i(0) = 0$, without loss of generality. Recall that

$$Q_i(x_i) = \int_{x_{-i}} q_i(x) f_{-i}(x_{-i}) \, \mathrm{d}x_{-i}.$$

Thus we have

$$\tilde{P} = \int x_i q_i(x) f(x) \, \mathrm{d}x - \int \left(\int_0^{x_i} Q_i(t) \, \mathrm{d}t \right) f_i(x_i) \, \mathrm{d}x_i.$$

We can now change the order of integration in the last integral:

$$\int \left(\int_0^{x_i} Q_i(t) \, \mathrm{d}t \right) f_i(x_i) \, \mathrm{d}x_i = \int \int_t^{\bar{v}} Q_i(t) f_i(x_i) \, \mathrm{d}x_i \, \mathrm{d}t$$

$$= \int Q_i(t)(1 - F_i(t)) \, \mathrm{d}t$$

$$= \int q_i(x)(1 - F_i(t)) f_{-i}(x) \, \mathrm{d}x_{-i} \, \mathrm{d}t$$

$$= \int q_i(x) \frac{1 - F_i(x_i)}{f_i(x_i)} f(x) \, \mathrm{d}x.$$

In the last line we replaced t by x_i as the label of the variable of integration. Substituting this in the expression for $\tilde{P}_i$:

$$\tilde{P}_i = \int x_i q_i(x) f(x) \, \mathrm{d}x - \int q_i(x) \frac{1 - F_i(x_i)}{f_i(x_i)} f(x) \, \mathrm{d}x$$

$$= \int \left[x_i - \frac{1 - F_i(x_i)}{f_i(x_i)} \right] q_i(x) f(x) \, \mathrm{d}x.$$

This is i's expected payment in any incentive compatible direct mechanism. To find the seller's expected revenue we simply sum over all bidders:

$$R = \int \sum_{i=1}^n \left[x_i - \frac{1 - F_i(x_i)}{f_i(x_i)} \right] q_i(x) f(x) \, \mathrm{d}x. \qquad (6.11)$$

Note that

$$R \leq \int \max_{i=1,\ldots,n} \left[x_i - \frac{1 - F_i(x_i)}{f_i(x_i)} \right]^+ f(x) \, \mathrm{d}x,$$

where $[r]^+ = \max\{r, 0\}$, stands for the non-negative part of $[\cdot]$. We can now characterize the optimal auction when the expression inside the brackets is increasing.

Theorem 16 (optimal auction)   *Suppose that for every bidder i,*

$$J_i(x) = x - \frac{1 - F_i(x)}{f_i(x)} \tag{6.12}$$

is increasing. Then the optimal auction allocates the object to the individual with the highest $J_i(x_i)$ if $J_i(x_i) \geq 0$. Otherwise the auctioneer keeps the object. Specifically, the allocation rule, $(q_i^*(x))_{i=1}^n$, is given by

$$q_j^*(x) = \begin{cases} 0 & \text{if } j \notin W(x) \text{ or } J_j(x_j) < 0, \\ \frac{1}{\#W(x)} & \text{if } j \in W(x), \text{ and } J_j(x_j) \geq 0, \end{cases}$$

where $W(x) = \{j; J_j(x_j) = \max_{1 \leq i \leq n} J_i(x_i)\}$.

Remark 6   *The function $J_i(x_i)$ in (6.12) is referred to as the marginal valuation. This is due to an analogy with the monopolist's marginal revenue. See, for example, Bulow and Roberts (1989).*

The payments by the bidders associated with the allocation rule $(q_j^*)_{j=1}^n$ can be specified in several ways. See remark 5 above. The following corollary gives the optimal auction in the symmetric case:

Corollary 5   *If the distribution of types is the same for every bidder, that is, $F_i = F$ for every i, and if $x - (1 - F(x))/f(x)$ is strictly increasing, the optimal auction allocates the object with probability one to the individual with the highest type if his marginal valuation is non-negative at the highest type.*

Proof of Theorem 16   Define the set

$$W(x) = \left\{ 1 \leq j \leq n; J_j(x_j) = \max_{1 \leq i \leq n} J_i(x_i) \right\}.$$

For every j we define

$$q_j^*(x) = \begin{cases} 0 & \text{if } j \notin W(x) \text{ or } J_j(x_j) < 0. \\ \frac{1}{\#W(x)} & \text{if } j \in W(x), \text{ and } J_j(x_j) \geq 0. \end{cases}$$

First note that $q_j^*(x)$ is increasing in the variable x_j and therefore $Q_j^*(x_j) = \int q_j^*(x) \, dx_{-j}$ is also increasing. Thus if we define

$$P_j^*(x_i) = Q_i^*(x_i)x_i - \int_0^{x_i} Q_i^*(t) \, dt,$$

the resulting mechanism $(q_j^*, P_j^*)_{j \leq n}$ satisfies the individual rationality and incentive compatibility constraints. It remains to check that it maximizes the seller's expected revenue. So suppose the allocation rule $(q_i)_{i=1}^n$ is feasible.[1]

---

[1] See Definition 13.

From equation (6.11) we see that

$$R = \int \sum_{i=1}^{n} \left[x_i - \frac{1 - F_i(x_i)}{f_i(x_i)} \right] q_i(x) f(x) \, dx$$

$$\leq \int \max_i \left[x_i - \frac{1 - F_i(x_i)}{f_i(x_i)} \right] \sum_{i=1}^{n} q_i(x) f(x) \, dx$$

$$= \int \max_{1 \leq i \leq n} J_i(x_i) \left(\sum_{i=1}^{n} q_i(x) \right) f(x) \, dx$$

$$\leq \int \left(\max_{1 \leq i \leq n} J_i(x_i) \right)^{+} f(x) \, dx$$

$$= \int \sum_{i=1}^{n} \left[x_i - \frac{1 - F_i(x_i)}{f_i(x_i)} \right] q_i^{*}(x) f(x) \, dx. \qquad \square$$

We now give a direct proof of the corollary.

Proof: Define $J(x) = x - (1 - F(x))/f(x)$. We define $q_i^{*}(x) = 0$ if $x_i < \max_{j \neq i} x_j$. Therefore $Q_i(x_i) = F^{n-1}(x_i)$ is increasing. Thus the associated mechanisms satisfy (6.2) and (6.3) and for every feasible q:

$$R = \int \sum_{i=1}^{n} \left[x_i - \frac{1 - F(x_i)}{f(x_i)} \right] q_i(x) f(x) \, dx$$

$$\leq \int \max_i J(x_i) \sum_{i=1}^{n} q_i(x) f(x) \, dx$$

$$= \int \left(J \left(\max_{1 \leq i \leq n} x_i \right) \right)^{+} f(x) \, dx = \int \sum_{i=1}^{n} J_i(x_i) q_i^{*}(x) f(x) \, dx. \qquad \square$$

The next example illustrates how an optimally chosen reserve price can be used to increase the seller's expected revenue.

Example 14 *Suppose $f_i(x) = \frac{1}{10}$, $x \in [0, 10]$. Then $J(x) = x - \frac{1 - (x/10)}{1/10} = 2x - 10$. If $\max_i x_i < 5$ the auctioneer keeps the object. Otherwise, the object is allocated to the bidder with the highest x_i. The seller's expected revenue in a symmetric equilibrium of any auction that allocates the object to the highest bidder and with a reserve price of 5 is equal to:*

$$R = \int_{\max_i x_i \geq 5} \left(2 \max_{1 \leq i \leq n} x_i - 10 \right) \frac{1}{10^n} \, dx_1 \cdots dx_n$$

$$= \int_5^{10} (2y - 10) \frac{n y^{n-1}}{10^n} \, dy = \frac{10}{1 + n} (n - 1 + 2^{-n}).$$

The seller's expected revenue for the Vickrey auction without a reserve price is

$$R_2 = \int_0^{10} n(n-1) \left(\frac{y}{10}\right)^{n-1} \left(1 - \frac{y}{10}\right) \mathrm{d}y = 10 \left(\frac{n-1}{n+1}\right).$$

The difference is $R - R_2 = 10/2^n(1+n)$. *Thus if we have three bidders the difference is* $\frac{10}{32} = 0.31$, *which is about 6% of the maximum* R. *The full surplus is* $\int \max x_i \, \mathrm{d}x = \int_0^{10} \frac{ny^n}{10^n} \, \mathrm{d}y = \frac{10n}{n+1}$. *Thus the consumer's surplus is*

$$\frac{10n}{n+1} - \frac{10}{1+n}(n-1+2^{-n}) = \frac{10(1-2^{-n})}{n+1} \leq \frac{10}{n+1}.$$

We now show that the optimal auction, in the symmetric bidders case, can be seen as a second-price sealed-bid auction with a single reserve price.

In the symmetric case we have that $\max_i J(x_i) = J(\max_i x_i)$. Define $x^* = \max_i x_i$. If there is only one bidder j such that $x_j = x^*$ and $J(x_j) \geq 0$, this bidder wins the object. If there are m bidders in this situation each one wins the object with probability $1/m$. Now we define the following payment (see Remark 5 above):

$$P_j(x) = q_j(x)x_j - \int_0^{x_j} q_j(s, x_{-j}) \, \mathrm{d}s$$

$$= \begin{cases} \max_{j \neq i} x_j & \text{if } x_j = x^* > \max_{i \neq j} x_i \\ \dfrac{1}{\#\{l; x_l = x^*\}} x^* & \text{if } x_j = x^*. \end{cases}$$

Above we used that if $x_j > \max_{i \neq j} x_i$ then

$$q_j(x)x_j - \int_0^{x_j} q_j(s, x_{-j}) \, \mathrm{d}s = x_j - \left(x_j - \max_{i \neq j} x_i\right) = \max_{i \neq j} x_i.$$

That is, the winner's payment is equal to the largest of : (1) the maximum type amongst all other players or, (2) the optimal reserve price.

Example 15 *There are many probability distributions that satisfy the increasing marginal valuations assumption. For example, the uniform distribution* $F(x) = x$ *in* $[0, 1]$ *satisfies it since*

$$J(x) = x - \frac{1-x}{1} = 2x - 1$$

is strictly increasing. More generally if $F(x) = x^\theta$ *then*

$$J(x) = x - \frac{1 - x^\theta}{\theta x^{\theta-1}} = \frac{x(\theta+1) - x^{-\theta+1}}{\theta}$$

is increasing if $\theta \geq 1$ *since*

$$J'(x) = \frac{\theta + 1 - (1 - \theta)x^{-\theta}}{\theta} \geq 0.$$

in this case. If $\theta < 1$ then J is not increasing. For example $F(x) = \sqrt{x}$ then $J(x) = 3x - 2\sqrt{x}$ is plotted below:

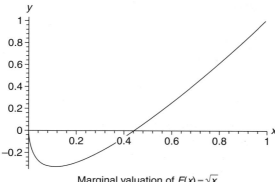

Marginal valuation of $F(x) = \sqrt{x}$

Remark 7 *If the density is increasing then the marginal valuation is increasing. To see this, differentiate $J(x)$:*

$$\frac{\mathrm{d}}{\mathrm{d}x} J(x) = 2 + \frac{(1 - F(x))f'(x)}{f^2(x)}$$

and, therefore, $f' \geq 0$ implies $J' > 0$. Thus, convex distributions have increasing marginal valuations.

Remark 8 *A simple but useful generalization of the optimal auction theorem can be obtained if instead of increasing marginal valuations we assume that $\{x, J(x) \geq 0\}$ is an interval and $J(\cdot)$ is increasing in this interval. The distributions $F(x) = x^\theta, 0 < \theta < 1$ are covered by this assumption.*

6.4   Some Extensions

6.4.1   Non-monotonic Marginal Valuation

In this section, we allow for marginal valuations that are not everywhere increasing. We begin by showing that there are many distributions with this property.

Proposition 4 *Suppose $h : [0,1] \to \mathbb{R}$ is a continuous function. Assume also that*

(*i*) $h(x) < x$ for every $x \in [0,1)$;
(*ii*) $h(1) = 1$;
(*iii*) $\int_0^1 \frac{\mathrm{d}y}{y - h(y)} = \infty$.

Then there exists a continuously differentiable distribution $F(r)$ such that for every $r \in [0,1)$,

$$r - \frac{1 - F(r)}{F'(r)} = h(r).$$

Proof: We first remark that the continuity of h and (i) imply that for every $x < 1$, $\min_{y \le x}(h(y) - y) > 0$. Thus, the integral $\int_0^x \frac{dy}{y - h(y)} > 0$ is finite.

Define $F \colon [0,1] \to \mathbb{R}$ by

$$F(x) = \begin{cases} 1 - \exp\left[-\int_0^x \frac{dy}{y - h(y)}\right], & \text{if } 0 \le x < 1, \\ 1, & \text{if } x = 1. \end{cases}$$

It is immediate that $0 \le F(x) < 1$ for every $x < 1$. From (iii) we have that $\lim_{x \to 1} F(x) = 1$. The density of F is given by

$$f(x) = F'(x) = \exp\left[-\int_0^x \frac{dy}{y - h(y)}\right] \frac{1}{x - h(x)} = \frac{1 - F(x)}{x - h(x)},$$

$0 \le x < 1$. Thus,

$$x - \frac{1 - F(x)}{f(x)} = x - (x - h(x)) = h(x), \quad 0 \le x < 1. \qquad \square$$

Remark 9　*A simple condition for the validity of (iii) above is $h'(1) > 1$.*

We see from the proposition above that practically any behavior on $(0,1)$ is possible for a marginal valuation $J(\cdot)$. And since there are no theoretical grounds to assume that the distribution of bidders' types has a monotonic marginal valuation, it is important to consider the general case of non-monotonic valuations.

We now return to the general development. Our aim is to compute the optimal auction when the marginal valuation is not monotonic. It is instructive to start with the simplest case.

One-bidder case

The seller allocates the object if and only if $t \ge t_0$ where t_0, is such that

$$\int_{t_0}^{\bar{v}} J(s)f(s)\, ds = \max_{t \in [0,\bar{v}]} \int_t^{\bar{v}} J(s)f(s)\, ds. \tag{6.13}$$

To see this, suppose $q(t) \in [0,1]$ is increasing. The seller maximizes

$$\int_0^{\bar{v}} q(t)J(t)f(t)\, dt.$$

Suppose first that $q(\cdot)$ is a step function. That is, $q(t) = a_i \in [0,1]$ if $t \in (t_i, t_{i+1}]$. Then, defining $b_i = \int_0^{t_i} J(t)f(t)\,\mathrm{d}t$, we obtain

$$\int_0^{\bar{v}} q(t)J(t)f(t)\,\mathrm{d}t = \sum_{i=0}^{n} a_i \int_{t_i}^{t_{i+1}} J(t)f(t)\,\mathrm{d}t$$

$$= \sum_{i=0}^{n} a_i(b_{i+1} - b_i) = \sum_{i=0}^{n} a_i b_{i+1} - \sum_{i=0}^{n} a_i b_i$$

$$= \sum_{j=1}^{n+1} a_{j-1}b_j - \sum_{j=1}^{n} a_j b_j = a_n \int_0^{\bar{v}} J(t)f(t)\,\mathrm{d}t - \sum_{j=1}^{n}(a_j - a_{j-1})b_j$$

$$\leq a_n \int_0^{\bar{v}} J(t)f(t)\,\mathrm{d}t - (a_n - a_0)\min_{j\geq 1} b_j$$

$$= a_n \max_{j\leq n} \int_{t_j}^{\bar{v}} J(t)f(t)\,\mathrm{d}t + a_0 \min_{j\geq 1} b_j$$

since

$$\sum_{j=1}^{n}(a_j - a_{j-1})b_j \geq \sum_{j=1}^{n}(a_j - a_{j-1})\min b_j = (a_n - a_0)\min_{j\geq 1} b_j.$$

The maximum in this case is attained for $a_0 = 0$ and $a_j = 1$ if $t_j \geq \bar{t}$. Thus, our solution maximizes expected revenue amongst the family of increasing step functions.

Now consider an increasing function $q(x) \in [0,1]$. Suppose $\epsilon > 0$ is given. Divide the interval $[0,1]$ in N parts where $1/N < \epsilon$. Define $I_j = (\frac{j}{N}, \frac{j+1}{N}]$, $j = 0, \ldots, N-1$. Then the inverse image $q^{-1}(I_j)$ is an interval (possibly empty). Also $\cup_j q^{-1}(I_j) = [0, \bar{v}]$. Thus, if we define $\tilde{q}(x) = \inf q(I_j)$ for $x \in q^{-1}(I_j)$ this function, $\tilde{q}$, is increasing, constant in the intervals $q^{-1}(I_j)$ and differs from q by no more than ϵ. Now note that $\int |J(t)|f(t)\,\mathrm{d}t < \infty$. Therefore if $\epsilon > 0$ is given and $q(x) \in [0,1]$ is increasing and $\tilde{q}$ is a step function distant from q by no more than ϵ then

$$\max_{t\in[0,\bar{v}]} \int_t^{\bar{v}} J(s)f(s)\,\mathrm{d}s \geq \int J(s)\tilde{q}(s)f(s)\,\mathrm{d}s$$

$$\geq \int J(s)f(s)(q(s) - \epsilon)\,\mathrm{d}s = \int J(s)f(s)q(s)\,\mathrm{d}s - \epsilon \int |J(s)|f(s)\,\mathrm{d}s.$$

Since ϵ is arbitrary we proved the general case.

Several-bidders case

In this section we need the concept of the Stjeltjes integral. Most readers may want to skip the proof and go directly to the examples below. First, we define

$$h_i(q) = J_i(F_i^{-1}(q)) = F_i^{-1}(q) - \frac{1 - q}{f_i(F_i^{-1}(q))}.$$

Second, define $H_i(q) = \int_0^q h_i(r)dr$. Now let $G_i(q)$ be the convex hull[2] of $H_i(q)$. By this we mean the largest convex function G_i such that $G_i \leq H_i$. Finally, define[3] $g_i(x) = (G_i)'_+(x)$ the right-hand derivative of G_i. The function g_i is increasing. Define $\bar{J}_i(t_i) = g_i(F_i(t_i))$. The optimal auction gives the object to the bidder with the greatest $\bar{J}_i(t_i)$ as will be seen in the proof of the following theorem.

Theorem 17 (optimal auction—general case)   *The optimal auction allocates the object to the bidder with the highest $\bar{J}_i(t_i)$ if this number is nonnegative. Otherwise, the auctioneer keeps the object. That is, the allocation rule is given by*

$$\bar{q}_i(t) = \begin{cases} \dfrac{1}{\#\bar{W}(t)} & \text{if } i \in \bar{W}(t) \text{ and } \bar{J}_i(t_i) \geq 0, \\ 0 & \text{if } i \notin \bar{W}(t). \end{cases}$$

where $\bar{W}(t) = \{j; \bar{J}_j(t_j) = \max_i \bar{J}_i(t_i)\}$.

First note that $\bar{Q}_i(t_i) = \int \bar{q}_i(t) f_{-i}(t_{-i}) \, dt_{-i}$ is increasing and therefore the mechanism defined by $(\bar{q}_i(t))_{i=1}^n$ is feasible. We now divide the proof into two lemmas.

Lemma 4   *The following inequality is true for every i:*

$$\int J_i(t_i) q_i(t) f(t) \, dt \leq \int \bar{J}_i(t_i) q_i(t) f(t) \, dt. \qquad (6.14)$$

Lemma 5   *Moreover, the equality is true if and only if*

$$\int_0^{\bar{v}} (H_i(F_i(t_i)) - G_i(F_i(t_i))) \, dQ_i(t_i) = 0. \qquad (6.15)$$

---

[2] See equation (D.1).
[3] See Appendix D.3.

Proof: First we have for every i that

$$\int J_i(t_i)q_i(t)f(t)\,\mathrm{d}t$$

$$= \int h_i(F_i(t_i))q_i(t)f(t)\,\mathrm{d}t$$

$$= \int (h_i(F_i(t_i)) - g_i(F_i(t_i)))q_i(t)f(t)\,\mathrm{d}t + \int \bar{J}_i(t_i)q_i(t)f(t)\,\mathrm{d}t$$

$$= \int (h_i(F_i(t_i)) - g_i(F_i(t_i)))Q_i(t_i)f_i(t_i)\,\mathrm{d}t_i + \int \bar{J}_i(t_i)q_i(t)f(t)\,\mathrm{d}t$$

$$= \int \left(\frac{\mathrm{d}}{\mathrm{d}t_i}H_i(F_i(t_i)) - \frac{\mathrm{d}}{\mathrm{d}t_i}G_i(F_i(t_i)) \right) Q_i(t_i)\,\mathrm{d}t_i + \int \bar{J}_i(t_i)q_i(t)f(t)\,\mathrm{d}t.$$

In the first line above we just used that $h_i(F_i(t_i)) = J_i(t_i)$. In the second line we used that $\bar{J}_i(t_i) = g_i(F_i(t_i))$. We now integrate by parts the first integral of the last line. Thus, writing $s = t_i$ and omitting the subscript i for conciseness:

$$\int_0^{\bar{v}} \left(\frac{\mathrm{d}}{\mathrm{d}s}H(F(s)) - \frac{\mathrm{d}}{\mathrm{d}s}G(F(s)) \right) Q(s)\,\mathrm{d}s$$

$$= (H(F(s)) - G(F(s)))Q(s)|_0^{\bar{v}} - \int_0^{\bar{v}} (H(F(s)) - G(F(s)))\,\mathrm{d}Q(s)$$

$$= - \int_0^{\bar{v}} (H(F(s)) - G(F(s)))\,\mathrm{d}Q(s) \le 0. \tag{6.16}$$

Above we used that that $H_i(1) = G_i(1)$ and $H_i(0) = G_i(0)$. Therefore, we have that

$$\int J_i(t_i)q_i(t)f(t)\,\mathrm{d}t \le \int \bar{J}_i(t_i)q_i(t)f(t)\,\mathrm{d}t.$$

It is also immediate from (6.16) that the equality is true if and only if

$$\int_0^{\bar{v}} (H_i(F_i(t_i)) - G_i(F_i(t_i)))\,\mathrm{d}Q_i(t_i) = 0. \qquad \qquad \square$$

Lemma 6 *For the mechanism $(\bar{q}_i(t))_{i=1}^n$ it is true that*

$$\bar{B}_i = \int_0^{\bar{v}} (H_i(F_i(t_i)) - G_i(F_i(t_i)))\,\mathrm{d}\bar{Q}_i(t_i) = 0. \tag{6.17}$$

Proof: Consider $t_i \in (0, \bar{v})$ such that

$$H_i(F_i(t_i)) > G_i(F_i(t_i)).$$

In this case G_i is linear in a neighborhood (see Lemma 14 in Appendix D) of $F_i(t_i)$. So $\bar{J}_i(s) = g_i(F_i(s))$ is constant in a neighborhood of t_i and finally we have that $\bar{Q}_i(s) = \bar{Q}_i(t_i)$ in the same neighborhood. Therefore we conclude that $\bar{B}_i = 0$. $\qquad\qquad\qquad\qquad\qquad\qquad\qquad\qquad\qquad\qquad\qquad\qquad\square$

We now prove the theorem.

Proof: It follows from (6.14) that for every feasible mechanism $(q_i(t))_{i=1}^n$,

$$\int \sum_{i=1}^n J_i(t_i)q_i(t)f(t)\,\mathrm{d}t \le \int \sum_{i=1}^n \bar{J}_i(t_i)q_i(t)f(t)\,\mathrm{d}t \le \int \sum_{i=1}^n \bar{J}_i(t_i)\bar{q}_i(t)f(t)\,\mathrm{d}t.$$

The last inequality above follows directly from the definition of $(\bar{q}_i(t))_{i=1}^n$. We now show that

$$\int \sum_{i=1}^n J_i(t_i)\bar{q}_i(t)f(t)\,\mathrm{d}t = \int \sum_{i=1}^n \bar{J}_i(t_i)\bar{q}_i(t)f(t)\,\mathrm{d}t$$

and we are done with the proof. This follows since to have equality in (6.14) it suffices that (6.15) is true. But (6.17) says exactly this. $\qquad\qquad\qquad\square$

We now apply the optimal auction theorem when the virtual valuation is not monotonic. We remark first that if $W : [0,1] \to [0,1]$ is strictly increasing and $W(0) = 0$, $W(1) = 1$ then its inverse W^{-1} is also strictly increasing. Thus, the inverse of a strictly increasing distribution $W : [0,1] \to [0,1]$ is also a (strictly increasing) distribution.

Example 16 *The function*

$$W(x) = \frac{3x - 8x^2 + 8x^3}{3}, \quad 0 \le x \le 1$$

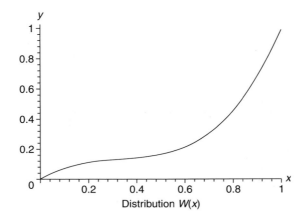

Distribution $W(x)$

is a strictly increasing distribution function. Thus $F(x) = W^{-1}(x)$ is a distribution. We can even write $F(x)$ explicitly as:

$$F(x) = \frac{z^{1/3} - 2z^{-1/3} + 4}{12} \tag{6.18}$$

$$z = z(x) = -44 + 324x + 18\sqrt{6 - 88x + 324x^2}.$$

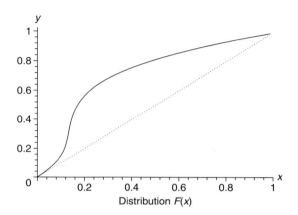

Distribution $F(x)$

If $J(x) = x - (1 - F(x))/F'(x)$ is the marginal valuation then

$$h(y) = J(F^{-1}(y)) = W(y) - \frac{1-y}{F'(W(y))} = W(y) - (1-y)W'(y)$$

$$= \frac{32y^3 - 48y^2 + 22y - 3}{3} = \frac{32}{3}\left(y - \frac{1}{4}\right)\left(y - \frac{1}{2}\right)\left(y - \frac{3}{4}\right).$$

This function is plotted below:

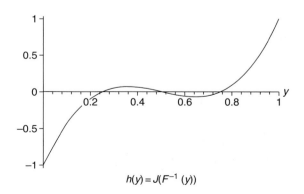

$h(y) = J(F^{-1}(y))$

The derivative of h is given by

$$h'(y) = \frac{1}{3}(96y^2 - 96y + 22) = 32\left(y - \frac{1}{2} - \frac{\sqrt{3}}{12}\right)\left(y - \frac{1}{2} + \frac{\sqrt{3}}{12}\right).$$

Thus, h has a local maximum at $\frac{1}{2} - \frac{1}{12}\sqrt{3} \approx 0.35$ and a local minimum at $\frac{1}{2} + \frac{1}{12}\sqrt{3} = 0.64$. The function h is increasing in $[0, \frac{1}{2} - \frac{1}{12}\sqrt{3}]$ and in $[\frac{1}{2} + \frac{1}{12}\sqrt{3}, 1]$. It is decreasing in $[\frac{1}{2} - \frac{1}{12}\sqrt{3}, \frac{1}{2} + \frac{1}{12}\sqrt{3}]$. Now we define $H(q) = \int_0^q h(y)\,dy = \frac{8}{3}q^4 - \frac{16}{3}q^3 + \frac{11}{3}q^2 - q$.

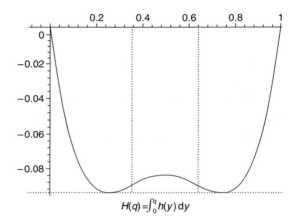

$$H(q) = \int_0^q h(y)\,dy$$

The function H is convex in the intervals $[0, \frac{1}{2} - \frac{1}{12}\sqrt{3}]$ and $[\frac{1}{2} + \frac{1}{12}\sqrt{3}, 1]$. We now have to find the greatest convex function that is pointwise less or equal to H. See the plot above. The vertical dotted lines indicate $x = \frac{1}{2} - \frac{1}{12}\sqrt{3}$ and $x = \frac{1}{2} + \frac{1}{12}\sqrt{3}$. The horizontal dotted line indicates the value of $H(\frac{1}{4}) = H(\frac{3}{4}) = -\frac{3}{32}$. From the graph it shall be clear that

$$G(x) = \begin{cases} H(x) & \text{if } 0 \leq x \leq \dfrac{1}{4} \\[2mm] -\dfrac{3}{32} & \text{if } \dfrac{1}{4} < x \leq \dfrac{3}{4} \\[2mm] H(x) & \text{if } \dfrac{3}{4} < x \leq 1 \end{cases}$$

is the convex hull of H. This is plotted below:

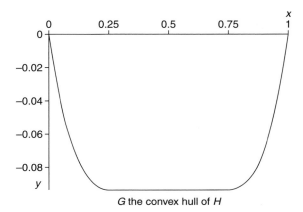

G the convex hull of H

We are almost done with the example. Now define $g(x) = (G')_+(x)$ the right-hand derivative of G. This is given by

$$g(x) = \begin{cases} \frac{1}{3}(32x^3 - 48x^2 + 22x - 3) & \text{if } 0 \le x \le \frac{1}{4} \\ 0 & \text{if } \frac{1}{4} < x \le \frac{3}{4} \\ \frac{1}{3}(32x^3 - 48x^2 + 22x - 3) & \text{if } \frac{3}{4} < x \le 1. \end{cases}$$

Finally, $\bar{J}(x) = g(F(x))$ is plotted below. For comparison we plot also the graph of J.

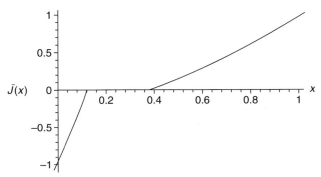

The marginal valuation $\bar{J}$

We see from the figure that no bidder with type $x_i < \frac{1}{4}$ receives the object. If the highest type is higher than $\frac{3}{4}$ then this bidder receives the object. If the highest type is between $\frac{1}{4}$ and $\frac{3}{4}$ and (say) there are m bidders with types in this range then each bidder receives the object with probability $1/m$.

Example 17 *We now consider another example where it will be more difficult to find the convex hull. Define the inverse distribution $F^{-1}(x) = \frac{1}{3}(4y - 10y^2 + 9y^3)$.*

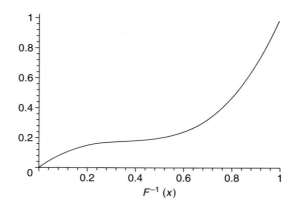

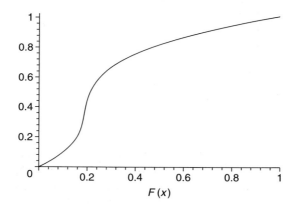

The distribution $F(x)$ is plotted above. It has an analytical expression similar to (6.18) and the reader will certainly forgive us for not explicitly writing it. If J is the marginal valuation for F then

$$h(x) = J(F^{-1}(x)) = F^{-1}(x) - (1-x)(F^{-1})'(x)$$

$$= -\frac{4}{3} + \frac{28x}{3} - 19x^2 + 12x^3$$

$$= 12\left(x - \frac{1}{4}\right)\left(x - \frac{2}{3}\right)^2.$$

This is plotted below.

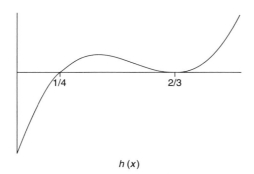

$h(x)$

Then, the function $H(x) = \int_0^x h(y)\,\mathrm{d}y = -\frac{4}{3}x + \frac{14}{3}x^2 - \frac{19}{3}x^3 + 3x^4$ *has the graph:*

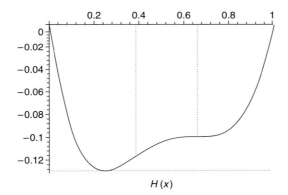

$H(x)$

To find the convex hull of H, *we first find the regions for which* $H'' \geq 0$, *that is, the regions for which* $h' \geq 0$. *The derivative of* h *is given by*

$$h'(x) = \frac{28}{3} - 38x + 36x^2 = 36\left(x - \frac{7}{18}\right)\left(x - \frac{2}{3}\right).$$

The vertical dotted lines in the graph above connects $\left(\frac{7}{18}, 0\right)$ *to* $\left(\frac{7}{18}, H\left(\frac{7}{18}\right)\right)$ *and* $\left(\frac{2}{3}, 0\right)$ *to* $\left(\frac{2}{3}, H\left(\frac{2}{3}\right)\right)$. *Thus,* h *is increasing in* $\left[0, \frac{7}{18}\right]$ *and in* $\left[\frac{2}{3}, 1\right]$. *So suppose* G *is the convex hull of* H. *To the left of the point* $x = 7/18 \approx 0.39$ *it must coincide with* H. *This follows since the function:*

$$\tilde{G}(x) = \begin{cases} H(x) & \text{if } x \leq \frac{1}{4} \\ H(1/4) & \text{if } \frac{1}{4} \leq x \leq 1 \end{cases}$$

is convex and less than or equal to H. *No point of the graph of* H *to the right of* $x = \frac{7}{18}$ *and to the left of* $\frac{2}{3}$ *belongs to the graph of* G *since* H *is concave in* *this region. So what we need to find are points $a \in \left(\frac{1}{4}, \frac{7}{18}\right)$ and $b \in \left(\frac{2}{3}, 1\right)$ such that the line connecting $(a, H(a))$ and $(b, H(b))$ satisfies the conditions:*

$$h(a) = H'(a)$$
$$H'(b) = h(b);$$
$$\frac{H(b) - H(a)}{b - a} = H'(a).$$

This gives a system:

$$12b^2 + (12a - 19)b + 12a^2 - 19a + \frac{28}{3} = 0,$$
$$3b^3 + \frac{9a - 19}{3}b^2 + \frac{14 - 19a + 9a^2}{3}b + \frac{-14a + 38a^2 - 27a^3}{3} = 0.$$

In the first equation above we solve for b and take the highest root (why?). This yields

$$b^* = \frac{19 - 12a + \sqrt{-87 + 456a - 432a^2}}{24}.$$

Substituting this in the second equation yields an equation in variable a:

$$-\frac{2041}{288}a - 9a^3 + \frac{57}{4}a^2 + \frac{3781 - 25\sqrt{-87 + 456a - 432a^2}}{3456} = 0.$$

Solving this equation we obtain:

$$a^* = \frac{19 - 5\sqrt{3}}{36} \approx 0.29,$$
$$b^* = \frac{19 + 5\sqrt{3}}{36} \approx 0.77.$$

The graph of the convex hull G is plotted below:

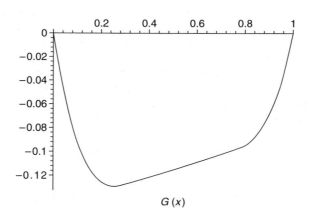

G (x)

Analytically, if $\omega(x) = -\frac{4}{3}x + \frac{14}{3}x^2 - \frac{19}{3}x^3 + 3x^4$ we have

$$G(x) = \begin{cases} \omega(x) & \text{if } x \leq \dfrac{19 - 5\sqrt{3}}{36} \\[2mm] -\dfrac{20449}{139968} + \dfrac{125}{1944}x & \text{if } \dfrac{19 - 5\sqrt{3}}{36} < x \leq \dfrac{19 + 5\sqrt{3}}{36} \\[2mm] \omega(x) & \text{if } \dfrac{19 + 5\sqrt{3}}{36} < x \leq 1. \end{cases}$$

We then find $g(x) = G'(x)$:

$$g(x) = \begin{cases} \dfrac{28x - 4}{3} - 19x^2 + 12x^3 & \text{if } x \leq \dfrac{19 - 5\sqrt{3}}{36} \\[2mm] \dfrac{125}{1944} & \text{if } \dfrac{19 - 5\sqrt{3}}{36} < x \leq \dfrac{19 + 5\sqrt{3}}{36} \\[2mm] \dfrac{28x - 4}{3} - 19x^2 + 12x^3 & \text{if } \dfrac{19 + 5\sqrt{3}}{36} < x \leq 1 \end{cases}$$

and the associated marginal valuation $\bar{J}(x) = g(F(x))$. Thus, if there are two bidders with types between $W((19 - 5\sqrt{3})/36) = F^{-1}((19 - 5\sqrt{3})/36)$ and $W((19 + 5\sqrt{3})/36)$ and all others have smaller types, those two bidders receive the object with 50 percent probability.

6.4.2 Correlated Values

The optimal auction result we presented above is very general when types are independent. If the marginal valuations are increasing and the bidders are ex-ante symmetric the optimal auction is a second-price sealed bid auction with an optimally chosen reserve price. The optimal auction can also be implemented as a first-price auction with a reserve price or through any other efficient auction format with an appropriately chosen reserve price.

However, the existence of correlation between types is also an important possibility. For example how much you appreciate a painting, a rare book or a fine wine is certainly a private matter but it is also naturally influenced by how much you think others appreciate them. What is the optimal auction if types are correlated? It turns out that, in general, it is not the Vickrey auction with a reserve price. It includes a Vickrey auction and also a lottery. This lottery will include auctioneer payments to the bidders! Before going into these details let us see where the approach used in the IPV case gets into difficulties. The main reason is that bidder's expected utility is not uniquely given as a function of the allocation rule. We saw this on the affiliated values chapter. First- and second-price auctions have the same allocation rule but give different expected revenue.

As before, we have n bidders with valuation $V_i = x_i$. Bidder i type varies in $x_i \in X_i = [0, \bar{v}]$. The set of joint types is $X = [0, \bar{v}]^n$ and the joint distribution of types has a continuously differentiable density $f : X \to \mathbb{R}_{++}$. The distribution of types of bidder i has density $f_i(x_i) = \int f(x)\,dx_{-i}$. The equality (6.1) is not valid since we do not have independence. If bidder i has type x_i, the distribution of x_{-i}, that is, the distribution of the other bidders' types has the conditional density given by

$$f(x_{-i} \,|\, x_i) = \frac{f(x_i, x_{-i})}{\int f(x)\,dx_{-i}}.$$

The incentive compatibility constraints (6.3) must be rewritten as

$$E[q_i(x)x_i - P_i(x) \,|\, x_i]$$

$$= \int (q_i(x)x_i - P_i(x)) f(x_{-i} \,|\, x_i)\,dx_{-i}$$

$$\geq E[q_i(\tilde{x})x_i - P_i(\tilde{x}) \,|\, x_i].$$

Here $\tilde{x} = (y, x_{-i})$ as before. Now defining,

$$Q_i(x_i) = E[q_i(x) \,|\, x_i] \quad \text{and} \quad \pi_i(x_i) = Q_i(x_i)x_i - E[P_i(x) \,|\, x_i]$$

the analogous equation to (6.5) is

$$\pi_i(x_i) - \pi_i(y) \geq Q_i(y)(x_i - y) + E[P_i(y, x_{-i}) \,|\, y] - E[P_i(y, x_{-i}) \,|\, x_i]$$

$$= Q_i(y)(x_i - y) + \int P_i(y, x_{-i})(f(x_{-i} \,|\, y) - f(x_{-i} \,|\, x_i))\,dx_{-i}.$$

If $x_i > y$ we have that

$$\frac{\pi_i(x_i) - \pi_i(y)}{x_i - y} \geq Q_i(y) - \int P_i(y, x_{-i}) \frac{f(x_{-i} \,|\, x_i) - f(x_{-i} \,|\, y)}{x_i - y}\,dx_{-i}.$$

Suppose now that $x_i < y$. Then

$$\frac{\pi_i(x_i) - \pi_i(y)}{x_i - y} \leq Q_i(y) - \int P_i(y, x_{-i}) \frac{f(x_{-i} \,|\, x_i) - f(x_{-i} \,|\, y)}{x_i - y}\,dx_{-i}.$$

Thus, if π_i is differentiable at y we have that

$$\pi_i'(y) = Q_i(y) - \int P_i(y, x_{-i}) \frac{\partial}{\partial y} f(x_{-i} \,|\, y)\,dx_{-i}. \tag{6.19}$$

We see from this equation that π_i is not a function only of q_i but of P_i as well. The next section shows how to characterize the optimal auction in general.

Full surplus extraction

For this part we rely on Cremer and MacLean (1988) and McAfee and Reny (1992). By surplus we mean the sum of the bidder's surplus and the seller's surplus. A bidder's surplus is his utility. The seller's surplus is the payment she receives. Thus, the total surplus is equal to $\max_i x_i$ if the bidder with the highest type receives the object. By full surplus extraction we mean that the seller receives on average $\max_i x_i$. Finally, by approximate full surplus extraction we mean that for every $\epsilon > 0$ there is an auction mechanism in which the seller surplus is at least $\max_i x_i - \epsilon$ in expectation. It is quite remarkable that, for a reasonably general class of density functions approximate full surplus extraction is possible. The key condition for approximate full surplus extraction is sufficient variability of the conditional density.

Discrete case

We begin our analysis with a simple discrete model. There are two bidders and two types. Say bidder $i = 1, 2$ can be of type $t_i = 1$ or $t_i = 2$. Let us suppose the following probability distribution of types:

$$\begin{pmatrix} \Pr(1,1) & \Pr(1,2) \\ \Pr(2,1) & \Pr(2,2) \end{pmatrix} = \begin{pmatrix} a & b \\ b & d \end{pmatrix},$$

where $a, b, d > 0$ and $a + 2b + d = 1$ and $ad - b^2 \neq 0$. That is $\Pr(t_1, t_2)$ is the probability that bidder 1 is of type $t_1 \in \{1, 2\}$ and bidder 2 is of type $t_2 \in \{1, 2\}$. The model is symmetric since $\Pr(t_1, t_2) = \Pr(t_2, t_1)$. The conditional probabilities are given in matrix form below:

$$\begin{pmatrix} \Pr(1\,|\,1) & \Pr(2\,|\,1) \\ \Pr(1\,|\,2) & \Pr(2\,|\,2) \end{pmatrix} = \begin{pmatrix} \dfrac{a}{a+b} & \dfrac{b}{a+b} \\ \dfrac{b}{b+d} & \dfrac{d}{b+d} \end{pmatrix}.$$

For example, $\Pr(1\,|\,1)$, the conditional probability that bidder two is of type 1 given that bidder 1 is of type 1, is equal to

$$\frac{\Pr(1,1)}{\Pr(1,1) + \Pr(1,2)} = \frac{a}{a+b}.$$

Let us specify the mechanism that extracts the full surplus. There is nothing special about the allocation rule, if both bidders announce 1, the auctioneer assigns the object to one of the bidders. If both announces 2 the auctioneer allocates the object to either one of the bidders. In this case, each bidder receives the object with probability 50 percent. If only one bidder announces 2, this bidder receives the object. The novelty is in the payment rule:

$$\begin{pmatrix} x^1(1,1) & x^1(1,2) \\ x^1(2,1) & x^1(2,2) \end{pmatrix} = \begin{pmatrix} \frac{1}{2} & 0 \\ 1 & 1 \end{pmatrix} + \begin{pmatrix} -\dfrac{b^2}{ad - b^2} & \dfrac{ab}{ad - b^2} \\ -\dfrac{b^2}{ad - b^2} & \dfrac{ab}{ad - b^2} \end{pmatrix}.$$

The first matrix after the equality corresponds to the payments in the second-price sealed bid auction. The second matrix is a lottery that depends on the other bidder's announcement. For example, if bidder 1 is of type 1, then with probability $\Pr(1\,|\,1) = a/(a+b)$ he receives a payment $b^2/(ad - b^2)$ and with probability $\Pr(2\,|\,1) = b/(a+b)$ he pays $ab/(ad-b^2)$. The expected value of this lottery is

$$-\frac{a}{a+b}\frac{b^2}{ad-b^2} + \frac{b}{a+b}\frac{ab}{ad-b^2} = 0.$$

If bidder 1 is of type 2, his lottery has an expected value given by

$$-\frac{b}{b+d}\frac{b^2}{ad-b^2} + \frac{d}{b+d}\frac{ab}{ad-b^2} = \frac{b}{b+d}.$$

Hence, a bidder with type 1 has an expected utility of 0. A bidder with type 2 has an expected utility equal to

$$\Pr(1\,|\,2)(2-1) + \Pr(2\,|\,2)(1-1) - \frac{b}{b+d} = 0.$$

We leave as an exercise to check the incentive compatibility constraints. That is, the reader needs to check that given the allocation and payment rules, a bidder will find it in his interest to report his true valuation when his opponent does the same. We now calculate the auctioneer's expected revenue.

$$R = \sum_{i\in\{1,2\}}\sum_{j\in\{1,2\}} \Pr(i,j)(x^1(i,j) + x^2(i,j))$$

$$= a\left(1 - \frac{2b^2}{ad-b^2}\right) + 2b\left(1 + \frac{ab-b^2}{ad-b^2}\right) + d\left(2 + \frac{2ab}{ad-b^2}\right)$$

$$= 4b + a + 2d = E[\max\{t_1, t_2\}].$$

Remark 10 *One curious aspect of the full surplus extracting auction is that in one case ($t_1 = t_2 = 1$) the auctioneer makes a net payment to bidders. For example if $2b^2/(ad-b^2) - 1 > 2$ (i.e., if $5b^2 > 3ad$), the seller makes a net payment to bidders higher than the object's valuation. This may favor bidders' collusion.*

Before we proceed to the continuum of types case, let us see what happens if the seller's information about the distribution is imprecise while the bidders know the correct distribution. Thus, we suppose that due to estimation errors, imperfect knowledge, or any other related reason, the seller assumes that the distribution of types is given by

$$\begin{pmatrix} \Pr'(1,1) & \Pr(1,2) \\ \Pr(2,1) & \Pr'(2,2) \end{pmatrix} = \begin{pmatrix} a+\epsilon & b \\ b & d-\epsilon \end{pmatrix}, \quad \epsilon \neq 0,$$

which implies that the conditional distribution is as follows:

$$
\begin{pmatrix} \Pr'(1\,|\,1) & \Pr'(2\,|\,1) \\ \Pr'(1\,|\,2) & \Pr'(2\,|\,2) \end{pmatrix} = \begin{pmatrix} \dfrac{a+\epsilon}{a+b+\epsilon} & \dfrac{b}{a+b+\epsilon} \\[2mm] \dfrac{b}{b+d-\epsilon} & \dfrac{d-\epsilon}{b+d-\epsilon} \end{pmatrix}.
$$

Define $\delta(\epsilon) = (a+\epsilon)(d-\epsilon) - b^2$. The seller then announces the allocation rule as before and the payment rule is given by:

$$
\begin{pmatrix} x^1(1,1) & x^1(1,2) \\ x^1(2,1) & x^1(2,2) \end{pmatrix} = \begin{pmatrix} \frac{1}{2} & 0 \\ 1 & 1 \end{pmatrix} + \begin{pmatrix} -\dfrac{b^2}{\delta(\epsilon)} & \dfrac{(a+\epsilon)b}{\delta(\epsilon)} \\[2mm] -\dfrac{b^2}{\delta(\epsilon)} & \dfrac{(a+\epsilon)b}{\delta(\epsilon)} \end{pmatrix}.
$$

This mechanism is incentive compatible as before. Let us check the participation constraints. Suppose bidder 1 has a type $t_1 = 1$. His expected utility is

$$
\Pr(1\,|\,1)\left(\frac{1}{2} - \frac{1}{2} + \frac{b^2}{\delta(\epsilon)}\right) + \Pr(2\,|\,1)\left(-\frac{(a+\epsilon)b}{\delta(\epsilon)}\right) = -\epsilon\frac{b^2}{(a+b)\delta(\epsilon)}.
$$

Now if $t_1 = 2$, his expected utility is

$$
\Pr(1\,|\,2)\left(2 - 1 + \frac{b^2}{\delta(\epsilon)}\right) + \Pr(2\,|\,2)\left(1 - 1 - \frac{(a+\epsilon)b}{\delta(\epsilon)}\right) = -\epsilon\frac{b(a+\epsilon)}{(b+d)\delta(\epsilon)}.
$$

Hence, if $\delta(\epsilon) > 0$ and $\epsilon > 0$, the participation constraints are not satisfied for any type of bidder! That is, by using a full-extracting surplus auction, a misinformed seller can end up receiving zero-revenue.

Continuum case

For simplicity we analyze only the two-bidder case. For every $b \in [0, \bar{v}]$, define the function $f_b : [0, \bar{v}] \to \mathbb{R}$ by $f_b(x) = f(b\,|\,x) = f(b,x)/f_2(x)$. Analogously, for every $a \in [0, \bar{v}]$, we define $f^a(y) = f(a\,|\,y) = f(a,y)/f_1(y)$. Here $f_1(a) = \int f(a,y)\mathrm{d}y$ and $f_2(b) = \int f(x,b)\mathrm{d}x$. The following lemma provides necessary and sufficient conditions for full surplus extraction. These conditions determine the allocation and payment rules.

Lemma 7 *Suppose (q, P) is an incentive compatible, voluntary participation direct mechanism. Then (q, P) extracts the full surplus if and only if for all a and b except on a measure zero set:*

1. $Q_1(a)a - E[P_1(a,b)\,|\,a] = 0$ and $Q_2(b)b - E[P_2(a,b)\,|\,b] = 0$;
2. If $a > b$ then $q_1(a,b) = 1$ and if $b > a$, $q_2(a,b) = 1$.

Proof: We prove first the "only if" part. Voluntary participation implies that

$$
Q_1(a)a - E[P_1(a,b)\,|\,a] \geq 0 \quad \text{and} \quad Q_2(b)b - E[P_2(a,b)\,|\,b] \geq 0. \tag{6.20}
$$

That is, the expected profits from participation must be non-negative. Taking the expectations and adding the two expressions above we obtain:

$$
E[P_1 + P_2] = \int E[P_1(a,b)|\,a]f_1(a)\,\mathrm{d}a + \int E[P_2(a,b)|\,b]f_2(b)\,\mathrm{d}b
$$

$$
\leq \int Q_1(a)af_1(a)\,\mathrm{d}a + \int Q_2(b)bf_2(b)\,\mathrm{d}b
$$

$$
= \int q_1(a,b)af(a,b)\,\mathrm{d}a\,\mathrm{d}b + \int q_2(a,b)bf(a,b)\,\mathrm{d}a\,\mathrm{d}b
$$

$$
= \int (q_1(a,b)a + q_2(a,b)b)f(a,b)\,\mathrm{d}a\,\mathrm{d}b
$$

$$
\leq \int \max\{a,b\}f(a,b)\,\mathrm{d}a\,\mathrm{d}b.
$$

On the other hand since the seller is extracting all the surplus, $E[P_1 + P_2] = \int \max\{a,b\}f(a,b)\,\mathrm{d}a\,\mathrm{d}b$. Hence we must have equality in (6.20). Moreover, we must have also that $\max\{a,b\} = q_1(a,b)a + q_2(a,b)b$ except on a set of types that occurs with probability zero. It is an immediate consequence that $q_1(a,b) = 1$ if $a > b$ and $q_2(a,b) = 1$ if $b > a$. The "if" part is immediate since we have equalities in place of inequalities above. □

Example 18 *Suppose the density function is $f(a,b) = (1 + 4ab)/2$. Then it is not possible to extract all the surplus. To prove this by contradiction, assume that the incentive compatible mechanism (q, P) extracts all surplus. Then the voluntary participation and incentive compatibility constraints can be written respectively, as:*

$$
a\int_0^a f(b\,|\,a)\,\mathrm{d}b - \int P_1(a,b)f(b\,|\,a)\,\mathrm{d}b
$$

$$
= a\int q_1(a,b)f(b\,|\,a)\,\mathrm{d}b - \int P_1(a,b)f(b\,|\,a)\,\mathrm{d}b
$$

$$
= aQ_1(a) - E[P_1(a,b)|\,a] = 0.
$$

and

$$
0 \geq a\int_0^y f(b\,|\,a)\,\mathrm{d}b - \int P_1(y,b)f(b\,|\,a)\,\mathrm{d}b
$$

$$
= aQ_1(y) - E[P_1(y,b)|\,a], y \in [0, \bar{v}].
$$

Since $f(b\,|\,a) = f(a,b)/f_1(a)$ we may multiply both equations by $f_1(a)$ and rewrite them as:

$$
\int P_1(a,b)\left(\frac{1 + 4ab}{2}\right)\mathrm{d}b = a\int_0^a \frac{1 + 4ab}{2}\,\mathrm{d}b
$$

and

$$\int P_1(y,b)\left(\frac{1+4ab}{2}\right)\,db \geq a\int_0^y \frac{1+4ab}{2}\,db.$$

Define $\phi_1(y) = \int P_1(y,b)\,db$ and $\phi_2(y) = \int P_1(y,b)b\,db$. Then the last equality and inequality can be rewritten as:

$$\frac{\phi_1(a)}{2} + 2a\phi_2(a) = a\int_0^a \frac{1+4ab}{2}\,db = \frac{a^2}{2} + a^4$$

and

$$\phi_1(y) + 2a\phi_2(y) \geq a\int_0^y \frac{1+4ab}{2}\,db = \frac{ay}{2} + a^2 y^2.$$

Subtracting $\phi_1(y) + 2y\phi_2(y) = (y^2/2) + y^4$ from both sides of the last inequality we obtain:

$$2(a-y)\phi_2(y) \geq \frac{ay}{2} + a^2 y^2 - \frac{y^2}{2} - y^4$$

$$= \frac{(a-y)y}{2} + (a-y)(a+y)y^2.$$

Hence, we have that $(a-y)[2\phi_2(y)-(y/2)-(a+y)y^2] \geq 0$ for every y and a. If we make a decrease to y we have that $2\phi_2(y)-(y/2)-2y^3 \geq 0$. Now make a increase to y to obtain $2\phi_2(y) - (y/2) - 2y^3 \leq 0$ and, therefore, $\phi_2(y) = (y/4) + y^3$. This yields $\phi_1(y) = (y^2/2) + y^4 - 2y((y/4) + y^3) = -y^4$. Now we go back to the incentive compatibility constraints

$$-y^4 + 2a\left(\frac{y}{4} + y^3\right) \geq \frac{ay}{2} + a^2 y^2 \tag{6.21}$$

for every y and a. However, $a = 0$ implies $y = 0$: a contradiction.

Remark 11 *It shall be clear that if $f(a,b) = \sum_{l=1}^n g_l(a)h_l(b)$ is a density, it will not be possible, in general, to extract the full surplus.*

To present a positive result we need some definitions.

Definition 14 *Let $C([0,\bar{v}])$ denote the set of continuous functions $g : [0,\bar{v}] \to \mathbb{R}$. The set $\mathcal{G} \subset C([0,\bar{v}])$ is dense if for every continuous $h : [0,\bar{v}] \to \mathbb{R}$ and every $\epsilon > 0$ there exists $g \in \mathcal{G}$ such that*

$$\sup_{x \in [0,\bar{v}]} |h(x) - g(x)| < \epsilon.$$

Thus, the vector space generated by $\mathcal{G} \subset C([0, \bar{v}])$, namely[4]

$$\langle \mathcal{G} \rangle := \left\{ \sum_{l=1}^{n} \lambda_i g_i; n \in \mathbb{N}, \lambda_i \in \mathbb{R}, g_i \in \mathcal{G}, 1 \leq i \leq n \right\}$$

is dense if for every continuous $h : [0, \bar{v}] \to \mathbb{R}$ and every $\epsilon > 0$ there exist $n \in \mathbb{N}$, $g_1, \ldots, g_n \in \mathcal{G}$ and real numbers $\lambda_1, \ldots, \lambda_n$ such that

$$\sup_{x \in [0, \bar{v}]} \left| h(x) - \sum_{l=1}^{n} \lambda_l g_l(x) \right| < \epsilon.$$

Example 19 *A classical example of a dense set is the set of polynomial functions. That is, the vector space generated by set $\mathcal{G} = \{x^n; n \in \mathbb{N} \cup \{0\}\} \subset C([0, \bar{v}])$. This is a consequence of the Stone–Weierstrass theorem. Another classical example is the set of trigonometric functions: $\{\sin kx, k \in \mathbb{N}\} \cup \{\cos kx; k \in \mathbb{N} \cup \{0\}\}$. In contrast, if $\mathcal{G} = \{x^{2n}; n \in \mathbb{N} \cup \{0\}\}$ the vector space generated by $\mathcal{G}$ is not dense since it contains only even functions.*

The following is true.

Theorem 18 *Suppose the density $f(a, b)$ is symmetric and that the vector space generated by the functions*

$$\left\{ a \to \int_0^{\bar{v}} z(b) f(b \,|\, a) \, \mathrm{d}b; z(\cdot) \in C([0, \bar{v}]) \right\} \tag{6.22}$$

is dense in the space of the continuous functions on $[0, \bar{v}]$. Then there is approximate full surplus extraction.

Proof: We consider bidder 1 first. Suppose $\epsilon > 0$ is given. We will show that it is possible to extract bidder 1 surplus with an error of at most ϵ. Define the allocation rule as in Lemma 7(ii). Define the payment function as

$$P_1(a, b) = \begin{cases} b + z(b) & \text{if } a \geq b, \\ z(b) & \text{if } a < b. \end{cases}$$

---

[4] That is, the vector space generated by a set $\mathcal{G}$ is the smallest set of continuous functions that is closed for addition and multiplication by scalars.

The function $z(\cdot)$ will be defined below. The expected utility of bidder 1 is given by

$$aQ_1(a) - E[P_1(a,b) \mid a]$$

$$= a \int_0^a f(b \mid a) \, db - \int_0^a (b + z(b)) f(b \mid a) \, db - \int_a^{\bar{v}} z(b) f(b \mid a) \, db$$

$$= \int_0^a (a - b) f(b \mid a) \, db - \int_0^{\bar{v}} z(b) f(b \mid a) \, db.$$

The incentive compatibility constraint is satisfied for any $z(\cdot)$ since for every y, $\int_0^a (a - b) f(b \mid a) \, db \geq \int_0^y (a - b) f(b \mid a) \, db$ and therefore:

$$\int_0^a (a - b) f(b \mid a) \, db - \int_0^{\bar{v}} z(b) f(b \mid a) \, db$$

$$\geq aQ_1(y) - E[P_1(y,b) \mid a]$$

$$= \int_0^y (a - b) f(b \mid a) \, db - \int_0^{\bar{v}} z(b) f(b \mid a) \, db.$$

The function $h(a) = \int_0^a (a - b) f(b \mid a) \, db$ is continuous. Hence, by the density assumption, there exists a $\tilde{z}(\cdot) \in C([0,1])$ such that

$$\sup_a \left| h(a) - \int_0^{\bar{v}} \tilde{z}(b) f(b \mid a) \, db \right| < \frac{\epsilon}{2}.$$

Now define $z(b) = \tilde{z}(b) - \epsilon/2$ and since

$$h(a) - \int_0^{\bar{v}} z(b) f(b \mid a) \, db = h(a) - \int_0^{\bar{v}} \tilde{z}(b) f(b \mid a) \, db + \frac{\epsilon}{2} \in \left(-\frac{\epsilon}{2}, \frac{\epsilon}{2} \right) + \frac{\epsilon}{2} = (0, \epsilon),$$

the voluntary participation constraint is satisfied and the surplus is extracted except at most for ϵ. $\qquad \square$

Remark 12 *Note that the mechanism constructed above has two parts. The part constituted by $z(\cdot)$ corresponds to a lottery—it is analogous to the discrete case. This lottery can be implemented in the following way. The auctioneer receives bidders' types (a, b) and charges bidder 1, 0 or b according to whether $a < b$. This corresponds to a Vickrey auction. Additionally, the auction charges bidder 1, an amount equal to $z(b)$. This is the lottery part. The lottery is drawn from the density $f(b \mid a)$.*

Remark 13 *In the independent case the range of (6.22) is one-dimensional since $\int z(b) f(b \mid a) \, db$ is constant with a. Thus, the density assumption in (6.22) is as far as possible from the independence assumption.*

Let us now see that the condition (6.22) is not empty. To this purpose we provide an example of a density that has a dense range and therefore almost full surplus extraction is possible. This is accomplished by choosing a set of orthogonal polynomials. If we define for $f, g \in C([0, 1])$ the function $\langle f, g \rangle = \int_0^1 f(x)g(x)\,\mathrm{d}x$ is an internal product in $C([0, 1])$. Thus two functions f, g are orthogonal if $\langle f, g \rangle = \int f(x)g(x)\,\mathrm{d}x = 0$. If f and g are not orthogonal we may choose $r \in \mathbb{R}$ such that f and $g - rf$ are orthogonal by choosing r such that

$$\int_0^1 f(x)(g(x) - rf(x))\,\mathrm{d}x = \langle f, g \rangle - r\langle f, f \rangle = 0.$$

That is $r = \langle f, g \rangle / \langle f, f \rangle$. In general the Gram–Schmidt orthogonalization method applied to a linearly independent set of functions $(f_n)_n$ results in a linearly independent set $(g_n)_n$ such that if $n \neq m$, $\langle g_n, g_m \rangle = 0$. If we apply this orthogonalization method to $\{1, x, x^2, \ldots, x^n, \ldots\}$ we obtain a set of orthogonal polynomials,

$$\mathcal{P} = \{P_0(x), P_1(x), \ldots, P_n(x), \ldots\}.$$

For example,

$$P_0(x) = 1, P_1(x) = 2x - 1, P_2(x) = 6x^2 - x + 1.$$

Example 20   *We take $\bar{v} = 1$. For every $P \in \mathcal{P}$ define $|P|_\infty = \max\{|P(x)|; 0 \leq x \leq 1\}$. For conciseness define $r_n = 1/2n(n+1)|P_n|_\infty^2$. We may now define our density function:*

$$f(a, b) = 1 + \sum_{n=1}^{\infty} r_n P_n(a) P_n(b).$$

We have that $f(a, b) \geq \frac{1}{2}$, since

$$\left| \sum_{n=1}^{\infty} r_n P_n(a) P_n(b) \right| \leq \sum_{n=1}^{\infty} r_n |P_n(a) P_n(b)|$$

$$= \sum_{n=1}^{\infty} \frac{1}{2n(n+1)} \frac{|P_n(a) P_n(b)|}{|P_n|_\infty^2}$$

$$\leq \sum_{n=1}^{\infty} \frac{1}{2n(n+1)} = \frac{1}{2} \sum_{n=1}^{\infty} \left(\frac{1}{n} - \frac{1}{n+1} \right) = \frac{1}{2}.$$

Now from $\int P_n(b)\,\mathrm{d}b = \langle P_n, P_0 \rangle = 0$, we have that

$$\int_0^1 f(a, b)\,\mathrm{d}b = 1 + \sum_{n=1}^{\infty} r_n P_n(a) \int_0^1 P_n(b)\,\mathrm{d}b = 1.$$

Therefore $f(b \mid a) = f(a,b)/\int_0^1 f(a,b)\,\mathrm{d}b = f(a,b)$. To show approximate full surplus extraction we use Theorem 18. For any integer $m \geq 1$,

$$\int_0^1 P_m(b)f(b \mid a)\,\mathrm{d}b$$

$$= \int_0^1 P_m(b)\left(1 + \sum_{n=1}^{\infty} r_n P_n(a)P_n(b)\right)\mathrm{d}b$$

$$= \int_0^1 P_m(b)\,\mathrm{d}b + \sum_{n=1}^{\infty} r_n P_n(a)\int_0^1 P_m(b)P_n(b)\,\mathrm{d}b$$

$$= \left(r_m \int_0^1 P_m^2(b)\,\mathrm{d}b\right)P_m(a).$$

Thus for every $m \geq 1$, by choosing $z(b) = P_m(b)/(r_m \int_0^1 P_m^2(b)\,\mathrm{d}b)$ we obtain that $\int_0^1 z(b)f(b \mid a)\,\mathrm{d}b = P_m(a)$. Thus the set

$$R = \left\{a \to \int z(b)f(b \mid a); z \in C([0,1])\right\} \supset \{P_m(x); m \geq 1\}.$$

But R also contains P_0 (for $z \equiv 1$) and therefore R is dense. $\qquad\square$

One question that arises is whether we can say anything about the optimal auction in the intermediate case when the range in (6.22) is not dense and is not unidimensional. We consider only dominant strategy optimal auctions (defined below). Note that the Vickrey auction and the auction in Theorem 18 are dominant strategy auctions. We will maintain the restriction to a two-bidder symmetric model.

Definition 15 *Suppose (q,P) is a direct mechanism. It is a dominant strategy mechanism if for every type a of bidder 1 and every type b of bidder 2 it is true that*

$$q_i(a,b)a - P_i(a,b) \geq q_i(a',b)a - P_i(a',b), \quad \forall a'. \tag{6.23}$$

Thus, regardless of bidder 2's bid, bidder 1 is better off (weakly better off at least) telling the truth than to pretend to be of type a'. We say that (q,P) is incentive compatible if

$$\int (q_i(a,b)a - P_i(a,b))f(b \mid a)\,\mathrm{d}b \geq 0.$$

That is, the incentive compatibility constraint is the same as before. Define $T(a,b) = q_i(a,b)a - P_i(a,b)$. The following proposition is analogous to Proposition 3.

Proposition 5 *For every b, $a \to q_i(a, b)$ is increasing.*

Proof: The incentive compatibility constraint implies for every a',

$$T(a, b) \geq q_i(a', b)a - P_i(a', b) = q_i(a', b)(a - a') + T(a', b).$$

Therefore, we have that

$$T(a, b) - T(a', b) \geq (a - a')q_i(a', b).$$

Analogously, we have that

$$T(a', b) - T(a, b) \geq (a' - a)q_i(a, b).$$

Adding both inequalities we obtain

$$0 \geq (a' - a)(q_i(a, b) - q_i(a', b))$$

and therefore if $a' > a$, then $q_i(a', b) \geq q_i(a, b)$. $\square$

In a similar fashion to the proof of (6.7) we may have the following.

Proposition 6 *For every b, it is true that*

$$T(a, b) = T(0, b) + \int_0^a q_i(s, b)\,\mathrm{d}s.$$

From this proposition we conclude that the payment satisfies the following:

$$P_i(a, b) = q_i(a, b)a - \left(T(0, b) + \int_0^a q_i(s, b)\,\mathrm{d}s\right)$$

$$= q_i(a, b)a - \int_0^a q_i(s, b)\,\mathrm{d}s - T(0, b). \tag{6.24}$$

Let $z(b)$ be a function and define $T(0, b) = z(b)$. Hence (q, P), with P_i defined by (6.24) and q is increasing in each variable. Then (q, P) is a dominant strategy mechanism. It is also incentive compatible if and only if

$$\int \left(z(b) + \int_0^a q_i(s, b)\,\mathrm{d}s\right) f(b\,|\,a)\,\mathrm{d}b \geq 0, \quad \forall a.$$

The auctioneer's expected revenue is given by:

$$R = R_1 + R_2,$$

$$R_1 = \int P_1(a, b) f(a, b)\,\mathrm{d}a\,\mathrm{d}b$$

$$= \int \left(q_1(a, b)a - \int_0^a q_1(s, b)\,\mathrm{d}s - z_1(b)\right) f(a, b)\,\mathrm{d}a\,\mathrm{d}b,$$

the expression for R_2 being analogous.

We now make an additional restriction. We restrict our mechanisms to efficient mechanisms. That is, mechanisms that satisfy (2) of Lemma 7. Thus $\int_0^a q_1(s, b) \, ds = (a-b)^+$. Also $\int_0^b q_2(a, s) \, ds = (b-a)^+$. The revenue from bidder 1 can be rewritten as

$$R_1 = \int a \left(\int_0^a f(a, b) \, db \right) da$$
$$- \int (a-b)^+ f(a, b) \, da \, db - \int z_1(b) f(a, b) \, da \, db.$$

And $z_1(b)$ satisfies the restriction:

$$\int (z_1(b) + (a-b)^+) f(a, b) \, db \geq 0, \quad \forall a.$$

Note that we used the fact that $f(b \mid a) = f(a, b) / \int f(a, b) \, db$. Define $\phi_1(a) = \int (a-b)^+ f(a, b) \, db$. Therefore to maximize revenue the auctioneer must choose $z_1(b)$ such that

$$\int z_1(b) f(a, b) \, db + \phi_1(a) \geq 0, \; \forall a, \quad \text{and} \quad \iint z_1(b) f(a, b) \, db \, da$$

is minimized.

Example 21 *We now fulfill our promise and find the optimal auction in a case in which the range is a two-dimensional vector space. Suppose the density is $f(a, b) = (1 + 4ab)/2$. The function*

$$\phi_1(a) = \int (a-b)^+ f(a, b) \, db = \int_0^a (a-b) \frac{1 + 4ab}{2} \, db = \frac{a^4}{3} + \frac{a^2}{4}.$$

The integral

$$\int z_1(b) f(a, b) \, db = \int z_1(b) \frac{1 + 4ab}{2} \, db = \frac{\int z_1(b) \, db}{2} + 2a \int z_1(b) b \, db.$$

Thus the set

$$\left\{ a \to \int z(b) f(b \mid a) \, db \right\} = \left\{ a \to \frac{\mu_1}{2} + 2\mu_2 a; \mu_i \in \mathbb{R} \text{ and exists } z(\cdot), \right.$$
$$\left. \int z(b) b^l \, db = \mu_l, l = 0, 1 \right\}$$

Define $\lambda_1 = \int z_1(b) \, db$ and $\lambda_2 = \int z_1(b) b \, db$. Then we want to find λ_1 and λ_2 such that

$$\frac{\lambda_1}{2} + 2a\lambda_2 + \frac{a^4}{3} + \frac{a^2}{4} \geq 0, \quad \forall a,$$

and

$$\gamma := \frac{\lambda_1}{2} + \lambda_2 = \int \left(\frac{\lambda_1}{2} + 2a\lambda_2 \right) \, da$$

is a minimized. Choosing $a = 0$ we see that necessarily $\lambda_1 \geq 0$. Since $\lambda_1 = \lambda_2 = 0$ is a possibility we see that $\gamma \leq 0$ and we may suppose without loss of generality that $\lambda_2 < 0$. The function

$$v(a) = 2a\lambda_2 + \frac{a^4}{3} + \frac{a^2}{4}$$

is convex in $[0, 1]$ and decreases in a neighborhood of $a = 0$. If $v'(1) \leq 0$ then

$$v'(1) = 2\lambda_2 + \frac{4}{3} + \frac{1}{2} \leq 0, \quad and \quad \frac{\lambda_1}{2} + 2\lambda_2 + \frac{1}{3} + \frac{1}{4} \geq 0.$$

The first inequality implies $\lambda_2 \leq -\frac{11}{12}$. The second implies $\gamma \geq -\lambda_2 - \frac{7}{12} \geq \frac{4}{12} > 0$. Suppose now that $v'(1) > 0$. Then there exists $x \in (0, 1)$ such that $v'(x) = 0$. From this we have that $2\lambda_2 = -(\frac{4x^3}{3} + \frac{x}{2})$ and hence

$$\frac{\lambda_1}{2} - x \left(\frac{4x^3}{3} + \frac{x}{2} \right) \frac{x^4}{3} + \frac{x^2}{4} \geq 0.$$

This inequality is equivalent to $\lambda_1 \geq \frac{8}{9}x^8 + \frac{1}{3}x^6 - \frac{1}{2}x^2$ and therefore,

$$\gamma = \frac{\lambda_1}{2} + \lambda_2 \geq \frac{4}{9}x^8 + \frac{1}{6}x^6 - \frac{1}{4}x^2 - \frac{2}{3}x^3 - \frac{1}{4}x.$$

The minimum of the right-hand side is at $x \approx 0.9023$. If now we choose

$$\lambda_2 = -\frac{1}{2} \left(\frac{4(0.9023)^3}{3} + \frac{0.9023}{2} \right) = -0.715,$$

$$\lambda_1 = \frac{8}{9}(0.9023)^8 + \frac{1}{3}(0.9023)^6 - \frac{1}{2}(0.9023)^2 = 0.163$$

$\gamma = \frac{0.163}{2} - 0.715 = -0.6335$ is minimum. To finish note that $z_1(b) = 4.942 - 9.558b$ is such that

$$\int z_1(b) \, db = \lambda_1 \quad and \quad \int z_1(b)b \, db = \lambda_2.$$

What conclusion can we drawn from the full surplus extraction results? Although the independent private values model plays a central role in the development of theory, it is reasonable to expect that bidders' types will exhibit some degree of correlation. However, auctions with random payments, if they exist at all, will be rare. This is true both in traditional auction settings, such as those used to sell houses, paintings, and wine, but also of the new engineered auctions such as the famous airwaves auctions. Below are some possible explanations for the nonexistence of these complex auctions involving lotteries, none of which has been formalized in the existing literature:

1. Too much information about the primitives (distribution of values, number of bidders, etc.) is needed to design the lottery;
2. The lottery might involve large payments from the auctioneer/bidders to provide bidders with the right incentives. In practice, bidders and the seller might be cash constrained;
3. Bidders have better things to do than participate in unprofitable auctions;
4. A risk averse seller might not be willing to risk making net payments to bidders; and
5. A full surplus extraction auction might encourage bidders' collusion.

Nevertheless, this is clearly an area that deserves more research.

6.4.3 Several Objects

We now return to the IPV set up. We will obtain a revenue equivalence result for the case where there are several identical objects for sale.

We suppose that there are $K > 1$ objects to sell and n bidders. Bidders only want one object each. If bidder i has type $t_i \in [0, 1]$ and receives object k his utility is $t_i \alpha_{ik}$ where $\alpha_{ik} > 0$ is given. Define the vector $\alpha_i = (\alpha_{i1}, \ldots, \alpha_{iK})$. Thus, if q_{ik} is the probability that bidder i receives object k then his utility is

$$t_i \cdot (q_i \cdot \alpha_i) = t_i \sum_{k=1}^{K} q_{ik} \alpha_{ik}.$$

We denote by $\mathbb{A}$ the set of possible allocations of the objects amongst the bidders. Thus,

$$\mathbb{A} = \{(a_1, \ldots, a_n); a_i \in \{0, 1, \ldots, K\}, \#\{i \leq n; a_i = k\} \leq 1 \quad \text{or } k = 0\}.$$

That is, each bidder receives at most one of the K existing objects. A direct mechanism, $(q, P) = (q, P_1, \ldots, P_n)$, is therefore given by

$$q(t) = (q_a(t))_{a \in \mathbb{A}}, q_a(t) \geq 0, \sum_{a \in \mathbb{A}} q_a(t) \leq 1;$$

and $P^i(t) \in \mathbb{R}$ is the payment of bidder i. The probability that i receives object k is therefore, $q_{ik}(t) = \sum_{a \in \mathbb{A}, a_i = k} q_a(t)$. The expected utility of i under the mechanism is

$$\pi_i(t_i) = t_i E_{-i} \left[\sum_{k=1}^{K} q_{ik}(t) \alpha_{ik} \right] - E_{-i}[P^i(t)]$$

$$= t_i E_{-i}[q_i(t) \cdot \alpha_i] - E_{-i}[P^i(t)].$$

If we define $Q^i(t_i) = (Q_1^i(t_i), \ldots, Q_K^i(t_i)), Q_k^i(t_i) = E_{-i}[q_{ik}(t)]$, we may write the incentive compatibility constraints as

$$\pi_i(t_i) \geq t_i Q^i(t') \cdot \alpha_i - E_{-i}[P^i(t')], \quad \forall t'.$$

From this we obtain the inequality

$$\pi_i(t_i) \geq (t_i - t') Q^i(t') \cdot \alpha_i + \pi_i(t').$$

Thus, following the same method as in the one-object case, we may prove that

$$\pi_i(t_i) = \pi_i(0) + \int_0^{t_i} Q^i(s) \cdot \alpha^i \, ds.$$

Hence, the bidder's expected payment is

$$E_{-i}[P^i(t)] = t_i E_{-i}[q_i(t) \cdot \alpha_i] - \pi_i(t_i)$$

$$= t_i E_{-i}[q_i(t) \cdot \alpha_i] - \int_0^{t_i} Q^i(s) \cdot \alpha^i \, ds - \pi_i(0).$$

Accordingly the following result holds:

Theorem 19 *Assume bidders demand only one object in a multi-object auction with IPV. Assume that (q, P) and $(\bar{q}, \bar{P})$ are two individually rational incentive compatible mechanisms such that:*

1. *The allocation rule is the same, that is, $q = \bar{q}$*
2. *The lowest type has the same expected utility in both mechanism, that is,*

$$E_{-i}[P^i(0, t_{-i})] = E_{-i}[\bar{P}^i(0, t_{-i})].$$

Then, the bidders' expected payments and the seller's expected revenue are the same in both auctions respectively. That is,

$$E_{-i}[P^i(t)] = E_{-i}[\bar{P}^i(t)] \quad and$$

$$E\left[\sum_{i=1}^n P^i(t)\right] = E\left[\sum_{i=1}^n \bar{P}^i(t)\right].$$

Proof: The proof is easy. Note that $E_{-i}[P^i(0, t_{-i})] = E_{-i}[\bar{P}^i(0, t_{-i})]$ implies that $E_{-i}[P^i(t)] = E_{-i}[\bar{P}^i(t)]$ which is the expected payment of a type t_i bidder. The seller expected revenue is

$$E\left[\sum_i P^i(t)\right] = \sum_i E[P^i(t)] = \sum_i E_i[E_{-i}[P^i(t)]]$$

$$= \sum_i E_i[E_{-i}[\bar{P}^i(t)]] = \sum_i E[\bar{P}^i(t)] = E\left[\sum_i \bar{P}^i(t)\right]. \qquad \square$$

6.4.4   Common Values Auction

In this section, we show that the Revenue Equivalence Theorem is also true in the common value independent signals[5] case. We will be even more general. We consider interdependent valuations possibly distinct for each bidder. So instead of supposing that a bidder with signal x_i values the object as x_i we suppose his valuation is $V^i = u^i(x_1, \ldots, x_n)$ where x_j is bidder j's signal. Naturally bidder i does not know the other bidders' signals. Let us rewrite the incentive compatibility and individual participation constraints. If (q, P) is a direct mechanism then it is incentive compatible if

$$E_{-i}[u^i(x)q_i(x) - P_i(x)] \geq E_{-i}[u^i(x, x_{-i})q_i(\tilde{x}) - P_i(\tilde{x})], \quad \forall x_i',$$

where $\tilde{x} = (x_i', x_{-i})$. The mechanism is individually rational if

$$E_{-i}[u^i(x)q_i(x) - P_i(x)] \geq 0.$$

We begin with a lemma.

Lemma 8   *If we define* $T_i(x_i) = E_{-i}[u^i(x)q_i(x) - P_i(x)]$ *then for every* x_i':

$$T_i(x_i) - T_i(x_i') \geq E_{-i}[(u^i(x) - u^i(x_i', x_{-i}))q_i(x_i', x_{-i})].$$

Proof: Rewrite the incentive compatibility constraint as

$$T_i(x_i) \geq E_{-i}[u^i(x)q_i(x_i', x_{-i}) - P_i(x_i', x_{-i})]$$
$$= E_{-i}[(u^i(x) - u^i(x_i', x_{-i}))q_i(x_i', x_{-i})] + T_i(x_i').$$

Therefore, we conclude that

$$T_i(x_i) - T_i(x_i') \geq E_{-i}[(u^i(x) - u^i(x_i', x_{-i}))q_i(x_i', x_{-i})]. \qquad \square$$

We want to prove the following lemma:

Lemma 9   *Suppose* u^i *is continuously differentiable. Then,*

$$T_i(x_i) = T_i(0) + \int_0^{x_i} E_{-i}\left[\frac{\partial u^i}{\partial x_i}(s, x_{-i})q_i(s, x_{-i})\right] ds.$$

Proof: For a given $n \in \mathbb{N}$, define the partition $\{0, \frac{x_i}{n}, \frac{2x_i}{n}, \ldots, x_i\}$. For each $j = 1, 2, \ldots, n$ there exists a $\xi_j \in \left(\frac{(j-1)x_i}{n}, \frac{jx_i}{n}\right)$ such that

$$u^i\left(\frac{jx_i}{n}, x_{-i}\right) - u^i\left(\frac{(j-1)x_i}{n}, x_{-i}\right) = \frac{\partial u^i}{\partial x_i}(\xi_j, x_{-i})\frac{x_i}{n}.$$

---

[5] Recall that in the common value model we prefer to use "signal" for "types".

Therefore,

$$T_i\left(\frac{jx_i}{n}\right) - T_i\left(\frac{(j-1)x_i}{n}\right) \geq E_{-i}\left[\frac{\partial u^i}{\partial x_i}(\xi_j, x_{-i})\frac{x_i}{n}q_i\left(\frac{(j-1)x_i}{n}x_{-i}\right)\right],$$

$j = 1, \ldots, n$. Adding all terms we obtain,

$$T_i(x_i) - T_i(0) \geq \sum_{j=1}^{n}\frac{x_i}{n}E_{-i}\left[\frac{\partial u^i}{\partial x_i}(\xi_j, x_{-i})q_i\left(\frac{(j-1)x_i}{n}x_{-i}\right)\right].$$

As n approaches ∞, the right-hand side converges to

$$\int_0^{x_i} E_{-i}\left[\frac{\partial u^i}{\partial x_i}(s, x_{-i})q_i(s, x_{-i})\right]\mathrm{d}s.$$

Therefore

$$T_i(x_i) - T_i(0) \geq \int_0^{x_i} E_{-i}\left[\frac{\partial u^i}{\partial x_i}(s, x_{-i})q_i(sx_{-i})\right]\mathrm{d}s.$$

The reverse inequality is proved in an analogous way. Hence, we have established the following. $\qquad\square$

Theorem 20 (general revenue equivalence) *If (q, P) and $(\bar{q}, \bar{P})$ are incentive compatible and individually rational mechanisms such that $q = \bar{q}$ and a bidder with the lowest signal has the same expected utility in both mechanisms then the expected payments and the sellers' expected revenue are the same for both mechanisms. That is*

$$E_{-i}[P_i(t)] = E_{-i}[\bar{P}_i(t)] \quad and \quad E\left[\sum_{i=1}^{n}P_i(t)\right] = E\left[\sum_{i=1}^{n}\bar{P}_i(t)\right].$$

Proof: If a_i is the expected payment of a bidder type $x_i = 0$ for (q, P) and $\bar{a}_i$ is the expected payment for $(\bar{q}, \bar{P})$ then if $a_i = \bar{a}_i$ it is true that

$$E_{-i}[P_i(x)] = E_{-i}[u^i(x)q_i(x)] - T_i(x_i)$$

$$= E_{-i}[u^i(x)q_i(x)] - a_i - \int_0^{x_i} E_{-i}\left[\frac{\partial u^i}{\partial x_i}(s, x_{-i})q_i(s, x_{-i})\right]\mathrm{d}s$$

$$= E_{-i}[u^i(x)\bar{q}_i(x)] - \bar{a}_i - \int_0^{x_i} E_{-i}\left[\frac{\partial u^i}{\partial x_i}(s, x_{-i})\bar{q}_i(s, x_{-i})\right]\mathrm{d}s$$

$$= E_{-i}[\bar{P}_i(x)].$$

Thus bidders' expected payments are the same for each bidder type. Moreover, the auctioneer' expected revenue is the same as well since $E[P_i(x)] = E_i[E_{-i}[P_i(x)]]$. $\qquad\square$

6.5 Exercises

1. (a) Show that if $f : \mathbb{R} \to \mathbb{R}$ and $g : \mathbb{R} \to \mathbb{R}$ are convex functions then $\max\{f, g\}$ is also a convex function.

   (b) Generalize the above result to show that if $\{f_i; i \in I\}$ is a family of convex functions and $\sup_{i \in I} f_i(x) < \infty$ for every x then $\sup_{i \in I} f_i$ is also a convex function. Conclude that if $H : \mathbb{R} \to \mathbb{R}$ is a function then there exists the largest convex function G such that $G(x) \leq H(x)$ for every x.

2. Prove the assertions on Remark 8.

3. Show that t_0 that solves (6.13) is such that $J(t_0) = 0$. Moreover show also that the optimum exists and is interior.

4. Find the optimal auction revenue if the individual distribution is uniform in $[0, 1]$ and there are n bidders. Compare it with the revenue of first-price sealed bid auctions (without reserve prices). How many bidders are necessary so that the auction without reserve prices generates more revenue than the optimal auction?

5. Repeat the last exercise if the individual distribution, instead of uniform, is any continuously differentiable distribution.

6. Prove the assertion on remark 9. Show also that if we want the distribution to have a continuous density on $[0, 1]$ it is necessary that $h'(1) = 2$.

7. An all-pay auction is an auction in which every bidder pays his bid whether or not receiving the object. In terms of mechanisms this means that $P_i(x)$ depends only on x_i. Suppose we have private values but types are correlated. Find the optimal auction amongst the class of all-pay auctions.

8. Suppose the utility of bidder i with type x_i is $u_i(x_i) = x_i^2$. Reduce this case to the case $u_i(x_i) = x_i$. Suggestion: if x_i^2 has density $f(x_i)$ find first the density of x_i. If x_i^2 is uniformly distributed what is the distribution of x_i. If x_i is uniformly distributed what is the distribution of x_i^2?

9. Do the same calculation of Example 20 if

$$f(a, b) = 1 + \sum_{n=1}^{\infty} a_n \frac{P_n(a) P_n(b)}{|P_n|_\infty^2}, \quad \sum_{n=1}^{\infty} |a_n| < 1.$$

10. The formalization of the English auction we presented is designed to cover the correlated values case. If types are independent, a much simpler strategy set can be used. Find one such simplified set up.

11. Suppose we have two bidders and the distribution is uniform. Show that if the auction is efficient the following payment rule is a possible one:

$$P(v, y) = \begin{cases} \dfrac{v}{2} + \dfrac{1}{\sqrt{v}} - \dfrac{1}{2\sqrt{y}} & \text{if } v > y \\ 0 & \text{otherwise.} \end{cases}$$

Show that the seller's payments are unbounded.

12. Find the war of attrition equilibrium for two bidders using the revenue equivalence theorem.

7

Multiple Objects

In this chapter we consider the sale of several objects. The objective of this chapter is not to generalize the theory developed in previous chapters to cover the sale of several objects. Instead, the purpose of this chapter is to illustrate several difficulties that arise when developing a general theory of auctions of multiple objects.

The reason for these difficulties does not come from the nature of the valuations (independent private values versus affiliated values) but rather from the additional strategic considerations when bidding for multiple objects—an individual's bid for one object might influence the allocation (price and likelihood of winning) not only of this particular object but also of other objects. Thus, unlike in the single-object case where a bidder's only concern was the bid of the opponent with the highest type, in a multi-object setting, bidders have to take into account several bids.

Suppose there are $K = 2$ objects for sale. These objects can be sold either sequentially or simultaneously. The objects are identical in the sense that bidders only care about how many objects they obtain. Bidders may demand one or more units. We consider the symmetric, Independent Private Values model. Thus every bidder i receives a type $x \in [0, 1]$ distributed with density $f(x)$. If the bidder with type x receives one object his utility is $U_1(x) = x$. If he receives 2 objects his utility is $U_2(x) = \alpha_2 x$. We assume that $\alpha_2 \geq 1$. Thus if the bidder demands at most one object, $\alpha_2 = 1$. If $\alpha_2 > 2$ we say that there is positive synergy since two objects together generate more utility than twice the utility generated from a single object. If $1 \leq \alpha_2 < 2$, we say that there is negative synergy.

This chapter is organized as follows. Section 7.1 examines sequential second-price auctions. Section 7.2 studies discriminatory and uniform auctions. Finally, we characterize the optimal auction and compare its expected revenue with that of standard auction formats.

7.1   Sequential Auctions

For convenience, let us define $r = \alpha_2 - 1$. Thus, if $r > 1$ there is positive synergy and if $r < 1$ negative synergy.

Sequential auctions present a complication that does not arise in simultaneous auctions; the first auction generates information about bidders' types that can be used in the second auction. For example, if strategies are strictly increasing in the first auction and the winning bid is announced (this is a minimum requirement) then bidders may infer the highest type. It may not be in the interest of the winner that this inference be made. Note that if all bids are announced then there is a complete revelation of all bidders' types. This possibility of information revelation makes the analysis more interesting but much harder. Thus, in this section we look only at Second-price sequential auctions. The reason that it is easier to examine second-price auctions than first-price auctions is the fact that second-price auctions in this context are Vickrey auctions—the revelation of types is a dominant strategy. Thus, the information that is revealed in the first round of a sequence of second-price auctions does not interact strategically with the information to be used in the second round.

Let us find equilibrium bidding strategies for a sequence of two second-price auctions. The equilibrium bidding strategy in the second auction is easy to calculate. If bidder i does not win one object in the first auction he bids $b_i^2(x) = x$ in the second auction. If he does win one object in the first auction he bids $b_i^2(x_i) = \alpha_2 x_i - x_i = (\alpha_2 - 1)x_i = rx_i-$ his value for an additional unit, in the second auction.

Now let us find equilibrium bidding strategies in the first auction. Assume that bidder i, $i = 2, \ldots, n$ bids according to the strictly increasing strategy $b(x)$ in the first auction. Define $Y = \max\{x_j; j \geq 2\}$. We also need to define Y^2, the second highest among $\{x_j; j \geq 2\}$. Thus, if bidder 1, with type x, bids $b(z)$ his expected utility is:

$$\phi(z) = E[(x - b(Y) + (rx - Y)^+)I_{z>Y}] + E[(x - \max\{rY, Y^2\})^+ I_{z<Y}].$$
$$(7.1)$$

If player 1's type is higher than Y, then he wins the first object and bids rx in the second auction. This is the first part of (7.1). The term $\max\{rY, Y^2\}$ in the second part appears for the following reason. If bidder 1 does not win the first object his type is smaller than Y. The bidder with type Y wins the first object and therefore bids rY in the second auction. (Ties occur with zero probability). The non-winning bidders bid their types, the highest of which is Y^2, in the second auction. If we have positive synergy then $rY \geq Y \geq Y^2$ and $\max\{rY, Y^2\} = rY$. If we have negative synergy, then this maximum can be equal to Y^2. (For example, consider the limiting case where $\alpha_2 = 1$.) We will consider both cases together. To write (7.1) in terms of f_Y, the density of Y, consider

$$\psi(y) = E[(x - \max\{rY, Y^2\})^+ \,|\, Y = y],$$

the conditional expectation of $(x - \max\{rY, Y^2\})^+$ given Y. The expected utility (7.1) can be rewritten as

$$\phi(z) = \int_0^z (x - b(y) + (rx - y)^+) f_Y(y)\,\mathrm{d}y + \int_z^1 \psi(y) f_Y(y)\,\mathrm{d}y.$$

In the last summand we used iterated expectations. That is, $E[\psi(Y) I_{z<Y}] = E[(x - \max\{rY, Y^2\})^+ I_{z<Y}]$. Differentiating we obtain,

$$\phi'(z) = \{x - b(z) + (rx - z)^+ - \psi(z)\} f_Y(z). \tag{7.2}$$

Thus if $z = x$ maximizes ϕ, then $\phi'(x) = 0$:

$$x + (r - 1)^+ x - \psi(x) = b(x).$$

Substituting this $b(\cdot)$ into (7.2) yields

$$\begin{aligned}
\frac{\phi'(z)}{f_Y(z)} &= x - z - (r - 1)^+ z + (rx - z)^+ \\
&= \begin{cases} x - z + (rx - z)^+ & \text{if } \alpha_2 \leq 2; \\ x - rz + (rx - z)^+ & \text{if } \alpha_2 > 2. \end{cases}
\end{aligned}$$

We examine the different possible cases.

(i) $r \leq 1$ In this case, if $z < x$ then $\phi'(z) > 0$. Suppose now that $z > x$. Then $(rx - z)^+ = 0$ and $\phi'(z) < 0$. Therefore $z = x$ maximizes ϕ.

(ii) $r > 1$ If $z < x$ then $rx > x > z$ and

$$\frac{\phi'(z)}{f_Y(z)} = x - rz + rx - z = \alpha_2(x - z) > 0.$$

Finally if $z > x$ then $\phi'(z) < 0$ when $(rx - z)^+ = 0$ and if $rx - z \geq 0$ then

$$\frac{\phi'(z)}{f_Y(z)} = x - rz + rx - z = \alpha_2(x - z) < 0.$$

Hence, in all cases $z = x$ is the optimum. We summarize our conclusions as follows.

Proposition 7   *The equilibrium bidding strategy for the first of the two sequential second-price auction of identical goods is given by:*

$$b(x) = x + (r - 1)^+ x - E[(x - \max\{rY, Y^2\})^+ \,|\, Y = x].$$

In particular,

1. *If there is positive synergy, then*
$$b(x) = rx.$$

2. *If there is negative synergy, then*
$$b(x) = E[\max\{rx, Y^2\} \mid Y = x].$$

Note that if bidders demand only one object, then the bid in the first auction is $b(x) = E[Y^2 \mid Y = x]$. In what follows we present a numerical example where we can explicitly compute equilibrium bidding strategies and the seller's expected revenue.

Example 22 *Suppose there are two bidders, the types are distributed uniformly on $[0, 1]$ and the synergy is negative, say $\alpha_2 = \frac{3}{2}$. Define $X^1 = \max\{x_1, x_2\}$ and $X^2 = \min\{x_1, x_2\}$. With two bidders, $Y^2 = 0$ and thus $b(x) = x/2$. The seller's expected revenue is*

$$E\left[b(X_1) + \frac{X_1}{2}I_{X_1>2X_2} + X_2I_{X_1<2X_2}\right]$$

$$= 2\int_{x_1>x_2}\left(b(x_1) + \frac{x_1}{2}I_{x_1>2x_2} + x_2I_{x_1<2x_2}\right)dx_2\,dx_1$$

$$= 2\int_0^1 \frac{x_1^2}{2}\,dx_1 + 2\int_0^1\left(\frac{x_1}{2}\right)^2 dx_1 + 2\int_{x_1>x_2} x_2I_{x_1<2x_2}\,dx_1\,dx_2$$

$$= \frac{1}{3} + \frac{1}{6} + 2\int_0^1\int_{x_{1/2}}^{x_1} x_2\,dx_2\,dx_1 = \frac{3}{4}.$$

Example 23 *If there is positive synergy, then the bidder with the highest type wins both objects. Thus, the sequential auction is efficient and the Revenue Equivalence Theorem holds. If there is negative synergy and when $X^2 > rX^1$, where X^1 is the highest type and X^2 is the second highest, then the bidder with the highest type may not win both objects. In this case, the revenue equivalence theorem breaks down.*

7.2   Simultaneous Auctions

We now consider the simultaneous sale of two objects. Simultaneous auctions have attracted a lot of attention as governments usually sell Treasury bills in this way. There are two common types: discriminatory and uniform-price auctions. In the former, all winning bidders pay their bids. In the latter, all the winning bidders pay the same amount—either the highest losing bid or the lowest winning bid. Below we analyze these two types of auction formats.

7.2.1   Discriminatory Auctions

In the discriminatory auction each bidder i bids a vector of K bids,

$$\left(b_1^i, \ldots, b_K^i\right), b_1^i \geq b_2^i \geq \cdots \geq b_K^i.$$

The $K's$ higher bids among $\left\{b_k^i; 1 \leq i \leq n, 1 \leq k \leq K\right\}$ are the winning bids. If bidder i has one bid amongst the winning bids his payment is b_i. If he has k bids among the winning bids his payment is $b_1^i + \cdots + b_k^i$ and he receives k objects. (The uniform-price auction is similar except in the payment; every winning bidder pays the same unitary price, which is equal either to the $K+1$th highest bid or to the Kth highest bid.) While the discriminatory auction is similar to the the first-price auction (you pay your bid), the uniform-price auction is similar to the second-price auction. This analogy, however, is imperfect as bidders in general will not bid their true valuations in a simultaneous uniform-price auction for strategic reasons (see next section).

We now consider a simple example with two bidders and two objects. If there is positive synergy, then the discriminatory auction has a simple equilibrium. The bidders bid as they were bidding in a first-price auction for a object with utility $\alpha_2 x$. The reason is that in an increasing, symmetric equilibrium, the individual with the highest type wins both objects. This individual pays the sum of his bids. This is equivalent to bidding for a single object that is worth $\alpha_2 x$. Below we formalize this intuition. We denote by $b(\cdot)$ the symmetric bidding function for the first object and by $c(\cdot)$ the symmetric bidding for the second object.

Theorem 21   *If $\alpha_2 \geq 2$, then a symmetric equilibrium strategy in the discriminatory auction of two objects is to bid the same amount for each object, $b(x) = c(x)$, where*

$$b(x) = \frac{\alpha_2}{2} \frac{\int_0^x y f_Y(y)\,\mathrm{d}y}{F_Y(x)}. \tag{7.3}$$

We first note that $b(x)$ defined in (7.3) satisfies the differential equation

$$b'(x)F_Y(x) + b(x)f_Y(x) = \frac{\alpha_2}{2} x f_Y(x). \tag{7.4}$$

If bidder 1 bids $b \geq c$ for the first and second object his expected utility is given by

$$\phi(b,c) = (\alpha_2 x - b - c)\Pr(c > b(Y)) + (x - b)\Pr(b > b(Y) > c).$$

Note that any bid $c > b(1)$ can be profitably reduced to $c = b(1)$. Any bid $b > b(1)$ can be profitably reduced as well. Thus, we may suppose that $b = b(\alpha)$ and $c = b(\beta)$, where $1 \geq \alpha \geq \beta \geq 0$. As a result, we can rewrite the expected utility as

$$\psi(\alpha, \beta) = (\alpha_2 x - b(\alpha) - b(\beta)) \Pr(\beta > Y) + (x - b(\alpha)) \Pr(\alpha > Y > \beta)$$
$$= (\alpha_2 x - b(\alpha) - b(\beta)) F_Y(\beta) + (x - b(\alpha))(F_Y(\alpha) - F_Y(\beta))$$
$$= ((\alpha_2 - 1)x - b(\beta)) F_Y(\beta) + (x - b(\alpha)) F_Y(\alpha).$$

The constrained maximization problem

$$\max_{\alpha \geq \beta} \psi(\alpha, \beta)$$

may be solved using Kuhn–Tucker. If λ is the Kuhn–Tucker multiplier then

$$\frac{\partial \psi}{\partial \alpha} = -b'(\alpha) F_Y(\alpha) + (x - b(\alpha)) f_Y(\alpha) = \lambda;$$

$$\frac{\partial \psi}{\partial \beta} = -b'(\beta) F_Y(\beta) + ((\alpha_2 - 1)x - b(\beta)) f_Y(\beta) = -\lambda;$$

$$\lambda \cdot (\alpha - \beta) = 0.$$

The differential equation (7.4) allows us to rewrite $\partial \psi / \partial \alpha$ and $\partial \psi / \partial \beta$ to obtain

$$\left(x - \frac{\alpha_2 \alpha}{2}\right) f_Y(\alpha) = \lambda; \tag{7.5}$$

$$\left((\alpha_2 - 1)x - \frac{\alpha_2 \beta}{2}\right) f_Y(\beta) = -\lambda; \tag{7.6}$$

$$\lambda \cdot (\alpha - \beta) = 0.$$

At the optimum we must have $\alpha = \beta$. To see why, suppose not; then $\lambda = 0$. Thus, $x - (\alpha_2 \alpha / 2) = 0$ and

$$0 = (\alpha_2 - 1)x - \frac{\alpha_2 \alpha}{2} = (\alpha_2 - 2)x > 0.$$

Hence, $\alpha = \beta$. Adding (7.5) and (7.6) we obtain

$$\left(x - \frac{\alpha_2 \alpha}{2} + (\alpha_2 - 1)x - \frac{\alpha_2 \alpha}{2}\right) f_Y(\alpha) = 0$$

and this yields $\alpha = x = \beta$, ending the proof.

The task of finding equilibrium strategies under negative synergy is harder. We will obtain the solution as a pair of differential equations. Suppose bidder 2 bids according to the strictly increasing continuous strategies $(b(\cdot), c(\cdot)), b(\cdot) \geq c(\cdot)$. If bidder 1 bids $(\bar{b}, \bar{c}), \bar{b} \geq \bar{c}$ his expected utility is

$$\psi(\bar{b}, \bar{c}) = (\alpha_2 x - \bar{b} - \bar{c}) \Pr(\bar{c} > b(Y)) + (x - \bar{b}) \Pr(\bar{b} > c(Y), b(Y) > \bar{c}).$$

The first summand corresponds to winning two objects and the second one to winning one of the objects only. Now note that a bid $\bar{b} > c(1)$ can be reduced to $c(1)$, increasing utility. Therefore, we suppose without loss of generality that $\bar{b} \leq c(1)$. An analogous reasoning allows us to suppose that $\bar{c} \leq b(1)$.

If equilibrium exists, $\bar{c} = c(1)$ and $\bar{b} = b(1)$ will be the choices when $x = 1$. Therefore, necessarily $c(1) \leq b(1)$ and $b(1) \leq c(1)$ implying $b(1) = c(1)$. Hence, a necessary condition for equilibrium is that $b(1) = c(1)$. We may rewrite

$$\Pr(\bar{c} > b(Y)) = \Pr(b^{-1}(\bar{c}) > Y) = F(b^{-1}(\bar{c})).$$

We have also that

$$\Pr(\bar{b} > c(Y), b(Y) > \bar{c}) = \Pr(c^{-1}(\bar{b}) > Y > b^{-1}(\bar{c}))$$
$$= F(c^{-1}(\bar{b})) - F(b^{-1}(\bar{c})).$$

The maximization problem can be reduced to the problem of

$$\max_{\bar{b},\bar{c}} (\alpha_2 x - \bar{b} - \bar{c}) F(b^{-1}(\bar{c})) + (x - \bar{b}) F(c^{-1}(\bar{b})) - F(b^{-1}(\bar{c}))$$

subject to $\bar{b} \geq \bar{c}$.
To see that it is always true that $c^{-1}(\bar{b}) \geq b^{-1}(\bar{c})$, write $\bar{b} = b(\alpha)$ and $\bar{c} = c(\beta)$. Then

$$c^{-1}(\bar{b}) = c^{-1}(b(\alpha)) \geq c^{-1}(c(\alpha)) = \alpha \text{ and } c^{-1}(\bar{b}) \geq c^{-1}(\bar{c}) = \beta.$$

Thus $c^{-1}(\bar{b}) \geq \max\{\alpha, \beta\}$. Analogously $\min\{\alpha, \beta\} \geq b^{-1}(\bar{c})$. Simplifying the last equation we have

$$\psi(\bar{b}, \bar{c}) = ((\alpha_2 - 1)x - \bar{c}) F(b^{-1}(\bar{c})) + (x - \bar{b}) F(c^{-1}(\bar{b})). \qquad (7.7)$$

The first-order conditions for optimum at $\bar{b} = b(x)$, and $\bar{c} = c(x)$ are:

$$\frac{\partial \psi}{\partial \bar{b}}\Big|_{\bar{b}=b(x)} = -F(c^{-1}(b(x))) + (x - b(x))f(c^{-1}(b(x)))(c^{-1})'(b(x)) = 0; \qquad (7.8)$$

$$\frac{\partial \psi}{\partial \bar{c}}\Big|_{\bar{c}=c(x)} = -F(b^{-1}(c(x))) + ((\alpha_2 - 1)x - c(x))f(b^{-1}(c(x)))(b^{-1})'(c(x)) = 0.$$

If we make a change of variables $y = b(x)$ in the first equation and $y = c(x)$ in the second equation, we have the system of differential equations:

$$-F(c^{-1}(y)) + (b^{-1}(y) - y)f(c^{-1}(y))(c^{-1})'(y) = 0;$$
$$-F(b^{-1}(y)) + ((\alpha_2 - 1)c^{-1}(y) - y)f(b^{-1}(y))(b^{-1})'(y) = 0.$$

We have just proved the necessity part of the following theorem.

Theorem 22 *The discriminatory price auction has a unique strictly increasing differentiable equilibrium. The strategies $(b(\cdot), c(\cdot))$ are equilibrium bidding*

*strategies of the discriminatory price auction if and only if $b^{-1}(\cdot)$ and $c^{-1}(\cdot)$
satisfy the system of differential equations:*

$$(c^{-1})'(y) = \frac{F(c^{-1}(y))}{(b^{-1}(y) - y)f(c^{-1}(y))};$$

$$(b^{-1})'(y) = \frac{F(b^{-1}(y))}{((\alpha_2 - 1)c^{-1}(y) - y)f(b^{-1}(y))},$$

(7.9)

and the initial conditions

$$b(1) = c(1);$$

$$b(0) = 0 = c(0).$$

Let us now prove the sufficiency part. Thus, suppose we have a solution
(b^{-1}, c^{-1}) of (7.9) such that $b(1) = c(1)$ and $b(0) = 0 = c(0)$. From (7.8) we
see that

$$\frac{\partial \psi}{\partial \bar{b}} = -F(c^{-1}(\bar{b})) + (x - \bar{b})f(c^{-1}\bar{b})(c^{-1})'(\bar{b})$$

$$= -F(c^{-1}(\bar{b})) + (x - \bar{b})f(c^{-1}(\bar{b}))\frac{F(c^{-1}(\bar{b}))}{(b^{-1}(\bar{b}) - \bar{b})f(c^{-1}(\bar{b}))}$$

$$= F(c^{-1}(\bar{b}))\frac{-b^{-1}(\bar{b}) + x}{(b^{-1}(\bar{b}) - \bar{b})}.$$

Thus, ψ is decreasing if $b^{-1}(\bar{b}) > x$ and is increasing if $b^{-1}(\bar{b}) < x$. Therefore
$\bar{b} = b(x)$ is the optimum. Analogously, we prove that $\bar{c} = c(x)$ is optimum.   □

We will not prove, however, that the differential equations system has a
solution. For this we refer the reader to Lebrun and Tremblay (2003).

Remark 14 *A system of two differential equations depends on two constants
which are the initial conditions. For example if $x_0 \in (0, 1)$ and C_1 and C_2 are
constants then the initial conditions have the form*

$$c^{-1}(x_0) = C_1;$$ (ic)

$$b^{-1}(x_0) = C_2.$$

*The condition $b(1) = c(1)$ is not of this form. To write as (ic) define $\bar{y} = b(1) =
c(1)$. Then $b^{-1}(\bar{y}) = 1$ and $c^{-1}(\bar{y}) = 1$. Thus, instead of having two arbitrary
constants we have $C_1 = C_2 = 1$ but $\bar{y}$ is also to be found. The additional
condition is to choose $\bar{y}$ so that $c^{-1}(0) = 0 = b^{-1}(0)$. All this is needed since
we cannot simply choose $x_0 = 0$ as (7.9) is not defined for $y = 0$.*

Remark 15 *There are methods to numerically approximate solutions of differential equations. These methods, however, are not applied directly to systems*

of the form (ic). Instead, we have to look in the parametrized family of solutions $(b_k^{-1}(\cdot), c_k^{-1}(\cdot))$ with initial condition $b_k^{-1}(k) = 1 = c_k^{-1}(1)$, and one that satisfies also $b_k^{-1}(0) = 0 = c_k^{-1}(0)$.

Below we solve this system for an example with the uniform-$[0, 1]$ distribution.

Example 24 *Suppose there are two bidders. Suppose $\alpha_2 = 3/2$ and $F(x) = x$. Write $\phi(y) = c^{-1}(y)$ and $\psi(y) = b^{-1}(y)$. Let us solve the system*

$$\phi'(y) = \frac{\phi(y)}{\psi(y) - y},$$

$$\psi'(y) = \frac{\psi(y)}{\phi(y)/2 - y}.$$

Eliminating the denominator in both equations we obtain,

$$\phi'(y)\psi(y) = y\phi'(y) + \phi(y) = (y\phi(y))' \text{ and } \psi'(y)\phi(y) = 2(y\psi(y))'.$$

Adding both equations yields

$$(\phi(y)\psi(y))' = (y\phi(y))' + 2(y\psi(y))'.$$

Therefore, by the Fundamental Calculus Theorem, $\phi(y)\psi(y) = y\phi(y) + 2y\psi(y) + C$. Considering $y = 0$, we see that $C = 0$. Thus, we have that

$$\phi(y) = \frac{2y\psi(y)}{\psi(y) - y}. \tag{7.10}$$

Substituting this result into the equation for ψ we obtain:

$$\psi'(y) = \frac{\psi(y)(\psi(y) - y)}{y^2}.$$

Define $z(y)$ by $yz(y) = \psi(y)$ and substituting this into the last equation we obtain an equation for z':

$$yz'(y) = z(y)(z(y) - 2).$$

Using that $1/z(z - 2) = -1/2z + 1/2(z - 2)$ we rewrite the last equation as

$$-\frac{z'(y)}{2z(y)} + \frac{z'(y)}{2(z(y) - 2)} = \frac{1}{y} \tag{7.11}$$

which is easily integrated to yield

$$\frac{z(y) - 2}{z(y)} = Ky^2.$$

Hence $z(y) = 2/(1 - Ky^2)$ and $\psi(y) = 2y/(1 - Ky^2)$. Using (7.10) we obtain that $\phi(y) = 4y/(1 + Ky^2)$. We are almost done now. To determine K we have to solve (why? Hint: $\bar{y}$ gives us $b(1)$),

$$\phi(\bar{y}) = \psi(\bar{y}) = 1.$$

The equality $\phi(\bar{y}) = \psi(\bar{y})$ gives $\bar{y} = 1/\sqrt{3K}$. Substituting this in the last equality we find $K = 3$. This gives $b^{-1}(y) = 2y/(1 - 3y^2)$. One can now easily check that the equilibrium bidding strategies are:

$$b(x) = \frac{x}{1 + \sqrt{1 + 3x^2}}; \quad c(x) = \frac{x}{2 + \sqrt{4 - 3x^2}}.$$

7.2.2 Uniform price Auctions

Uniform-price auctions have been suggested as an alternative format for the sale of Treasury bills and are currently used in electricity spot markets around the globe. Given that the debate on which auction format is superior (discriminatory versus uniform), our aim in this section is modest. Our objective here is to illustrate that, in the context of the sale of multiple objects, auction formats matter quite considerably in terms of bidding behavior and the seller's expected revenue.

As above, we concentrate on the Independent Private Values model and on the sale of K objects. Each bidder i bids a vector of bids $(b_1^i, \ldots, b_K^i)$, $b_1^i \geq \cdots \geq b_K^i$. The winners are the Kth highest bidders. The payment for each object will be the same for the winning bidders. This payment is either equal to the $K + 1$th highest bid (that is, the highest losing bid) or the Kth highest bid (that is, the lowest winning bid). Both types occur in practice. We consider both cases below.

Winning bidders pay the highest losing bid.
It is tempting to conclude that this auction format is similar to the Vickrey auction and that bidding one's true valuation for each object is an equilibrium. Such a conclusion would be flawed. This auction format has properties that are distinct from those of the Vickrey auction as illustrated below for the case of negative synergies.

We consider again $K = 2$ and first we examine the positive synergy case. The next result should come as no surprise. With positive synergies, in any increasing, symmetric equilibrium, the individual with the highest type receives both objects. Thus, it does not matter if the two objects are sold together or separately. In the former setting, the equilibrium bidding strategy is such where a player with value x bids $\alpha_2 x$. In the latter, this individual's bids for both objects are identical and equal to $(\alpha_2/2)x$ as we show below. In this case, the analogy with the Vickrey auction is precise.

Theorem 23 *The uniform price auction of two objects with positive synergy($\alpha_2 \geq 2$) has as equilibrium strategies $b(x) = c(x) = (\alpha_2/2)x$.*

Proof: Suppose bidders $i = 2, \ldots, n$ bid according to $(b(\cdot), c(\cdot))$, $b(x) = c(x) = rx$, $r = \alpha_2/2$. Let us find bidder 1's best response. If he bids $(b, c), b \geq c \geq 0$ his expected utility is given by

$$\phi(b, c) = E[(2r(x - Y))I_{c>rY} + (x - rY)I_{b>rY>c}]$$

$$= 2r \int_0^{c/r} (x - y)f_Y(y)\, dy + \int_{c/r}^{b/r} (x - ry)f_Y(y)\, dy.$$

Note that the payment in case $b > rY > c$ is rY since rY is the third highest bid. The constrained maximization problem

$$\max_{b \geq c} \phi(b, c) \tag{7.12}$$

has a Kuhn–Tucker multiplier $\lambda \in \mathbb{R}$ so that at the optimum (b, c).

$$\frac{\partial \phi}{\partial b} = \lambda$$

$$\frac{\partial \phi}{\partial a} = -\lambda$$

$$\lambda(b - c) = 0.$$

Thus

$$(x - b)f_Y(b/r)\frac{1}{r} = \lambda$$

$$((2r - 1)x - c)f_Y\left(\frac{c}{r}\right)\frac{1}{r} = -\lambda$$

$$\lambda(b - c) = 0.$$

If $b > c$ then $\lambda = 0$ and $x = b$. But, then, $(2r - 1)x - c \geq x - c > x - b = 0$, a contradiction. Therefore, at the optimum $b = c$ and from

$$((2r - 1)x - c + x - c)f_Y\left(\frac{c}{r}\right)\frac{1}{r} = 0,$$

we conclude that $c = rx$. $\qquad \square$

The following limiting case is of interest. Suppose that there is no synergy, that is, $\alpha_2 = 2$. Then $b(x) = c(x) = x$ is an equilibrium. If bidders want only one object ($\alpha_2 = 1$) then $(x, 0)$ is an equilibrium. We consider now the negative synergy case. That is, consider $1 < \alpha_2 < 2$ and that bidder $i, i = 2, \ldots, n$ bids according to strictly increasing, continuous bidding strategies $(b(\cdot), c(\cdot))$. We will find bidder 1's best response. We begin with a lemma.

Lemma 10   *To maximize his expected utility, bidder 1 can restrict his bids to* $b = x$ *and* $c \leq x$.

Proof: If bidder 1 bids $b \geq c$ we may write the expected utility as

$$\psi(b,c) = E[(\alpha_2 x - 2b(Y))I_{c>b(Y)} + (x - \max\{c, c(Y)\})I_{b>c(Y),b(Y)>c}].$$

If $c > x$, bidder 1's expected utility is negative when only one object is won: $x - \max\{c, c(Y)\} \leq x - c < 0$. This is always true when two objects are won if $c > b(Y) \geq x$. Thus, reducing to $c = x$ increases or at least does not decrease his expected utility. If $b > x \geq c$, reducing b to x does not alter the first summand but it increases the second summand since it eliminates the cases in which $b > c(Y) > x$. Now if $x > b \geq c$, increasing b to x does not reduce and may increase the second summand by including the cases where $x > c(Y) \geq b$.

The conclusion to draw from the lemma above is that we shall look for an equilibrium with $b(x) = x \geq c(x)$. We take this into account in $\psi(b,c)$ and rewrite it as

$$\begin{aligned}
\bar{\phi}(c) &= \psi(x,c) \\
&= E[(\alpha_2 x - 2Y)I_{c>Y} + (x - \max\{c, c(Y)\})I_{x>c(Y),Y>c}].
\end{aligned} \tag{7.13}$$

Define $\bar{k} = 1$ if $x > c(1)$ and $\bar{k} = c^{-1}(x)$ otherwise. To obtain first-order conditions we now restrict ourselves to the case where $c = c(\beta) \leq x$. This is equivalent to $\beta \leq \bar{k}$. Thus, the expected utility may be written as

$$\begin{aligned}
\phi(\beta) &= \int_0^{c(\beta)} (\alpha_2 x - 2y) f_Y(y) \, dy + \int_{c(\beta)}^{\bar{k}} (x - \max\{c(\beta), c(y)\}) f_Y(y) \, dy \\
&= \int_0^{c(\beta)} (\alpha_2 x - 2y) f_Y(y) \, dy + \int_{c(\beta)}^{\bar{k}} (x - c(\max\{\beta, y\})) f_Y(y) \, dy \\
&= \int_0^{c(\beta)} (\alpha_2 x - 2y) f_Y(y) \, dy + \int_{c(\beta)}^{\beta} (x - c(\beta)) f_Y(y) \, dy \\
&\quad + \int_{\beta}^{\bar{k}} (x - c(y)) f_Y(y) \, dy \\
&= \int_0^{c(\beta)} (\alpha_2 x - 2y) f_Y(y) \, dy + (x - c(\beta))(F_Y(\beta) - F_Y(c(\beta))) \\
&\quad + \int_{\beta}^{\bar{k}} (x - c(y)) f_Y(y) \, dy.
\end{aligned} \tag{7.14}$$

Differentiating we obtain

$$
\begin{aligned}
\phi'(\beta) &= (\alpha_2 x - 2c(\beta)) f_Y(c(\beta)) c'(\beta) - c'(\beta)(F_Y(\beta) - F_Y(c(\beta))) \\
&\quad + (x - c(\beta))(f_Y(\beta) - f_Y(c(\beta)) c'(\beta)) - (x - c(\beta)) f_Y(\beta) \\
&= f_Y(c(\beta)) c'(\beta) \{ rx - c(\beta) \} - c'(\beta)(F_Y(\beta) - F_Y(c(\beta))) \\
&= c'(\beta) [f_Y(c(\beta)) \{ rx - c(\beta) \} - (F_Y(\beta) - F_Y(c(\beta)))].
\end{aligned}
$$

Thus if $\beta = x$ is to be the optimum:

$$
c'(x) \left[f_Y(c(x)) \{ rx - c(x) \} - (F_Y(x) - F_Y(c(x))) \right] = 0.
$$

Therefore, whenever $c'(x) > 0$,

$$
(rx - c(x)) f_Y(c(x)) + F_Y(c(x)) = F_Y(x). \tag{7.15}
$$

For example, if $F(x) = x$ this equation implies that $\alpha_2 = 2$. If $F(x) = \sqrt{x}$, there is a solution:

$$
c(x) = \left(3 - \alpha_2 - 2\sqrt{2 - \alpha_2} \right) x.
$$

The first-order condition above suggests that perhaps we should look at a constant equilibrium, that is, $c' = 0$. So, to this effect, suppose $(x, 0)$ is the bid submitted by bidders $i = 2, \ldots, n$. If bidder 1 bids $(x, c), x \geq c$ his expected utility is (see equation (7.13)):

$$
\begin{aligned}
\bar{\phi}(c) &= E[(\alpha_2 x - 2Y) I_{c>Y} + (x - c) I_{Y>c}] \\
&= \int_0^c (\alpha_2 x - 2y) f_Y(y)\, dy + (x - c)(1 - F_Y(c)).
\end{aligned}
$$

Thus,

$$
\begin{aligned}
\bar{\phi}'(c) &= (\alpha_2 x - 2c) f_Y(c) - (1 - F_Y(c)) - f_Y(c)(x - c) \\
&= ((\alpha_2 - 1)x - c) f_Y(c) - (1 - F_Y(c)). \qquad \square
\end{aligned}
$$

The following theorem is now easy to prove. Recall that $r = \alpha_2 - 1$.

Theorem 24 *Suppose the synergy is negative. Suppose also that $f_Y(0) < \infty$, and $f_Y'(y) \geq 0$ for every $y < r$. Then, $(x, 0)$ is a symmetric equilibrium bidding strategy.*

Proof: If $0 < c < rx$ then $\bar{\phi}''(c) = (rx - c) f_Y'(c) \geq 0$. Therefore $\bar{\phi}'$ is increasing. Thus,

$$
\bar{\phi}'(c) \leq \bar{\phi}'(rx) = -(1 - F(rx)) \leq 0.
$$

Therefore, $\bar{\phi}(c) \leq \bar{\phi}(0)$. This ends the proof. $\qquad \square$

Note that with negative synergies bidders do not bid their true valuations! Indeed, this auction format can perform poorly in terms of the seller's expected revenue. The seller's expected revenue in the symmetric equilibrium is equal to zero as shown in the next example.

Example 25   *We can apply the theorem to $F_Y(x) = x^t$ if $t \geq 1$. If $F_Y(x) = F^n(x)$, $n \geq 2$ then $f_Y(0) = nF^{n-1}(0)f(0) = 0$ if $f(0) < \infty$.*

Bidders pay the lowest winning bid
An alternative formulation is for winning bidders to pay the lowest winning bid as the constant per unit price. The reader might conjecture that such a small change will not impact much on the analysis. It turns out that such a conjecture would be wrong as we show next.

Suppose $(b(\cdot), c(\cdot))$ is a symmetric, strictly increasing equilibrium. If bidders $2, \ldots, n$ bid according to $(b(\cdot), c(\cdot))$ and bidder 1 bids $(\bar{b}, \bar{c})$, $\bar{b} \geq \bar{c}$ his expected utility is

$$\psi(\bar{b}, \bar{c}) = E[(\alpha_2 x - 2\bar{c})I_{\bar{c} > b(Y)} + (x - \min\{\bar{b}, b(Y)\})I_{\bar{b} > c(Y), b(Y) > \bar{c}}].$$

We can assume without loss of generality that $\bar{c} \leq \alpha_2/2$. We can also assume that $\bar{b} \leq x$. Note that $\bar{b}$ can be strictly less than x. Moreover, if $\bar{b} > c(1)$, bidder 1 can reduce $\bar{b}$ without reducing his expected utility to $\bar{b} = c(1)$. Since $\bar{b} = b(1)$ is the choice if $x = 1$, we have in equilibrium $b(1) = c(1)$. As before, we may rewrite ψ as

$$\psi(\bar{b}, \bar{c}) = (\alpha_2 x - 2\bar{c})F(b^{-1}(\bar{c})) + \int_{b^{-1}(\bar{c})}^{c^{-1}(\bar{b})} (x - \min\{\bar{b}, b(y)\})f(y)\,dy$$

$$= (\alpha_2 x - 2\bar{c})F(b^{-1}(\bar{c})) + \int_{b^{-1}(\bar{c})}^{b^{-1}(\bar{b})} (x - b(y))f(y)\,dy$$

$$+ \int_{b^{-1}(\bar{b})}^{c^{-1}(\bar{b})} (x - \bar{b})f(y)\,dy$$

$$= (\alpha_2 x - 2\bar{c})F(b^{-1}(\bar{c})) + \int_{b^{-1}(\bar{c})}^{b^{-1}(\bar{b})} (x - b(y))f(y)\,dy$$

$$+ (x - \bar{b}) \int_{b^{-1}(\bar{b})}^{c^{-1}(\bar{b})} f(y)\,dy.$$

If $\bar{b} > \bar{c}$, the first-order conditions for the optimum (i.e., $\partial \psi / \partial \bar{b} = 0$ and $\partial \psi / \partial \bar{c} = 0$, respectively) are (collecting terms in $(x - \bar{b})$ and simplifying):

$$(x - \bar{b})(F \circ c^{-1})'(\bar{b}) - (F(c^{-1}(\bar{b})) - F(b^{-1}(\bar{b}))) = 0;$$

$$-2F(b^{-1}(\bar{c})) + (\alpha_2 x - 2\bar{c})(F \circ b^{-1})'(\bar{c}) - (x - \bar{c})f(b^{-1}(\bar{c}))(b^{-1})'(\bar{c}) = 0.$$

Substituting $\bar{b} = b(x)$ and $\bar{c} = c(x)$ we obtain:

$$(x - b(x))(F \circ c^{-1})'(b(x)) - (F(c^{-1}(b(x))) - F(x)) = 0;$$
$$- 2F(b^{-1}(c(x))) + (\alpha_2 x - 2c(x))(F \circ b^{-1})'(c(x))$$
$$- (x - c(x))f(b^{-1}(c(x)))(b^{-1})'(c(x)) = 0.$$

Changing variables ($y = b(x)$ in the first line and $y = c(x)$ in the second line) yields:

$$(b^{-1}(y) - y)(F \circ c^{-1})'(y) - (F(c^{-1}(y)) - F(b^{-1}(y))) = 0;$$
$$- 2F(b^{-1}(y)) + (\alpha_2 c^{-1}(y) - 2y)(F \circ b^{-1})'(y)$$
$$- (c^{-1}(y) - y)f(b^{-1}(y))(b^{-1})'(y) = 0.$$

We now use that $(F \circ c^{-1})' = (f \circ c^{-1})(c^{-1})'$ and $(F \circ b^{-1})' = (f \circ b^{-1})'(b^{-1})'$ to get

$$(c^{-1})'(y) = \frac{F(c^{-1}(y)) - F(b^{-1}(y))}{(b^{-1}(y) - y)f(c^{-1}(y))};$$

$$(b^{-1})'(y) = \frac{2F(b^{-1}(y))}{((\alpha_2 - 1)c^{-1}(y) - y)f(b^{-1}(y))}; \qquad (7.16)$$

$$b(1) = c(1).$$

Example 26   Let us find the equilibrium for the uniform distribution without synergy ($\alpha_2 = 2$). In this case we have to solve,

$$(c^{-1})'(y) = \frac{c^{-1}(y) - b^{-1}(y)}{b^{-1}(y) - y};$$

$$(b^{-1})'(y) = \frac{2b^{-1}(y)}{c^{-1}(y) - y};$$

$$b(1) = c(1).$$

To simplify the notation, denote by $\phi = \phi(y) = c^{-1}(y)$ and $\psi = \psi(y) = b^{-1}(y)$:

$$\phi' = \frac{\phi - \psi}{\psi - y};$$

$$\psi' = \frac{2\psi}{\phi - y}.$$

Eliminating the denominator in both equations, we get:

$$\phi'\psi = y\phi' + \phi - \psi = (y\phi)' - \psi,$$
$$\psi'\phi = y\psi' + 2\psi = (y\psi)' + \psi.$$

Adding both equations we obtain that $(\phi\psi)' = (y\phi)' + (y\psi)'$ *and thus*

$$\phi = \frac{y\psi}{\psi - y}.$$

Substituting this in the equation for ψ' *we get*

$$\psi' = \frac{2\psi}{y\psi/(\psi - y) - y} = \frac{2\psi(\psi - y)}{y^2}.$$

Now define $yz = \psi$ *to obtain the following equation for* z:

$$z' = \frac{z(2z - 3)}{y}.$$

The decomposition in partial fractions $\frac{1}{z(2z-3)} = -\frac{1}{3z} + \frac{2}{3(2z-3)}$ *yields*

$$-\frac{z'}{3z} + \frac{2z'}{3(2z - 3)} = \frac{1}{y}.$$

There is, therefore, a constant $T > 0$ *such that* $(2z - 3)/z = Ty^3$, *which gives*

$$z(y) = \frac{3}{2 - Ty^3}, \quad \psi(y) = \frac{3y}{2 - Ty^3} \quad and \quad \phi(y) = \frac{3y}{1 + Ty^3}.$$

To find T *we solve the system* $\phi(\bar{y}) = \psi(\bar{y}) = 1$ *which gives* $T = 4$. *Finally the equilibrium strategies are obtained by inverting* ϕ *and* ψ, $c(x) = \phi^{-1}(x)$ *and* $b(x) = \psi^{-1}(x)$. *The expressions are cumbersome. For example the solution for* $b(x)$:

$$b(x) = \frac{1}{2} \frac{\left(2x + 4x^{5/2}/(\sqrt{1 + 4x^3} + 1)\right)\left(\left(2x^{3/2} + \sqrt{1 + 4x^3}\right)^{1/3} + 1\right)}{\left(2x^{3/2} + \sqrt{1 + 4x^3}\right)^{1/3} + \left(2x^{3/2} + \sqrt{1 + 4x^3}\right)^{2/3} + 2x^{3/2} + \sqrt{1 + 4x^3}}.$$

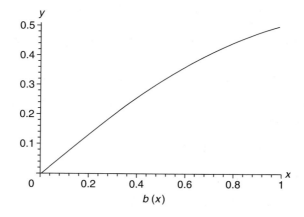

7.3 Optimal Auction

When there are multiple objects for sale but bidders demand only one object, the Revenue Equivalence Theorem holds; both the uniform-price auctions and the discriminatory auction are efficient and yield the same expected revenue. The reader is invited to find the equilibrium bidding functions for these auction formats in this case.

In this section, we look for the optimal auction in the presence of synergy. For simplicity, we consider only two objects and symmetric bidders. Suppose a bidder has type $x \in [0, 1]$. Then if q_{ik} is the probability that bidder i receives k objects, $k = 0, 1, 2$, and his payment is P^i, then his utility is

$$x(q_{i1} + q_{i2}\alpha_2) - P^i.$$

There are several possible ways of allocating the objects amongst the bidders. This set is given by

$$\mathbb{A} = \left\{ (k_1, \ldots, k_n); k_i \in \{0, 1, 2\}, \sum_{i=1}^{n} k_i \leq 2 \right\}.$$

If bidder 1 receives two objects, then the allocation is $(2, 0, \ldots, 0)$. If bidder 1 receives one object and bidder 3 the other the allocation is $(1, 0, 1, \ldots, 0)$ and so on.

A direct mechanism to sell the two objects is $(q, P) = (q(t), P^1(t), \ldots, P^n(t))_{t \in [0,1]^n}$ such that

$$q(t) = (q_a(t))_{a \in \mathbb{A}}, \quad q_a(t) \in \mathbb{R}_+, \sum_{a \in \mathbb{A}} q_a(t) \leq 1;$$

$P^i(t) \in \mathbb{R}$ is the expected payment of bidder i.

That is, $q_a(t)$ represents the probability of occurrence of the allocation a that determines how many objects each bidder will win. The probability that bidder i wins one object is therefore $q_{i1} = q_{i1}(t) = \sum_{a \in \mathbb{A}, a_i = 1} q_a(t)$. The probability that i wins two objects is $q_{i2} = q_{i2}(t) = \sum_{a \in \mathbb{A}, a_i = 2} q_a(t)$.

Define the expected utility of i under this mechanism as:

$$\pi_i(t_i) = t_i E_{-i}[q_{i1}(t) + q_{i2}(t)\alpha_2] - E_{-i}[P^i(t)]. \tag{7.17}$$

If we define $Q^i(t_i) = (Q_1^i(t_i), Q_2^i(t_i))$, $Q_k^i(t_i) = E_{-i}[q_{ik}(t)]$ we may write the incentive compatibility constraints as

$$\pi_i(t_i) \geq t_i(Q_1^i(t') + Q_2^i(t')\alpha_2) - E_{-i}[P^i(t', t_{-i})], \quad t' \in [0, 1].$$

From this we obtain the inequality

$$\pi_i(t_i) \geq (t_i - t_i')\left(Q_1^i(t') + Q_2^i(t')\alpha_2\right) + \pi_i(t_i').$$

Thus, following the same method as in the one object case, we can prove that

$$\pi_i(t_i) = \pi_i(0) + \int_0^{t_i} (Q_1^i(s) + Q_2^i(s)\alpha_2)\,\mathrm{d}s. \tag{7.18}$$

Combining (7.17) and (7.18) we have that

$$E_{-i}[P^i(t)] = t_i E_{-i}[q_{i1}(t) + q_{i2}(t)\alpha_2] - \pi_i(t_i)$$

$$= t_i E_{-i}[q_{i1}(t) + q_{i2}(t)\alpha_2] - \pi_i(0) - \int_0^{t_i} (Q_1^i(s) + Q_2^i(s)\alpha_2)\,\mathrm{d}s.$$

Hence the seller's expected revenue is

$$R = \sum_{i=1}^n \int P^i(t) f(t)\,\mathrm{d}t = \sum_{i=1}^n \int E_{-i}[P^i(t)] f(t_i)\,\mathrm{d}t_i$$

$$= -\sum_{i=1}^n \pi_i(0) + \sum_{i=1}^n \int \left(t_i E_{-i}[q_{i1}(t) + q_{i2}(t)\alpha_2] \right.$$

$$\left. - \int_0^{t_i} (Q_1^i(s) + Q_2^i(s)\alpha_2)\mathrm{d}s \right) f(t_i)\,\mathrm{d}t_i.$$

Therefore, the Revenue Equivalence Theorem generalizes to multiple objects. That is, if $q(t)$ is the same in two auction formats and the lowest type has a zero expected utility (i.e., $\pi_i(0) = 0$) then the seller's expected revenue is the same in the two auctions. In particular, all efficient auction formats yielding the lowest type zero expected utility have the same expected revenue.

Let us now find the optimal auction. Voluntary participation means that $\pi_i(t_i) \geq 0$ for every type. In particular $\pi_i(0) \geq 0$. Thus, we choose $\pi_i(0) = 0$ for all i. As before we can write

$$\int \left(\int_0^{t_i} (Q_1^i(s) + Q_2^i(s)\alpha_2)\,\mathrm{d}s \right) f(t_i)\,\mathrm{d}t_i$$

$$= \int \frac{1 - F(t_i)}{f(t_i)} (q_{i1}(t) + q_{i2}(t)\alpha_2) f(t)\,\mathrm{d}t.$$

Thus, to maximize revenue we have to choose mechanisms (q, P) that are incentive compatible and maximize

$$\sum_{i=1}^n \int \left(t_i [q_{i1}(t) + q_{i2}(t)\alpha_2] - \frac{1 - F(t_i)}{f(t_i)} (q_{i1}(t) + q_{i2}(t)\alpha_2) \right) f(t)\,\mathrm{d}t$$

$$= \int \sum_{i=1}^n \left(t_i - \frac{1 - F(t_i)}{f(t_i)} \right) (q_{i1}(t) + q_{i2}(t)\alpha_2) f(t)\,\mathrm{d}t.$$

Define

$$
l_a^i = \begin{cases} 1 & \text{if } a_i = 1 \\ 0 & \text{otherwise} \end{cases} \quad \text{and} \quad m_a^i = \begin{cases} 1 & \text{if } a_i = 2 \\ 0 & \text{otherwise.} \end{cases}
$$

Define also $J(t_i) = t_i - (1 - F(t_i))/f(t_i)$. In this notation we have that $q_{i1}(t) = \sum_{a \in \mathbb{A}} l_a^i q_a(t)$ and $q_{i2}(t) = \sum_{a \in \mathbb{A}} m_a^i q_a(t)$. Then, the revenue can be written as

$$
\int \sum_{i=1}^{n} \left(t_i - \frac{1 - F(t_i)}{f(t_i)} \right) (q_{i1}(t) + q_{i2}(t)\alpha_2) f(t) \, dt
$$

$$
= \int \sum_{i=1}^{n} J(t_i) \sum_{a \in \mathbb{A}} q_a(t)(l_a^i + \alpha_2 m_a^i) f(t) \, dt
$$

$$
= \int \sum_{a \in \mathbb{A}} q_a(t) \sum_{i=1}^{n} J(t_i) \left(l_a^i + \alpha_2 m_a^i \right) f(t) \, dt \tag{mr}
$$

$$
\leq \int \max_{a \in \mathbb{A}} \sum_{i=1}^{n} J(t_i) \left(l_a^i + \alpha_2 m_a^i \right) f(t) \, dt. \tag{7.19}
$$

Finally, define for each $t \in [0, 1]^n$ the set

$$
S(t) = \left\{ a^* \in \mathbb{A}; \sum_{i=1}^{n} J(t_i) \left(l_{a^*}^i + \alpha_2 m_{a^*}^i \right) = \max_{a \in \mathbb{A}} \sum_{i=1}^{n} J(t_i) \left(l_a^i + \alpha_2 m_a^i \right) \right\}.
$$

Define

$$
q_a^*(t) = \begin{cases} \frac{1}{\#S(t)} & \text{if } a \in S(t), \\ 0 & \text{otherwise.} \end{cases}
$$

We want to establish the following result that characterizes the optimal auction.

Theorem 25 *Suppose $J(t_i)$ is increasing. Then the optimal auction allocates the objects accordingly to $(q_a^*(t))_{a \in \mathbb{A}}$ and charges*

$$
P^i(t) = t_i[q_{i1}(t) + q_{i2}(t)\alpha_2] - \int_0^{t_i} q_{i1}(s, t_{-i}) \, ds - \int_0^{t_i} q_{i2}(s, t_{-i})\alpha_2 \, ds.
$$

Proof: We have to check the incentive compatibility and voluntary participation constraints. First note that

$$
E_{-i}[P^i(t)] = t_i \left(Q_1^i(t_i) + \alpha_2 Q_2^i(t_i) \right) - \int_0^{t_i} \left(Q_1^i(s) + \alpha_2 Q_2^i(s) \right) \, ds.
$$

A bidder's expected utility is given by

$$\pi_i(t_i) = t_i E_{-i}[q_{i1}(t) + q_{i2}(t)\alpha_2] - E_{-i}[P^i(t)]$$

$$= t_i \left(Q_1^i(t_i) + \alpha_2 Q_2^i(t_i)\right) - t_i \left(Q_1^i(t_i) + \alpha_2 Q_2^i(t_i)\right)$$

$$+ \int_0^{t_i} \left(Q_1^i(s) + \alpha_2 Q_2^i(s)\right) ds$$

$$= \int_0^{t_i} \left(Q_1^i(s) + \alpha_2 Q_2^i(s)\right) ds \geq 0.$$

Thus voluntary participation is assured. Let us check incentive compatibility. If bidder i being of type t_i declares type u under the mechanism his expected utility is

$$t_i \left(Q_1^i(u) + \alpha_2 Q_2^i(u)\right) - E_{-i}[P^i(u, t_{-i})]$$

$$= t_i \left(Q_1^i(u) + \alpha_2 Q_2^i(u)\right) - \left(u \left(Q_1^i(u) + \alpha_2 Q_2^i(u)\right)\right.$$

$$\left. - \int_0^u \left(Q_1^i(s) + \alpha_2 Q_2^i(s)\right) ds\right)$$

$$= (t_i - u) \left(Q_1^i(u) + \alpha_2 Q_2^i(u)\right) + \int_0^u \left(Q_1^i(s) + \alpha_2 Q_2^i(s)\right) ds. \qquad (7.20)$$

We need to compare the last number with $\pi_i(t_i)$. Subtracting $\pi_i(t_i)$ from (7.20) we obtain

$$\int_0^{t_i} \left(Q_1^i(s) + \alpha_2 Q_2^i(s)\right) ds - (t_i - u) \left(Q_1^i(u) + \alpha_2 Q_2^i(u)\right)$$

$$- \int_0^u \left(Q_1^i(s) + \alpha_2 Q_2^i(s)\right) ds$$

$$= \int_u^{t_i} \left(Q_1^i(s) + \alpha_2 Q_2^i(s)\right) ds - (t_i - u) \left(Q_1^i(u) + \alpha_2 Q_2^i(u)\right).$$

We only have to show that $q_{i1}(s, t_{-i}) + \alpha_2 q_{i2}(s, t_{-i})$ is increasing in s. This will imply that $Q_1^i(s) + \alpha_2 Q_2^i(s)$ is increasing as well and this will end the proof. Recall how q^* is defined. It allocates the objects according to the maximum of $\sum_{i=1}^n J(t_i) \left(l_a^i + \alpha_2 m_a^i\right)$. Now note that

$$\left\{\sum_{i=1}^n J(t_i) \left(l_a^i + \alpha_2 m_a^i\right); a \in \mathbb{A}\right\} = J^1 \cup J^2 \cup J^3,$$

where

$$J^1 = \{J(t_i); 1 \leq i \leq n\},$$

$$J^2 = \{J(t_i) + J(t_j); i, j \leq n, i \neq j\}$$

and

$$J^3 = \{\alpha_2 J(t_i); 1 \leq i \leq n\}.$$

If for some s, $q_{i1}(s, t_{-i}) = 0$ and $q_{i2}(s, t_{-i}) = 0$ then any other s will not yield less than 0. Suppose bidder i receives one object. Suppose also without loss of generality that $J(s) > 0$. There must be another bidder receiving an object too (why? This is left as an exercise). If $J(s) + J(t_j)$ is the maximum, then either $J(s') + J(t_j)$ is the maximum when i's type increases to s' or $\alpha_2 J(s')$ is the new maximum. In either case, bidder i receives two objects and $q_{i1}(s', t_{-i}) + q_{i2}(s', t_{-i})\alpha_2 = \alpha_2$. If bidder i is already receiving two objects, increasing s only increases his expected utility.   □

Remark 16   *The specification of payments, $P^i(t)$ is of course not unique. Any specification that yields the same $E_{-i}[P^i(t)]$ is correct.*

Example 27   *As an example let us consider $K = 2$ and the uniform distribution. And suppose $\alpha_2 = \frac{3}{2}$. We calculate the optimal revenue and allocation. Note that $J(t) = t - (1-t) = 2t - 1$. If $\{t_1, t_2, \ldots, t_n\}$ is the realization of types and $Z = \max t_i$ and Z^2 the second highest, then the objects are allocated to the bidder with the highest marginal valuation amongst*

$$\left\{ 0, 2t_i - 1, 2t_i - 1 + 2t_j - 1, \tfrac{3}{2}(2t_i - 1), i, j \leq n, i \neq j \right\},$$

or equivalently, amongst

$$\left\{ 0, 2Z - 1, 2Z + 2Z^2 - 2, \tfrac{3}{2}(2Z - 1) \right\}.$$

However, note that if $2t - 1 \geq 0$ then $\frac{3}{2}(2t - 1) \geq 2t - 1$. Therefore, the optimal auction is such that it never happens that only one object is allocated. It may happen that no objects are allocated. This is so if $Z \leq \frac{1}{2}$. If $Z > \frac{1}{2}$, the highest type bidder receives two objects if

$$\tfrac{3}{2}(2Z - 1) > 2Z + 2Z^2 - 2.$$

That is if $Z > 2Z^2 - \frac{1}{2}$. If $Z > \frac{1}{2}$ and $Z \leq 2Z^2 - \frac{1}{2}$, the bidder with the highest and second highest signals receives one object each. We now suppose $n = 2$ and calculate the optimum revenue. From (mr), the optimal revenue is

$$\int \max_{a \in \mathbb{A}} \sum_{i=1}^{n} (2t_i - 1) \left(l_a^i + \alpha_2 m_a^i \right) \, dt_1 \, dt_2$$

$$= \int \max \left\{ 0, 2\max\{t_1, t_2\} - 1, 2(t_1 + t_2 - 1), 3\max\{t_1, t_2\} - \tfrac{3}{2} \right\} dt_1 \, dt_2$$

$$= 2 \int_{u>v} \max \left\{0, 2u - 1, 2(u + v - 1), 3u - \tfrac{3}{2}\right\} du\, dv$$

$$= 2 \int_{u>\frac{1}{2}} \int_{v=\frac{u}{2}+\frac{1}{4}}^{v=1} (2(u + v - 1))\, du\, dv + 2 \int_{u>1/2} \int_{v=0}^{v=\frac{u}{2}+\frac{1}{4}} \left(3u - \tfrac{3}{2}\right) du\, dv$$

$$= 2 \int_{1/2}^{1} \left(\tfrac{9}{4} u - \tfrac{5}{4} u^2 - \tfrac{9}{16}\right) du + 2 \int_{1/2}^{1} \left(\tfrac{u}{2} + \tfrac{1}{4}\right)\left(3u - \tfrac{3}{2}\right) du$$

$$= \frac{43}{48} = 0.89.$$

For the sake of comparison, consider the optimal auction with the requirement that the object is always delivered. In this case, the revenue is given by (why?)

$$R = \int \max \left\{2t_1 - 1 + 2t_2 - 1, \tfrac{3}{2}(2t_2 - 1), \tfrac{3}{2}(2t_1 - 1)\right\} dt_1\, dt_2.$$

We decompose R in four parts accordingly to whether $t_i \geq \tfrac{1}{2}$ or not, $i = 1, 2$. If $t_1 \leq \tfrac{1}{2}$ and $t_2 \leq \tfrac{1}{2}$ then the integrand is $2t_1 - 1 + 2t_2 - 1$. Thus

$$I_1 = \int_0^{1/2} \int_0^{1/2} (2u - 1 + 2v - 1)\, du\, dv = -\frac{1}{4}.$$

If $u \geq \tfrac{1}{2}$ and $v \geq \tfrac{1}{2}$ then since the cases $u \geq v$ and $v \geq u$ are symmetrical,

$$I_2 = 2 \int_{\frac{1}{2}}^{1} \int_{\frac{1}{2}}^{u} \max \left\{2u - 1 + 2v - 1, \tfrac{3}{2}(2u - 1)\right\} du\, dv$$

$$= 2 \int_{\frac{1}{2}}^{1} \int_0^{\frac{1}{2} + \frac{2u-1}{4}} \tfrac{3}{2}(2u - 1)\, du\, dv$$

$$+ 2 \int_{\frac{1}{2}}^{1} \int_{\frac{1}{2} + \frac{2u-1}{4}}^{u} (2u - 1 + 2v - 1)\, du\, dv = \frac{31}{48}.$$

It remains to consider the cases $u \geq \tfrac{1}{2} \geq v$ and $v \geq \tfrac{1}{2} \geq u$. From the symmetry both integrals will be equal. Thus

$$I_3 = I_4 = \int_{1/2}^{1} \int_0^{1/2} \max \left\{2u - 1 + 2v - 1, \tfrac{3}{2}(2u - 1)\right\} du\, dv$$

$$= \int_{1/2}^{1} \int_0^{1/2} \tfrac{3}{2}(2u - 1)\, dv\, du = \frac{3}{16}.$$

The total is $R = I_1 + I_2 + I_3 + I_4 = -\tfrac{1}{4} + \tfrac{31}{48} + \tfrac{6}{16} = \tfrac{37}{48} = 0.770$.

That is, to guarantee efficiency the seller has to give up some of its expected revenue. This is the same trade-off (expected revenue versus efficiency) that one faces in the one object auction model.

7.4   Exercises

1. Suppose there are three objects to sell. How much synergy is necessary so that in a symmetric equilibrium each bidder bids the same amount for each object?
2. Solve equation (7.11).
3. Suppose $0 < r < 1$ in Example 24. Check that the strategies

$$b(x) = \frac{rx}{r + \sqrt{r^2 + 1 - r^2 x^2}};$$

$$c(x) = \frac{rx}{1 + \sqrt{1 - x^2(1 - r^2)}},$$

   satisfy the differential equations (7.9) in the uniform $[0, 1]$ distribution case and that they are equilibrium bidding strategies.
4. In Theorem 23 we only checked the first-order conditions. Show that $b(x) = c(x) = rx$ are indeed optimal solutions of the expected utility maximization problem (7.12).
5. Check that (7.15) has no solution if $F_Y(x) = x^2$. More generally, show that it has no solution if $0 < f_Y'(0) < \infty$.
6. Consider the two-bidder two-object uniform-price auction. Suppose the distribution is uniform on $[0, 1]$ and that $c'(x) > 0$ for every x. Show that $(x, c(x))$ is a symmetric equilibrium when $\alpha_2 = 2$.
7. Calculate the seller's expected revenue in Example 24. Compare your result with the expected revenue of the sequential second-price auction.

8

What is Next?

The reader who has persevered with the book will now be fully versed in the mechanics of single-object auction theory and will also have developed an appreciation of the difficulties involved in analyzing the sale of two or more objects.

However, this reader will only have a limited understanding of the ongoing and potential research questions. This was our explicit choice. We chose instead to focus on the mechanics of basic theory rather than offer a broader (but less detailed) coverage of topics. To fill this gap, we suggest two complementary approaches.

The first approach we suggest is a conventional one. The reader can consult the excellent books by Krishna (2002), Klemperer (2004), and Milgrom (2004). These books, although perhaps offering a less detailed exposition of the mechanisms of the theory, are more comprehensive in their coverage of some of the recent research topics. This includes the auction of multiple objects, such as the analysis of recent designs including ascending clock auctions and hybrid—combining sealed-bid and ascending/descending stages—designs, as well as the analysis of topics such as entry, collusion, and the effects of the existence of budget-constrained bidders.

The second approach that can be followed by readers who want to be introduced to ongoing (and potential) research questions consists of reviewing the literature that confronts auction theory with practice. There are three streams of literature that are relevant for this approach. First, there is an increasing body of literature that empirically tests the various auction theory models. See, for example, the survey of Athey and Haile (2005). There is also an empirical literature that is more exploratory in nature and aims at uncovering auction phenomena that might not have been considered yet by the theoretical literature. Examples include the survey of empirical studies of art auctions undertaken by Ashenfelter and Graddy (2003) and the work of Jones, Menezes, and Vella (2004) on wool auctions in Australia. For example, the latter work documents violations of the law of one price—identical objects being auctioned for different prices—and has resulted in a stream of theoretical papers attempting to identify the reasons for the violation.

The experimental economics literature offers an alternative approach to testing auction theory. The survey by Kagel (1995) although somewhat dated provides a comprehensive review of the literature that tests auction theory in a laboratory. This is an important body of literature covering both classical results demonstrating more aggressive bidding (i.e., bids that are closer to the bidder's value) than suggested by theory, as well as tests of specific features and new auction designs.

The final stream of literature aims to reconcile theory with the actual practice of designing and running auctions. A very good reference in this stream is Klemperer (2004). Although we are not aware of a comprehensive survey of the difficulties encountered in the practice of auction design, many useful references can be found which are usually associated with policy-making initiatives. This is the case for the design of spectrum auctions in telecommunications and more recently the design of auctions to allocate CO_2 allowances under various initiatives to reduce greenhouse gas emissions. See, for example, Holt et al. (2007) and Evans and Peck (2007).

Reading this type of literature seems to us a necessity for any serious student of auction theory. In doing so one appreciates both the limitations as well as the value of the insights provided by the theory developed in this book. It becomes apparent that in many applications fundamental assumptions do not hold.

For example, the value that potential bidders assign to an object has both private and common components. An individual bidding for a residential property will have both an idiosyncratic value for the property and some common component related to the expected resale value and interest rates. A generator bidding to supply electricity will have considerations including its own costs (not necessarily known by other bidders), its expectations about the behavior of other generators and, importantly, common factors such as weather forecasts. The difficulty this poses is that valuations might not be affiliated—for example, the private and common components might move in opposite directions across individuals. Many results (e.g., ranking auctions according to the expected revenue they generate) do not necessarily hold in this case.

Similarly, there is no reason to expect that the distribution of types or valuations of a bidder is an interval of the real line as typically assumed. However, as is demonstrated in the next section, in this case one can still adapt the techniques and approaches developed above to obtain results that are more general in nature and to show that under some circumstances standard results do not hold for distributions without density.

A second observation that emerges from the practice of running and participating in auctions is that it is rare for an auction to involve the sale of only one object. Typically, similar (or identical) objects are sold either simultaneously or sequentially. Importantly, often bidders demand more than one object and are asymmetric in their demands. For example, the asymmetry might be along the lines of incumbent versus entrants or related to size or choice of technology. Auction practitioners are also often concerned with entry. Ensuring the participation of enough competitors can mitigate the exercise of market power by large bidders (who, for example, might bid less than their demand) or of collusion (tacit or otherwise).

Finally, literature concerning the practical design of auctions highlights that often there is enough flexibility for the auction designer to change some parameters generally considered fixed in theory. For example, consider the auction of the rights to access an essential input produced by a vertically integrated incumbent. Suppose further that even an efficient entrant requires two to three years of operation to recover the fixed costs of entry. The auction designer can propose to auction one-year contracts for each of the following three years— making the objects complementary—or to auction, for example, one-year and three-year supply contracts. In the latter case, objects are substitutes, which avoids the complications that emerge under complementarity.[1] The auction designer can also affect participation by choosing a platform making it easier for agents to bid or by setting appropriate penalties for non-compliance (e.g., in the case of auctions of licences). In addition, auction designers can influence the definition of the property right—for example, by including transferability or alienability of the right—so that a secondary market can help mitigate any inefficiencies that might arise from the auction allocation.

In summary, we highly recommend that the reader venture into the practice of designing, running, and participating in auctions; it is a sure way to understand the usefulness and limitations of the theory contained in this book and a quick path to the discovery of some very exciting research questions.

8.1 Distribution Hypotheses in Auction Theory[2]

In this book and in most of the economics literature the set of possible types or valuations of a bidder i is an interval $T := T_i = [a, b]$, $0 \leq a < b$. Let $F : \mathbb{R} \rightarrow [0, 1]$ be the distribution of types $t \in T$. That is: F is an increasing right-continuous function such that $F(a-) = 0$ and $F(b) = 1$. The distribution usually satisfies condition (M):

---

[1] Recall that in Chapter 7 we illustrated the difficulties involved when auctioning multiple objects with synergies. More generally, see Milgrom (2007).
[2] This section is based on Monteiro (2007) and Monteiro and fux Svaiter (2007).

Definition 16 *A distribution $F : \mathbb{R} \to \mathbb{R}$ satisfies condition (M) if there is a continuous function $f : [a, b] \to R_{++}$ such that*

$$F(x) = \int_a^x f(u)\, du, a \le x \le b.$$

That is, a distribution satisfies condition (M) if it has a continuous strictly positive density on its support $[a, b]$. There are, however, several economically meaningful examples that do not satisfy condition (M):

1. Suppose that in a population of potential bidders there are two types of bidders. Half of the bidders have possible types that are uniformly distributed in $[0, 1]$ and the other half are uniformly distributed in $[2, 3]$. If two bidders are drawn randomly from this distribution and it is not possible to distinguish from which part of the population they come, the distribution of types is given by

$$F(x) = \begin{cases} \frac{x}{2} & \text{if } 0 \le x \le 1; \\ \frac{1}{2} & \text{if } 1 \le x \le 2; \\ \frac{x-1}{2} & \text{if } 2 \le x \le 3. \end{cases}$$

This distribution has density:

$$f(x) = \begin{cases} \frac{1}{2} & \text{if } 0 \le x \le 1; \\ 0 & \text{if } 1 < x < 2; \\ \frac{1}{2} & \text{if } 2 \le x \le 3. \end{cases}$$

Thus the density is not continuous in $\{1, 2\}$ and $f(x) = 0$, $1 < x < 2$.

2. More generally, if the set of types is a closed set such that $\{a, b\} \subset T \subsetneq [a, b]$, then the distribution of types F has a density in $[a, b] \setminus T$ but $f(x) = 0$ if $x \in [a, b] \setminus T$.

3. Suppose that types are drawn from a population such that half of the population has types uniformly distributed in $[0, 1]$. And the other half of the population is identical and has type $t = \frac{1}{2}$. The distribution of types in this case is

$$F(x) = \begin{cases} \frac{x}{2} & \text{if } 0 \le x < \frac{1}{2}; \\ \frac{3}{4} & \text{if } x = \frac{1}{2}; \\ \frac{x+1}{2} & \text{if } \frac{1}{2} \le x \le 1. \end{cases}$$

Thus the distribution has a size $1/2$ jump at $x = 1/2$.

What can we say about independent private value auctions, for a general distribution? We consider three topics:

a) Is the revenue equivalence theorem valid?
b) Can we characterize the optimal auction in this case?
c) What is the equilibrium of the first-price auction?

We begin addressing item (a). If we review section 6.2 we see that nothing changes if we define $Q_i(x) := \int q_i(x, x_{-i}) dF_{-i}(x_{-i})$ where $F_{-i} = \Pi_{j \neq i} F_j$. Thus, if (q, P) is an individually-rational, incentive-compatible mechanism then

$$E_{-i}[P_i(x)] := \int P_i(x) dF_{-i}(x_{-i}) = x_i Q_i(x_i) - a_i - \int_0^{x_i} Q_i(t) dt. \quad (8.1)$$

Thus, any such mechanism yields the same expected revenue. Let us examine this revenue equivalence from another perspective and, thus, consider the following distribution of types:

$$F(x) = \begin{cases} 0 & \text{if} \quad x < 0; \\ \frac{1}{2} & \text{if} \quad 0 \leq x < 1; \\ 1 & \text{if} \quad 1 \leq x. \end{cases} \quad (*)$$

That is, bidders are of type $t = 0$ or type $t = 1$ with equal probability. Types $t \in (0,1)$ have zero probability. If we only allow bidders to declare a type $t \in T = \{0,1\}$ we have in principle more leeway to define mechanisms since we do not have to worry about incentive compatibility for types $0 < t < 1$. Let us see an example.

Example 28 *Consider a second-price auction with two bidders of types $t_1, t_2 \in T = \{0,1\}$. Types are independent with distribution (*). In a second price auction we have the following allocation rule for bidder 1,*

$$\begin{pmatrix} q_1(0,0) & q_1(0,1) \\ q_1(1,0) & q_1(1,1) \end{pmatrix} = \begin{pmatrix} \frac{1}{2} & 0 \\ 1 & \frac{1}{2} \end{pmatrix}.$$

That is, in the case of bidder 1 and bidder 2 announcing the same type, there is a tie and the object is allocated to bidder 1 with 50% probability. The allocation rule for bidder 2 is $q_2(i,j) = 1 - q_1(i,j)$. Payment is given by:

$$\begin{pmatrix} P_1(0,0) & P_1(0,1) \\ P_1(1,0) & P_1(1,1) \end{pmatrix} = \begin{pmatrix} 0 & 0 \\ 0 & 1 \end{pmatrix} \quad (P1)$$

if the bidder receives the object. Thus expected payment is $P_1(0) = 0$ and $P_1(1) = \frac{1}{4}$.

Consider now the following expected payment rule:

$$\begin{pmatrix} P_2^*(0) = P_1^*(0) \\ P_2^*(1) = P_1^*(1) \end{pmatrix} = \begin{pmatrix} 0 \\ 1/2 \end{pmatrix}. \quad (P*)$$

Let us show that the allocation (q_1, q_2) above and payment $P^* = (P_1^*, P_2^*)$ satisfies both the incentive compatibility and voluntary participation constraints. If bidder 1 is of type 0 his expected utility is 0. If bidder 1 is of type 1 his expected utility is

$$\frac{3}{4} - \frac{2}{4} = \frac{1}{4} > 0.$$

Thus, voluntary participation is satisfied. A type-0 bidder will not announce his type as type 1 since this would yield expected utility equal to $-\frac{1}{2} < 0$. A type-1 bidder also has no incentive to announce his type as 0 since his expected utility from truthful revelation would be equal to $\frac{1}{4}$.

This example shows that revenue equivalence is not valid if $T = \{0, 1\}$. However if $T = [0, 1]$ and the distribution is the same, revenue equivalence is valid. The following theorem summarizes the relationship between the two setups.

Theorem 26 *Suppose $T_i \subset [0, 1]$ is the set of types of bidder $i, 1 \leq i \leq n$. Let F_i be the distribution of types $t_i \in T_i$ and suppose we have independent private values. If $(q, P) : \Pi_{i=1}^n T_i \to [0, 1]^n \times \mathbb{R}^n$ is a voluntary participation, incentive compatible mechanism then it is possible to extend (q, P) to a mechanism $(q', P') : [0, 1]^n \to [0, 1]^n \times \mathbb{R}^n$ that is incentive-compatible and satisfies voluntary participation. Moreover the expected payment implied by P' is completely specified as a function of q' and the utility of the lowest type as in (8.1).*

The reasoning above allows us to assume, without loss of generality, that the set of types is an interval. And as a bonus of extending the set of types to an interval, we restore revenue equivalence.

We now address question (b). The optimal auction studied in Chapter 6 relies on condition (M) and is not useful for an arbitrary distribution. Note that the allocation rule stated in Theorem 17 (Chapter 6) is not even defined if the distribution does not have a density or if the density exists but is null sometimes. In this case, it is possible to show that the following generalization holds:

Theorem 27 *Suppose the distribution of types of bidder i is $F_i : [0, 1] \to [0, 1]$, $1 \leq i \leq n$. Then there are $l_0 \equiv 0, l_1(\cdot), \ldots, l_n(\cdot)$ increasing functions such that the optimal mechanism is defined by $(\bar{q}, \bar{p})$ where $\bar{p}^i$ is defined by (8.3) and $\bar{q}(s) = (\bar{q}_1(s), \ldots, \bar{q}_I(s))$ by (8.2).*

Definition 17 *For each $s \in S$ let $H(s) = \{i \geq 1; l_i(s_i) = \max_{j \geq 0} l_j(s_j)\}$. Define*

$$\bar{q}_i(s) = \begin{cases} \frac{1}{\#H(s)} & if \quad i \in H(s); \\ 0 & if \quad i \notin H(s). \end{cases} \tag{8.2}$$

Definition 18 *The payment of bidder i is for $s \in S$ given by*

$$\bar{p}^i(s) = s_i \bar{q}_i(s) - \int_{a_i}^{s_i} \bar{q}_i(y, s_{-i}) \, dy. \tag{8.3}$$

It would take a great deal of effort to go through a formal and didactically appealing proof of this result. Instead, we illustrate the application of this theorem through a simple example:

Example 29   *Let the distribution of types of bidders $i = 1, 2$ be given by*

$$F\left(u\right) = \begin{cases} \frac{u}{3} & \text{if } 0 \le u < 1; \\ \frac{u+1}{3} & \text{if } 1 \le u \le 2. \end{cases}$$

This distribution has a jump of size $1/3$ at $u = 1$. The function $l_1 = l_2$ is given by

$$l_1\left(x\right) = \begin{cases} 2x - 3 & \text{if } 0 \le x < 1; \\ 2\left(\sqrt{2} - 1\right) & \text{if } 1 \le x \le \sqrt{2}; \\ 2\left(x - 1\right) & \text{if } \sqrt{2} \le x \le 2. \end{cases}$$

We now calculate the revenue of the second-price auction (with an optimal reserve price) and the optimal auction revenue to illustrate how the optimal auction differs from the standard case where the set of types is an interval. It should be clear that it is optimal to set $r = 1$ for a second-price auction. The expected revenue of such an auction can be calculated as follows:

$$2 \int_{x_1 \ge r > x_2} r dF\left(x_1\right) dF\left(x_2\right) + \int_{\min\{x_1, x_2\} \ge r} \min\left\{x_1, x_2\right\} dF\left(x_1\right) dF\left(x_2\right)$$

$$= 2F\left(1-\right)\left(1 - F\left(1-\right)\right) + \int_{x_1 \ge x_2 \ge 1} x_2 dF\left(x_1\right) dF\left(x_2\right)$$

$$+ \int_{x_2 > x_1 \ge 1} x_1 dF\left(x_1\right) dF\left(x_2\right) = \frac{4}{9} + \int_{x_2 \ge 1}\left(1 - F\left(x_2-\right)\right) x_2 dF\left(x_2\right)$$

$$+ \int_{x_1 \ge 1}\left(1 - F\left(x_1\right)\right) x_1 dF\left(x_1\right) = \frac{7}{9} + \int_{x_2 > 1}\left(1 - \frac{x_2 + 1}{3}\right)\frac{x_2}{3} dx_2$$

$$+ \int_{x_1 > 1}\left(1 - \frac{x_1 + 1}{3}\right)\frac{x_1}{3} dx_1 = \frac{7}{9} + \frac{2}{3} \int_1^2 \left(z - \frac{z^2 + z}{3}\right) dz$$

$$= \frac{7}{9} + \frac{2}{3} \int_1^2 \frac{2z - z^2}{3} dz = \frac{7}{9} + \frac{2}{9}\left(z^2 - \frac{z^3}{3}\right) |_1^2 = \frac{25}{27}.$$

In contrast, the revenue in the optimal auction can be calculated as follows:

$$\int \max\{l(x), l(y), 0\} \, dF(x) \, dF(y)$$

$$= \int_{\max\{x,y\}\geq 1} l(\max\{x,y\}) \, dF(x) \, dF(y) = \int_1^2 l(z) \, dF^2(z)$$

$$= l(1)\frac{1}{3} + \int_1^{\sqrt{2}} 2\left(\sqrt{2}-1\right) \frac{2(z+1)}{9} \, dz + \int_{\sqrt{2}}^2 2(z-1) \frac{2(z+1)}{9} \, dz$$

$$= 2\left(\sqrt{2}-1\right)\frac{1}{3} + 2\left(\sqrt{2}-1\right)\left(\frac{z^2}{9}+z\right)|_1^{\sqrt{2}} + \frac{4}{9}\left(\frac{z^3}{3}-z\right)|_{\sqrt{2}}^2$$

$$= 2\left(\sqrt{2}-1\right)\frac{1}{3} + 2\left(\sqrt{2}-1\right)\left(\frac{1}{9}+\sqrt{2}-1\right) + \frac{4}{9}\left(\frac{8}{3}-\frac{2\sqrt{2}}{3}-2+\sqrt{2}\right)$$

$$= 2\left(\sqrt{2}-1\right)\left(\sqrt{2}-\frac{5}{9}\right) + \frac{4}{9}\left(\frac{2}{3}+\sqrt{2}\frac{1}{3}\right) = \frac{3286}{2700} > \frac{2500}{2700}.$$

We now address question (c). Let us first consider a continuous distribution $F : [0,1] \to [0,1]$. Recall expression (3.10):

$$b^*(v) = v - \frac{\int_0^v F(x)^{n-1} \, dx}{F(v)^{n-1}}.$$

This is the equilibrium bid of the first-price auction when there are n bidders each with valuation distributed as F. The expression (3.10) was obtained under the assumption that F has a density. The density however does not appear in the definition of $b^*(\cdot)$. We will now prove that this expression works also if the distribution does not have a density. Suppose bidders $i = 2, \ldots, n$ bids according to $b^*(\cdot)$ and let us find the best response of bidder 1 with valuation $0 < v \leq 1$. We note first without proof that $b^*(\cdot)$ is strictly increasing. If bidder 1 bids $b^*(\omega)$ his expected utility is

$$(v - b^*(\omega)) \Pr\left(b^*(\omega) > \max\{b^*(v_2), \ldots, b^*(v_n)\}\right)$$

$$= (v - b^*(\omega)) F^{n-1}(\omega) = (v-\omega) F^{n-1}(\omega) + \int_0^\omega F(x)^{n-1} \, dx$$

$$= \int_\omega^v F^{n-1}(\omega) \, dx + \int_0^\omega F(x)^{n-1} \, dx.$$

If $\omega < v$ then

$$\int_\omega^v F^{n-1}(\omega) \, dx + \int_0^\omega F(x)^{n-1} \, dx = \int_0^v \min\{F^{n-1}(\omega), F^{n-1}(x)\} \, dx$$

$$< \int_0^v \min\{F^{n-1}(v), F^{n-1}(x)\} \, dx = \int_0^v F^{n-1}(x) \, dx.$$

And if $\omega > v$,

$$\int_{\omega}^{v} F^{n-1}(\omega)\, dx + \int_{0}^{\omega} F(x)^{n-1}\, dx = \int_{0}^{v} F^{n-1}(x)\, dx$$

$$+ \int_{v}^{\omega} \left[F^{n-1}(x) - F^{n-1}(\omega) \right] dx < \int_{0}^{v} F^{n-1}(x)\, dx.$$

This expression however is not valid if the distribution is not continuous. A pure strategy equilibrium does not exist if the distribution has jumps. Fortunately it is possible to combine the above expression and a generalization of the mixed equilibrium of section 3.4. The following theorem gives the symmetric equilibrium of the first-price auction for an arbitrary distribution $F : [0,1] \to [0,1]$.

Theorem 28 *The symmetric first-price auction equilibrium is a mixed-strategy equilibrium. It is a mixed strategy G_v with support $[b^*(v-), b^*(v)]$ if F is discontinuous at v and is the pure strategy $b^*(v)$ if F is continuous at v.*

The mixed strategy has support $[b(v-), b(v)]$ and is defined by

$$G_v(x) = \frac{F(v-)}{F(v) - F(v-)} \left(-1 + \left(\frac{v - b^*(v-)}{v - x} \right)^{\frac{1}{n-1}} \right). \qquad (8.4)$$

Appendix A

Probability

The requirements on probability theory for this book are modest. In this appendix, we collect the definitions and results needed in the book. Probability theory is an important area of mathematics with several and diverse applications in economics. A thorough understanding of probability theory requires measure theory and Lebesgue's integration theory. For this book we assume however that the reader is familiar with the Riemann integral that is taught in Calculus courses.

A.1 Probability Spaces

A probability space is defined by three objects: the sample space, the set of events and the probability measure. The sample space is the set formed of all possible results of an experiment. For example, if the throwing of a coin is the experiment, the sample space is the set $\{H, T\}$. If the experiment is the throwing of a dice the sample space is $\{1, 2, 3, 4, 5, 6\}$.

The sample space is not uniquely defined. For example, the throwing of a coin could have the sample space $\{1, 2\}$. We denote by Ω the sample space. Let us denote by $\mathcal{P}(\Omega)$ the set of subsets of Ω. That is,

$$\mathcal{P}(\Omega) = \{A; A \subset \Omega\}.$$

The next step is to define the set of events. A subset of Ω, say B, is an event if the probability of B is defined. Thus the set of events is the domain of the probability measure (to be defined below). Suppose $\mathcal{E} \subset \mathcal{P}(\Omega)$ is the set of events. If A and B are events, that is, if $A, B \in \mathcal{E}$, the union of the events $A \cup B$ is an event as well:

$$A \cup B = \{\omega \in \Omega; \omega \in A \text{ or } \omega \in B\} \in \mathcal{E}.$$

If A is an event then the complement of A is an event:

$$\text{If } A \in \mathcal{E} \text{ then } A^c = \{\omega \in \Omega; \omega \notin A\} \in \mathcal{E}.$$

If the set of events is closed for unions and complements, then it is closed for intersections as well since $(A \cap B)^c = A^c \cup B^c$ implies that $A \cap B = (A^c \cup B^c)^c$. In general, if the sample space is infinite we need to consider the general countable union of events.

Definition 19 (σ-algebra)   *A set $\mathcal{E} \subset \mathcal{P}(\Omega)$ is a sigma-algebra if*

1. *$\emptyset \in \mathcal{E}$;*
2. *for any $A \in \mathcal{E}$ then $A^c \in \mathcal{E}$;*
3. *for any family $A_n \in \mathcal{E}, n \geq 1$ then $\cup_{n=1}^{\infty} A_n \in \mathcal{E}$.*

We now define probability measure. We say that events A and B are disjoint (or mutually exclusive) if $A \cap B = \emptyset$. If $A_n, n \geq 1$ is a family of events, we say that they are pairwise disjoint if for every $n \neq m$ then $A_n \cap A_m = \emptyset$.

Definition 20 (probability measure)   *A probability measure, P, is a function $P \colon \mathcal{E} \to [0,1]$, $\mathcal{E} \subset \mathcal{P}(\Omega)$ a σ-algebra of events, such that:*

p-1 $P(\Omega) = 1$,
p-2 If $A, B \in \mathcal{E}$ are mutually exclusive (i.e. $A \cap B = \emptyset$) then $P(A \cup B) = P(A) + P(B)$,
p-3 If $A_n \in \mathcal{E}$ for every $n \geq 1$ are pairwise disjoint then $P(\cup_n A_n) = \sum_{n=1}^{\infty} P(A_n)$.

We can now formally define a probability space.

Definition 21 (probability space)   *A probability space is a triple $(\Omega, \mathcal{E}, P)$ such that $\mathcal{E} \subset \mathcal{P}(\Omega)$ is a σ-algebra and $P \colon \mathcal{E} \to [0,1]$ is a probability measure.*

If Ω is finite it is usually possible to assign a probability to every subset of Ω. The same is true if Ω is countable. However if Ω is uncountable it is not possible, in general, to assign a probability to every subset of Ω. The reason for this is technical and need not concern us here.

Example 30   *The finite and countably infinite sample space case.*
Suppose $\Omega = \{\omega_i; i \in \mathbb{N}\}$ is a countable set. If the sequence of non-negative real numbers, $r_i \geq 0$ has a sum $\sum_{i=1}^{\infty} r_i = 1$ we may define a probability space $(\Omega, \mathcal{P}(\Omega), P)$ by

$$P(A) = \sum_{i \,:\, \omega_i \in A} r_i \text{ if } A \subset \Omega. \tag{A.1}$$

A.2 Uncountable Sample Space Case

The case of uncountable sample spaces is very important. Uniform distributions, normal distributions, Brownian motions, etc. can only exist on uncountable sample spaces. On uncountable sample spaces it is not possible in general to define probability for every event. One approach is to try to have a probability defined for a large enough class of events. If $\mathcal{C} \subset \mathcal{P}(\Omega)$ is a class of events, there exists the smallest σ-algebra of events that contains $\mathcal{C}$. Suppose $\Omega = \mathbb{R}$. We say that $I \subset \mathbb{R}$ is a bounded interval if there exist a and b, with $a < b$ such that I is one of the sets

$$[a, b], (a, b], [a, b), (a, b).$$

If $\mathcal{C}^1 = \{I \subset \mathbb{R}; I \text{ is a bounded interval}\}$, the smallest σ-algebra that contains $\mathcal{C}^1$ is denoted by $\mathcal{B}^1$ and is called the Borelean σ-algebra on $\mathbb{R}$. Thus, a countable union of open intervals belongs to the Borelean σ-algebra. Since every open subset of $\mathbb{R}$ can be written as a countable union of open intervals, it is therefore also a Borelean set. The closed subsets are Borelean since a closed set is the complement of an open set.

Example 31 (uniform distribution)   *Suppose $\Omega = [0, 1]$. We want to formalize the experiment of taking a point $x \in [0, 1]$ at random. A natural beginning is to consider that the probability of an interval $[c, d] \subset [0, 1]$ is the length of the interval. Thus $P([c, d]) = d - c$. Hence $P(\Omega) = 1 - 0 = 1$.*

For instance, the probability of taking a point in the interval $\left[0, \frac{1}{2}\right]$ is $\frac{1}{2}$. The probability of taking a point in $\left[\frac{1}{3}, \frac{2}{3}\right]$ is $\frac{1}{3}$. We can also evaluate the probability of more complicated sets. Thus if I and J are disjoint intervals, $I \cup J \subset [0, 1]$ then $P(I \cup J) = P(I) + P(J)$. If we have a countable set of intervals $I_n \subset [0, 1]$ and the family $I_n, n \geq 1$ is pairwise disjoint then we define $P(\cup_n I_n) = \sum_{n=1}^{\infty} P(I_n)$.

A natural question is then when should we stop? Another important question is: Do we need to be restricted to sets that are obtained from intervals after a finite number of operations of union/complementation?

The answer to this last question is given in measure theory by Caratheodory's extension theorem. The application of Caratheodory's theorem to our example yields the existence of a unique probability measure $\lambda: \mathcal{B}^1 \to [0, 1]$ such that $\lambda([a, b]) = b - a$ whenever $0 \leq a \leq b \leq 1$. The Borelean σ-algebra contains all sets obtained from intervals after a countable number of operations of unions and complements. It is, however, not exhausted by these sets.

Instead of considering only intervals, we can consider the Cartesian product of intervals. Define

$$\mathcal{C}^n = \prod_{j=1}^{n} \mathcal{C}^1 = \left\{ \prod_{j=1}^{n} I_j; I_j \text{ is an interval} \right\}.$$

The smallest σ-algebra of $\mathbb{R}^n$ that contains $\mathcal{C}^n$ is denoted $\mathcal{B}^n$ and is called the Borel σ-algebra on $\mathbb{R}^n$. The more important examples of probability spaces are the probability spaces with density functions. The uniform and normal distributions have densities. We restrict ourselves in this book to continuous density functions. Thus suppose $K = \prod_{j=1}^{n} [a_i, b_i]$ is a product of intervals. A continuous density function is a continuous function $f\colon K \to \mathbb{R}$ such that

1. $f(k) \geq 0$ for every $k \in K$;
2. $\int_K f(x)\, \mathrm{d}x = \int_K f(x_1, x_2, \ldots, x_n)\, \mathrm{d}x_1\, \mathrm{d}x_2 \cdots \mathrm{d}x_n = 1$.

The following theorem—a particular case of Caratheodory's extension theorem—is proved in measure theory courses.

Theorem 28 *For any density function $f\colon K \to \mathbb{R}$, there is a unique probability measure $P\colon \mathcal{B}^n \to [0,1]$ such that:*

$$\text{If } \prod_{j=1}^{n} I_j \subset K \ \text{ then } P\left(\prod_{j=1}^{n} I_j\right) = \int_{\prod_{j=1}^{n} I_j} f(x)\, \mathrm{d}x.$$

For example if $f(k) = 1/\Pi_{j=1}^{n}(b_i - a_i)$, the probability that emerges from applying the theorem is called the uniform probability measure on K. It is therefore the unique probability measure defined on the Borelean σ-algebra such that $P\left(\Pi_{j=1}^{n} [c_j, d_j]\right) = \Pi_{j=1}^{n}(d_j - c_j)/(b_j - a_j)$ whenever $a_j \leq c_j \leq d_j \leq b_j$. Usually when we mention the uniform distribution we are referring to the uniform probability measure on $[0,1]$. If another type of uniform distribution is considered this will be explicitly mentioned.

A.3   Random Variables

Suppose $(\Omega, \mathcal{A})$ is given, where Ω is the sample space and $\mathcal{A}$ is a sigma-algebra of events in Ω. Usually if $\omega \in \Omega$ is drawn, we obtain as a measurement some real number $X(\omega)$. For example, if Ω is the set of all humans, $X(\omega)$ may be the height of human ω. In most experiments we only obtain functions of the sample space as a result. The following definition is important.

Definition 22 (random variable) *A function $X\colon \Omega \to \mathbb{R}$ is a random variable if for every interval (a,b) of real numbers, the set $\{\omega \in \Omega; a < X(\omega) < b\}$ is an event. That is, for a random variable, the probability of its value being in a given interval is well defined.*

Remark 17 *It is possible to show that if X is a random variable then the set $\{\omega \in \Omega; X(\omega) \in B\}$ is an event for every B in the Borelean σ-algebra. That is, for every B in the σ-algebra generated by the intervals.*

We need to introduce the following notation: If X is a random variable we denote the set $\{\omega \in \Omega; X(\omega) \in B\}$ by $[X \in B]$. That is we omit the ω in the notation.

If X is a random variable we may define its distribution function. This is one of the fundamental concepts in probability theory.

Definition 23 *The distribution function of a random variable $X: \Omega \to \mathbb{R}$ is the function $F_X: \mathbb{R} \to [0,1]$ defined by*

$$F_X(x) = P([X \le x]). \tag{A.2}$$

Thus, $F_X(x)$ is the probability that the random variable is less than or equal to x. The distribution function of a random variable is a particular case of the general concept of distribution functions.

Definition 24 (distribution)   *A function $F: \mathbb{R} \to [0,1]$ is a distribution function if:*

1. *F is non-decreasing, that is, $F(x) \le F(y)$ if $x \le y$.*
2. *F is right-continuous: I.e. $F(x+) := \lim_{y \downarrow x} F(y) = F(x)$.*
3. *$F(-\infty) := \lim_{x \to -\infty} F(x) = 0, F(\infty) := \lim_{x \to \infty} F(x) = 1$.*

Remark 18 *It is possible to show that for any distribution function F there is a probability space $(\Omega, \mathcal{A}, P)$ and a random variable $X: \Omega \to \mathbb{R}$ such that $F_X = F$. Thus in this sense distribution of random variables and distribution functions concepts coincide.*

Example 32 (uniform distribution)   *A random variable $U: \Omega \to \mathbb{R}$ such that its distribution is given by $F_U(x) = x$ for every $x \in [0,1]$ is said to have a uniform $[0,1]$ distribution. It shall be clear that $F(x) = 0$ if $x < 0$ and $F(x) = 1$ if $x \ge 1$.*

Definition 25 (density of a distribution)   *The distribution function F has a density if there is a (Riemann integrable) function $f: \mathbb{R} \to \mathbb{R}_+$ such that for every x we have that $F(x) = \int_{-\infty}^{x} f(u)\,du$.*

We remind the reader that a continuous function is Riemann integrable. If a function has a finite or infinite countable number of discontinuities it is also Riemann integrable. This is enough for our purposes. Reciprocally if the (Riemann integrable) function $f: \mathbb{R} \to \mathbb{R}$ is non-negative and $\int_{-\infty}^{\infty} f(x)\,dx = 1$ then defining $F(x) = \int_{-\infty}^{x} f(u)\,du$ we have that F is a distribution function.

Remark 19   *The Fundamental Calculus Theorem implies that at every point of continuity of $f(x)$ that $F'(x) = f(x)$. In this way we recover the density function f from the distribution F.*

The uniform distribution is a distribution with a density. Consider

$$f(x) = \begin{cases} 1 & \text{if } x \in [0,1], \\ 0 & \text{if } x \notin [0,1]. \end{cases}$$

Since $F(x) = \int_{-\infty}^{x} f(y)\,\mathrm{d}y = x$ if $x \in [0,1]$, $f(\cdot)$ is the density of the uniform distribution.

Definition 26   *The distribution has a bounded support if there is an interval $[a,b]$ such that $F(a-) = \sup_{x<a} F(x) = 0$ and $F(b) = 1$. Moreover, $F(x)$ is strictly increasing then the interval $[a,b]$ is the support of the distribution F.*

A.4   Random Vectors and their Distribution

A random variable is a function of the result of an experiment. Recall the example of the height of human ω. We could however obtain more information. We could measure the height and weight of human ω. In this case, we would have $X\colon \Omega \to \mathbb{R}^2$. We are, however, not limited to two measures. The general concept is that of a random vector.

Definition 27   *A function $X\colon \Omega \to \mathbb{R}^n$ is a random vector if $\{\omega \in \Omega; X(\omega) \in \Pi_{i=1}^{n}(a_i, b_i)\}$ is an event for every Cartesian product of intervals $\Pi_{i=1}^{n}(a_i, b_i) \subset \mathbb{R}^n$.*

It is possible to show that if X is a random vector then $[X \in B]$ is an event for every $B \subset \mathbb{R}^n$ Borelean. If we write $X = (X_1, \ldots, X_n)$, then X is a random vector if and only if $X_1, \ldots, X_n$ are random variables. It is convenient to define random vector distributions.

Definition 28   *The distribution of a random vector X is the function $F_X\colon \mathbb{R}^n \to [0,1]$ given by*

$$F_X(x_1, \ldots, x_n) = P([X_1 \le x_1, \ldots, X_n \le x_n]).$$

The distribution F_X has a density if there exists a Riemann integrable function $f\colon \mathbb{R}^n \to \mathbb{R}_+$ such that for every $x \in \mathbb{R}^n$,

$$F_X(x) = \int_{-\infty}^{x_1} \int_{-\infty}^{x_2} \cdots \int_{-\infty}^{x_n} f(y_1, y_2, \ldots, y_n)\,\mathrm{d}y_1\,\mathrm{d}y_2 \cdots \mathrm{d}y_n.$$

From the joint distribution of X we may obtain the distribution of each X_j (the marginal distribution). Simply note that

$$F_{X_1}(x_1) = P(X_1 \le x_1) = P(X_1 \le x_1, X_2 < \infty, \ldots, X_m < \infty)$$
$$= F_X(x_1, \infty, \ldots, \infty) = \lim_{x_2 \to \infty, \ldots, x_m \to \infty} F_X(x_1, x_2, \ldots, x_m).$$

If X has a density then X_1 has a density as well. This density is easily obtained: Since

$$F_{X_1}(x_1) = P(X_1 \le x_1, X_2 < \infty, \ldots, X_m < \infty)$$
$$= \int_{-\infty}^{x_1} \left(\int_{-\infty}^{\infty} \cdots \int_{-\infty}^{\infty} f(y_1, y_2, \ldots, y_n) \, dy_2 \cdots dy_n \right) dy_1$$

Thus $f_1(x_1) := \int_{-\infty}^{\infty} \cdots \int_{-\infty}^{\infty} f(x_1, y_2, \ldots, y_n) \, dy_2 \cdots dy_n$ is a density function for F_{X_1}. The following lemma gives an important property of distributions with density.

Lemma 11 *If the random vector $(X_1, X_2, \ldots, X_n)$ has a density then for every pair of indices $i \ne j$ we have that*

$$\Pr[X_i = X_j] = 0.$$

Proof: Let M be an upper bound of $\{f(x) ; x \in \mathbb{R}^n\}$. Let $N, m > 0$ be integers. For each $n \in \mathbb{Z}$ we divide the interval $[n, n+1]$ in N pairwise disjoint intervals, $\{I_n^k, k = 1, 2, \ldots, N\}$. Thus

$$\Pr\left[X_i \in I_n^k, X_j \in I_n^k, X_l \in [-m, m], l \notin \{i, j\}\right]$$
$$= \int_{x_i \in I_n^k} \int_{x_j \in I_n^k} \int_{x_l \in [-m,m]} f(x_i, x_j, x_{-l}) \, dx_i \, dx_j \, dx_{-l}$$
$$\le M(2m)^{n-2} \frac{1}{N^2}.$$

Hence

$$\Pr\left[X_i = X_j, X_i \in [n, n+1], |X_l| \le m, l \ne i, j\right]$$
$$\le \sum_{k=1}^{N} \Pr\left[X_i \in I_n^k, X_j \in I_n^k, X_l \in [-m, m], l \ne i, j\right]$$
$$\le M(2m)^{n-2} \frac{N}{N^2} = \frac{M(2m)^{n-2}}{N}.$$

Since this is true for every N we have that

$$\Pr[X_i = X_j, X_i \in [n, n+1], |X_l| \le m, l \ne i, j] = 0.$$

The countable union of sets with probability 0 has probability 0 therefore $\Pr[X_i = X_j] = 0$.   □

A.5   Independence of Random Variables

Suppose $X_i \colon \Omega \to \mathbb{R}$, $1 \le i \le m$ are random variables.

Definition 29   *We say that $X_1, X_2, \ldots, X_m$ are independent if for all $B_1, B_2, \ldots, B_m$, Borel subsets of $\mathbb{R}$, it is true that*

$$P([X_i \in B_i, \text{for all } i, 1 \le i \le m]) = P(X_1 \in B_1) \cdots P(X_m \in B_m). \quad \text{(A.3)}$$

To see that if $X_1, \ldots, X_m$ are independent then every sub-family is also independent, note that by choosing $B_j = \mathbb{R}$ the random variable X_j can be omitted from (A.3). If $X_1, \ldots, X_m$ are independent then

$$\begin{aligned}
F_X(x) &= P([X_1 \le x_1, \ldots, X_m \le x_m]) \\
&= P([X_1 \le x_1]) \cdots P([X_m \le x_m]) \\
&= F_{X_1}(x_1) \ldots F_{X_m}(x_m).
\end{aligned}$$

Reciprocally if $F_X(x) = F_{X_1}(x_1) \ldots F_{X_m}(x_m)$ then the random variables $X_1, \ldots, X_m$ are independent. As a corollary we have that if F_X has a density then the coordinates are independent if and only if $f(x) = f_1(x_1), \ldots, f_m(x_m)$. Thus we have the following proposition.

Proposition 8   *1. If X has a density $f(x)$ then X_i has a density f_i given by $f_i(x_i) = \int_{-\infty}^{\infty} \cdots \int_{-\infty}^{\infty} f(y_1, \ldots, y_{i-1}, x_i, y_{i+1}, \ldots, y_n) \, \mathrm{d}y_{-i}$.*
2. If the random variables $X_1, \ldots, X_n$ have density then $X_1, X_2, \ldots, X_n$ are independent if and only if the random vector $X = (X_1, \ldots, X_n)$ has density $f(x) = f_1(x_1), \ldots, f_n(x_n)$.

A.6   The Distribution of the Maximum of Independent Random Variables

We begin recalling the definition of the maximum. If a and b are real numbers the maximum of a and b, denoted $\max\{a, b\}$ is a if $a \ge b$. And it is b if $b \ge a$. More generally the maximum of the n real numbers, $a_1, a_2, \ldots, a_n$ is a_j such that $a_j \ge a_l$, $l = 1, 2, \ldots, n$. We write $\max\{a_1, a_2, \ldots, a_n\} = a_j$. Suppose $X_1, X_2, \ldots, X_n$ are independent random variables, identically distributed. That is, $F_{X_1} = F_{X_2} = \cdots = F_{X_n}$. To each $\omega \in \Omega$ define $\max\{X_1, \ldots, X_n\}(\omega) = \max\{X_1(\omega), \ldots, X_n(\omega)\}$. We want to find the distribution of the maximum of the n functions, $\max\{X_1,\ldots,X_n\}$. Call F the common distribution F_{X_1} and call G the distribution of $\max\{X_1,\ldots,X_n\}$. Thus,

$$G(r) = P(\{\omega \in \Omega; \max\{X_1(\omega),\ldots,X_n(\omega)\} \leq r\}) \tag{A.4}$$
$$= P([X_i \leq r, 1 \leq i \leq n]) = P(\cap_{i=1}^n [X_i \leq r])$$

$$= \prod_{i=1}^n P([X_i \leq r]) = \prod_{i=1}^n F(r) = F^n(r). \tag{A.5}$$

If F has a density, G has a density too (recall remark (19)):

$$g(r) = G'(r) = nF^{n-1}(r)f(r). \tag{A.6}$$

Example 33 *The maximum of n independent uniform random variables has a distribution with density $g(r) = nr^{n-1}, r \in [0,1]$.*

A.7 The Distribution of the Second Highest Value

Let us consider a finite group of numbers, $x_1, x_2, \ldots, x_m$. Let us re-order these numbers from the largest to the smallest, $y_1, y_2, \ldots, y_m$. Thus $y_1 \geq y_2 \geq \cdots \geq y_m$. If there is repetition among the $x'_j s$ there will be also repetition amongst the $y'_j s$. The number $y_1 = \max\{x_1, x_2, \ldots, x_m\}$ is the maximum. The number y_2 is the second largest and so on. The number y_m is the mth largest. For example, suppose our group is $1, 2, 2$. The $y_1 = 2 = y_2$, $y_3 = 1$.

We want to find the distribution of the second highest value of the independent, identically distributed random variables, $X_1, X_2, \ldots, X_m$. Call Y^2 the second highest and Y^1 the highest. We need to evaluate the probability that $Y^2 \leq r$ for a given real number r. If $Y^1 \leq r$ then a fortiori $Y^2 \leq r$. Suppose the maximum is $X_1(\omega) > r$. Then $Y^2 \leq r$ if and only if $X_j(\omega) \leq r, j \neq 1$. Also if the maximum is $X_k(\omega) > r$ then $Y^2 \leq r$ if and only if $X_j(\omega) \leq r$, for all $j \neq r$. Thus,

$$[Y^2 \leq r] = [Y^1 \leq r] \cup \cup_{k=1}^m \{X_k > r \geq X_j, \forall j \neq k\}. \tag{A.7}$$

The sets in (A.7) are pairwise disjoint. Therefore,

$$F_{Y^2}(r) = P([Y^1 \leq r]) + \sum_{k=1}^m P([X_k > r \geq X_j, \forall j \neq k]). \tag{A.8}$$

We know already that $P\left(\left[Y^1 \leq r\right]\right) = F^m\left(r\right)$. To evaluate the summands above we use independence:

$$P\left(\left[X_k > r \geq X_j, \forall j \neq k\right]\right) \tag{A.9}$$

$$= P\left(\left[X_k > r\right]\right) \cdot P\left(\left[r \geq X_j, \forall j \neq k\right]\right) \tag{A.10}$$

$$= P\left(\left[X_k > r\right]\right) \cdot \prod_{j \neq k} P\left(\left[r \geq X_j\right]\right) = \left(1 - F\left(r\right)\right) F^{m-1}\left(r\right) \tag{A.11}$$

Finally we have that $F_{Y^2}\left(r\right) = F^m\left(r\right) + \sum_{k=1}^{m}\left(1 - F\left(r\right)\right) F^{m-1}\left(r\right) = F^m\left(r\right) + m\left(1 - F\left(r\right)\right) F^{m-1}\left(r\right)$. If F has density f then the density of Y^2 is given by

$$f_{Y^2}\left(r\right) = m\left(m - 1\right)\left(1 - F\left(r\right)\right) F^{m-2}\left(r\right) f\left(r\right). \tag{A.12}$$

Let us find the joint distribution of the highest and second highest types. We have n bidders. Thus if $a \geq b$ then

$$\Pr\left(Y \leq a, Y^2 \leq b\right) = \Pr\left(Y \leq b\right) + \Pr\left(b < Y \leq a, Y^2 \leq b\right)$$

$$= F^n\left(b\right) + n(F\left(a\right) - F\left(b\right))F^{n-1}\left(b\right).$$

From this we get the density $f_{(Y,Y^2)}$ easily:

$$f_{(Y,Y^2)}\left(a,b\right) = nf\left(a\right)\left(n - 1\right) F^{n-2}\left(b\right) f\left(b\right), b \leq a.$$

A.8   Mean Value of Random Variables

Suppose we have n real numbers, $x_1, x_2, \ldots, x_n$. The mean of $x_1, x_2, \ldots, x_n$ is by definition $\sum_{i=1}^{n} x_i/n$. It is possible that some of the x_i are equal. Suppose that by omitting repetitions we obtain the set $y_1, y_2, \ldots, y_l$ of real numbers. And define $k_1 \in \mathbb{N}$ the number of times y_1 is repeated in $x_1, x_2, \ldots, x_n$, k_2 the number of times y_2 is repeated and so on until k_l the number of times y_l is repeated. By construction $\sum_{i=1}^{l} k_i = n$. Thus, the average of a collection of numbers with repetition is

$$\frac{\sum_{i=1}^{l} k_i y_i}{\sum_{i=1}^{l} k_i} = \sum_{i=1}^{l} \left(\frac{k_i}{\sum_{i=1}^{l} k_i}\right) y_i. \tag{A.13}$$

Let us consider now a discrete random variable. That is, a random variable $X : \Omega \to \mathbb{R}$ with a finite range, $X\left(\Omega\right) = \{y_1, y_2, \ldots, y_l\}$. The average of X is by definition

$$E\left[X\right] = \sum_{i=1}^{l} y_i P\left(\left[X = y_i\right]\right). \tag{A.14}$$

Comparing (A.13) with (A.14) we see that the discrete random variable means definition is natural. If the random variable is not discrete the definition of the mean is more complicated. A particularly important case is when the random variable has a distribution with density. If the random variable X has a distribution F_X with density f_X its mean is defined by

$$E[X] := \int_{-\infty}^{\infty} x f_X(x) \, dx. \tag{A.15}$$

This definition is also natural. Rewriting (A.14) as

$$E[X] = \sum_{i=1}^{l} y_i \left(P([X \le y_i]) - P([X \le y_{i-1}]) \right)$$

$$= \sum_{i=1}^{l} y_i \left(F_X(y_i) - F_X(y_{i-1}) \right),$$

we may consider (A.14) as a Riemann sum of the integral $\int_{-\infty}^{\infty} x f_X(x) \, dx$. Thus, if we use finer and finer partitions, the discrete mean will converge to (A.15). The general definition is given in terms of the Lebesgue integral $\int X(\omega) \, dP(\omega)$ and will not be used in this book. We summarize the discussion above in the following definition:

Definition 30 *The mean of the distribution F with density f is defined by $\int_{-\infty}^{\infty} x f(x) \, dx$. If the random variable X has distribution F_X with density f_X then the mean of X is defined by $E[X] := \int_{-\infty}^{\infty} x f_X(x) \, dx$.*

If X is a random variable and $h \colon \mathbb{R} \to \mathbb{R}$ is a continuous function the mean of $h \circ X$ can be proved to be equal to $\int_{-\infty}^{\infty} h(x) f_X(x) \, dx$. This result is true in much more generality for any $h(\cdot)$ which is measurable. That is, for any $h(\cdot)$ such that $h^{-1}((-\infty, a))$ is a Borelean set for any real number a. If $h(x) = x^p$ the mean $E[X^p]$ is the moment of order p. The variance of X is given by $E[(X - E[X])^2]$.

Example 34 *Let us calculate the mean of some random variables.*

1. *Given the uniform $[a, b]$ distribution. It has a density function $f(x) = 1/(b - a)$ if $a \le x \le b$ and $f(x) = 0$ otherwise. Thus if the random variable X has a uniform $[a, b]$ distribution its mean is*

$$E[X] = \int_{a}^{b} x \frac{1}{b - a} \, dx = \frac{b^2 - a^2}{2(b - a)} = \frac{b + a}{2}.$$

   The uniform $[0, 1]$ distribution has mean $\frac{1}{2}$.
2. *Consider now the power distribution: $F(x) = x^\gamma, \gamma > 0$. It is defined for $x \in [0, 1]$. If $x > 1$, $F(x) = 1$. If $x < 0$, $F(x) = 0$. Its density is easily calculated by $f(x) = F'(x) = \gamma x^{\gamma - 1}, x \in (0, 1)$. Since $f(\cdot)$ is continuous*

on $(0,1)$ *it is indeed the density of* F. *Hence, the mean of the power distribution* x^γ *is* $\int_0^1 x \left(\gamma x^{\gamma-1}\right) dx = \gamma \int_0^1 x^\gamma dx = \gamma/(\gamma+1)$.

3. *Another common distribution is the exponential distribution. It is given by* $F(x) = 1 - e^{-rx}, x \geq 0$, *with parameter* $r > 0$. *The exponential distribution has a continuous density* $f(x) = re^{-rx}$. *Thus, the mean is*

$$\int_0^\infty xre^{-rx}\,dx = \int_0^\infty \frac{y}{r}e^{-y}\,dy = \frac{\int_0^\infty ye^{-y}\,dy}{r} = \frac{1}{r}.$$

The last integral is calculated using integration by parts.

Example 35 *Let us calculate the mean of the maximum of independent uniformly distributed random variables. Suppose* X_1, X_2, X_3 *are independently uniformly distributed in* $[0,1]$. *From (A.6) we obtain the mean of the maximum:*

$$E\left[\max\{X_1, X_2, X_3\}\right] = \int x \left(3F^2(x) f(x)\right) dx \tag{A.16}$$

$$= \int_0^1 x \left(3x^2 \cdot 1\right) dx = \frac{3}{4}. \tag{A.17}$$

The generalization to any number of independently uniformly distributed random variables is immediate:

$$E\left[\max\{X_1, X_2, \ldots, X_m\}\right] = \int_0^1 xmx^{m-1}\,dx = \frac{m}{m+1}. \tag{A.18}$$

The mean of the second highest value can also be easily calculated using (A.12). We obtain

$$E\left[Y^2\right] = \int_0^1 m(m-1)(1-x)x^{m-1}\,dx = \frac{m-1}{m+1}.$$

The following proposition has an immediate proof using (A.6) and (A.12).

Proposition 9 *Suppose* $X_1, \ldots, X_m$ *is a sequence of independent identically distributed random variables. Suppose also that the common distribution* $F(\cdot)$ *has a density* $f(\cdot)$ *which is zero outside the interval* $[a,b]$. *Then the mean value of the maximum is* $\int_a^b rmF^{m-1}(r) f(r)\,dr$. *The mean value of the second highest value is* $\int_a^b rm(m-1)(1-F(r)) F^{m-2}(r) f(r)\,dr$.

A.9 Conditional Probability

Consider a probability space $(\Omega, \mathcal{A}, P)$ and suppose that the event $A \in \mathcal{A}$, $P(A) > 0$ is known to occur. We often want to know the probability of an event B given that A occurs. For example, when throwing a dice we may want to know the probability of number 2 occurring given that an even numbered side has occurred. The conditional probability of event B given the event A is by definition

$$P(B \mid A) = \frac{P(A \cap B)}{P(B)}. \tag{A.19}$$

Thus $P(A \mid A) = 1$. If B and C are disjoint events then $P(B \cup C \mid A) = P(B \mid A) + P(C \mid A)$. If we define $\mathbb{A} = \{B \cap A; B \in \mathcal{A}\}$ we have that $(A, \mathbb{A}, P(\cdot \mid A))$ is a probability space. The conditional probability is very simple if A and B are independent. In this case $P(B \mid A) = P(B)$. So knowing that A occurs doesn't affect the probability of the occurrence of B.

Let us now consider the case of conditioning for events with probability zero. This is a much harder case and the general answer needs the Radon–Nikodym theorem which is not covered here (see Chung's book, e.g.) If we restrict ourselves to distributions with density a definition can be made without much difficulty.

Suppose we have a random vector (X, Y) with distribution F and density $f(\cdot, \cdot)$. A natural definition of the conditional density $f_{X \mid Y=y}$ is $f_{X \mid Y=y}(x) = f(x, y)/f_Y(y)$. The conditional distribution $F_{X \mid Y=y}$ is

$$F_{X \mid Y=y}(x) = \int_{-\infty}^{x} f_{X \mid Y=y}(u) \, du = \int_{-\infty}^{x} \frac{f(u, y)}{\int_{-\infty}^{\infty} f(a, y) \, da} \, du.$$

Example 36 *Suppose $X_1, \ldots, X_m$ are independent, uniformly distributed in $[0, 1]$. Let us find the conditional distribution of Y^2 given Y^1. We first find the distribution of (Y^2, Y^1):*

$$F(y, z) = P\left(Y^2 \leq y, Y^1 \leq z\right).$$

If $z \leq y$ then $F(y, z) = P\left(Y^1 \leq z\right) = \int_0^z f_{Y^1}(u) \, du$. If $y < z$. Then $F(y, z) = P\left(Y^1 \leq y\right) + P\left(Y^2 \leq y < Y^1 \leq z\right)$. The last summand can be calculated using the reasoning in (A.7) and (A.8). It is $P\left(Y^2 \leq y < Y^1 \leq z\right) = m(z - y) y^{m-1}$. Thus $F(y, z) = y^m + m(z - y) y^{m-1}$. The density of F is $f(y, z) = \frac{\partial^2 F}{\partial y \partial z} = m(m - 1) y^{m-2}$ if $0 \leq y \leq z \leq 1$ and 0 otherwise. The conditional density is therefore

$$f_{Y^2 \mid Y^1=z} = \frac{m(m-1) y^{m-2}}{m z^{m-1}} = \frac{(m-1) y^{m-2}}{z^{m-1}} \quad \text{if } y \leq z.$$

The mean of Y^2 conditional on $Y^1 = z$ is

$$\int_0^z \frac{(m-1) y^{m-1}}{z^{m-1}} \, dy = z \frac{m-1}{m}.$$

Lemma 12 *Suppose $X = (X_1, \ldots, X_m)$ is a random vector with joint density $f_X(x)$. Suppose also that $u(x)$ is a Riemann integrable function. Then*

$$E\left[u(X)|X_1 = x_1\right] = E\left[E\left[u(X)|X_1, X_2\right]|X_1 = x_1\right].$$

Proof: If $f_{X_1}(x_1) = \int f_X(x)\,dx_2 \ldots dx_m$ is the marginal density of X_1 then

$$E\left[u(X)|X = x_1\right] = \int u(x_1, x_2, \ldots, x_m)\frac{f_X(x)}{f_{X_1}(x_1)}\,dx_2 \cdots dx_m.$$

Now if $f_{X_1 X_2}$ is the joint density of (X_1, X_2) we have that

$$E\left[u(X)|X_1 = x_1, X_2 = x_2\right] = \int u(x)\frac{f(x_1, x_2, x_3, \ldots, x_m)}{f_{X_1 X_2}(x_1, x_2)}\,dx_3 \cdots dx_m.$$

Thus

$$\int E\left[u(X)|X_1 = x_1, X_2 = x_2\right]\frac{f_{X_1 X_2}(x_1, x_2)}{f_{X_1}(x_1)}\,dx_2$$

$$= \int \left(\int u(x)\frac{f(x_1, x_2, x_3, \ldots, x_m)}{f_{X_1 X_2}(x_1, x_2)}\,dx_3 \cdots dx_m\right)\frac{f_{X_1 X_2}(x_1, x_2)}{f_{X_1}(x_1)}\,dx_2$$

$$= \int u(x)\frac{f(x_1, x_2, x_3, \ldots, x_m)}{f_{X_1}(x_1)}\,dx_2\,dx_3 \cdots dx_m = E\left[u(X)|X = x_1\right].$$

$$\square$$

In equation (3.6), we mentioned that the equilibrium bidding function of the first-price auction is the expected value of the second highest type given the highest type. The conditional density of Y^2 given $Y = a$ is

$$f_{Y^2|Y=a}(b) = \frac{(n-1)F^{n-2}(b)f(b)}{F^{n-1}(a)}, \quad b \le a.$$

Thus

$$E\left[Y^2|Y = v\right] = \int y f_{Y^2|Y=v}\,dy$$

$$= \int_0^v y\frac{(n-1)F^{n-2}(y)f(y)}{F^{n-1}(v)} = b^*(v). \tag{A.20}$$

Appendix B

Differential Equations

We collect here a few results on ordinary differential equations that are used in the text.

B.1 The Simplest Differential Equation

Suppose $f : \mathbb{R} \to \mathbb{R}$ is a continuous function. Let x_0 and A be given real numbers. If we want to find a differentiable function $y : \mathbb{R} \to \mathbb{R}$ such that

$$y'(x) = f(x), \quad \forall x \in \mathbb{R};$$
$$y(x_0) = A,$$

(B.1)

we say that we want to solve the differential equation $y' = f$ with initial condition $y(x_0) = A$. This equation is solved using the Fundamental Theorem of Calculus.

Theorem 29 Fundamental Theorem of Calculus   *If two differentiable functions $g(x)$ and $h(x)$ have the same derivative then they differ by a constant.*

To solve (B.1) consider $\psi(x) = A + \int_{x_0}^{x} f(y)\, dy$. Then note that $\psi(x_0) = A$ and $\psi'(x) = f(x)$ for every x since $f(\cdot)$ is continuous. Suppose now that $y(\cdot)$ solves (B.1). Then since $y'(x) = f(x) = \psi'(x)$ we have by the fundamental theorem of calculus that $\psi(x) = y(x) + C$ for some constant C. Choosing $x = x_0$ we see that $C = 0$.

B.2 Integrating Factor

The integrating factor is used to solve linear differential equations. It is used several times in this book. It can be applied to equations of the following form:

$$b'(x) + b(x)Q(x) = R(x).$$

To understand how it works note that the left-hand side of the above equation has a slight similarity to the derivative of a product: $(bp)' = b'p + bp'$. Suppose we multiply the left-hand side by a function $P(x)$. It becomes

$$b'(x)P(x) + b(x)P(x)Q(x).$$

If we can choose $P(x)$ such that $P'(x) = P(x)Q(x)$ (this P is called an integrating factor) we transform the left-hand side into the derivative of the product $b(x)P(x)$:

$$\begin{aligned}(b(x)P(x))' &= b'(x)P(x) + b(x)P'(x) \\ &= (b'(x) + b(x)Q(x))P(x) \\ &= R(x)P(x).\end{aligned}$$

Now to find P such that $P' = PQ$ is easy. Note that

$$(\log P)' = \frac{P'}{P} = Q.$$

Thus $P(x) = e^{\int Q(x)\,dx}$ is an integrating factor. And our differential equation has a solution:

$$b(x) = \frac{\int R(x)P(x)}{P(x)}.$$

The reader may wonder why we did not mention the initial condition. This will, however, be taken care of in the text each time we use the integrating factor.

Appendix C

Affiliation

Proposition 10 *Suppose that for every i, j, $p(\cdot)$ satisfies the monotone likelihood property for the variables (x_i, x_j). Then the density $p(\cdot)$ satisfies the multivariate monotone likelihood property.*

Proof: We follow the proof in Karlin and Rinott (1981) Proposition 2.1. We prove by induction on dimension n. Suppose it is true for n. Suppose p is defined on $X = \Pi_{i=1}^{n+1}[a_i, b_i]$ and satisfies the monotone likelihood property for any pair of variables. By the induction hypotheses it also satisfies the multivariate monotone likelihood for any set of n variables. Consider $x, y \in X$. Without loss of generality, we may suppose that $x = (x_1^*, \ldots, x_k^*, x_{k+1}, \ldots, x_{n+1})$, $y = (y_1, \ldots, y_k, y_{k+1}^*, \ldots, y_{n+1}^*)$ where $x_l^* \geq y_l, l = 1, \ldots, k$ and $y_l^* \geq x_l$ for the other coordinates. Then

$$
\frac{p(x \vee y)p(x \wedge y)}{p(x)p(y)}
$$

$$
= \frac{p(x_1^*, \ldots, x_k^*, y_{k+1}^*, \ldots, y_{n+1}^*)\ p(y_1, \ldots, y_k, x_{k+1}, \ldots, x_{n+1})}{p(x_1^*, \ldots, x_k^*, x_{k+1}, \ldots, x_{n+1})\ p(y_1, \ldots, y_k, y_{k+1}^*, \ldots, y_{n+1}^*)}
$$

$$
= \frac{p(x_1^*, \ldots, x_k^*, y_{k+1}^*, \ldots, y_{n+1}^*)\ p(x_1^*, y_2, \ldots, y_k, x_{k+1}, \ldots, x_{n+1})}{p(x_1^*, \ldots, x_k^*, x_{k+1}, \ldots, x_{n+1})\ p(x_1^*, y_2, \ldots, y_k, y_{k+1}^*, \ldots, y_{n+1}^*)}
$$

$$
\times \frac{p(x_1^*, y_2, \ldots, y_k, y_{k+1}^*, \ldots, y_{n+1}^*)\ p(y_1, \ldots, y_k, x_{k+1}, \ldots, x_{n+1})}{p(x_1^*, y_2, \ldots, y_k, x_{k+1}, \ldots, x_{n+1})\ p(y_1, \ldots, y_k, y_{k+1}^*, \ldots, y_{n+1}^*)} \geq 1.
$$

The term in the second line above is not less than one by the induction hypothesis—x_1^* is the variable that is fixed. In the third line above the same reasoning applies—$(y_2, \ldots, y_k)$ is fixed. $\qquad\square$

Lemma 13 *If $f_1(x)f_2(y) \leq f_3(x \vee y)f_4(x \wedge y)$ and $\phi_i(x) = \int f_i(x)\,dx_n$, $i = 1, 2, 3, 4$ then*

$$\phi_1(x)\phi_2(y) \leq \phi_3(x \vee y)\phi_4(x \wedge y). \tag{C.1}$$

Proof: Write $y = (x_1, \ldots, x_{n-1})$. To prove (C.1) is equivalent to prove that

$$\int f(y, a)f(y', b)\,da\,db \leq \int f(y \vee y', a)f(y \wedge y', b)\,da\,db.$$

Or rather that

$$\int_{a<b} [f(y, a)f(y', b) + f(y, b)f(y', a)]\,da\,db$$

$$\leq \int_{a<b} [f(y \vee y', a)f(y \wedge y', b) + f(y \vee y', b)f(y \wedge y', a)]\,da\,db.$$

Define

$$t_1 = f(y, a)f(y', b), \quad t_2 = f(y, b)f(y', a),$$

$$s_1 = f(y \vee y', a)f(y \wedge y', b), \quad s_2 = f(y \vee y', b)f(y \wedge y', a).$$

It is immediate that $t_1 \leq s_2, t_2 \leq s_2$. Moreover, $t_1 t_2 \leq s_1 s_2$. If $s_2 = 0$ then $t_1 = t_2 = 0$. If

$$s_2 > 0, \quad s_2[s_2 + s_1 - t_1 - t_2] = s_2^2 + s_2 s_1 - s_2 t_1 - s_2 t_2$$

$$= (s_2 - t_2)(s_2 - t_1) + (s_2 s_1 - t_1 t_2) \geq 0$$

imply that $s_2 + s_1 \geq t_1 + t_2$. $\square$

We now prove Theorem 9 repeated here for convenience:

Theorem 9 *Let f_1, f_2, f_3, and f_4 be non-negative functions on $\mathbb{R}^n$ such that for all $x, y \in \mathbb{R}^n$, $f_1(x)f_2(y) \leq f_3(x \vee y)f_4(x \wedge y)$. Then*

$$\int f_1(x)\,dx \int f_2(x)\,dx \leq \int f_3(x)\,dx \int f_4(x)\,dx.$$

Proof: The proof is by induction on the dimension n. For $n = 1$ the result is true if

$$\int_{x<y} (f_1(x)f_2(y) + f_1(y)f_2(x))\,dx\,dy$$

$$\leq \int_{x<y} (f_3(x)f_4(y) + f_3(y)f_4(x))\,dx\,dy.$$

Define

$$a = f_1(x)f_2(y); \quad b = f_1(y), \quad d = f_3(y)f_4(x).$$

It is straight forward to verify that the following inequalities hold $a \leq d, b \leq d$ and $ab \leq cd$. The inequality $c + d \geq a + b$ follows from the inequality $d(c + d - a - b) = (d - a)(d - b) + cd - ab \geq 0$. Suppose now the result is true for dimension $n - 1$. If $f_1(x)f_2(y) \leq f_3(x \vee y)f_4(x \wedge y)$ then integrating in x_n the resulting function

$$\phi_i(x_{-n}) = \int f_i(x)\, \mathrm{d}x_n$$

also satisfies the same inequality. See the Lemma 13. Thus,

$$\int \phi_1(x)\, \mathrm{d}x_{-n} \cdot \int \phi_2(x)\, \mathrm{d}x_{-n} \leq \int \phi_3(x)\, \mathrm{d}x_{-n} \cdot \int \phi_4(x)\, \mathrm{d}x_{-n}.$$

And now the result is immediate since $\int \phi_i(x)\, \mathrm{d}x_{-n} = \int f_i(x)\, \mathrm{d}x$. $\qquad\square$

Appendix D

Convexity

In this section, we consider a few results on convex functions that are used in Chapter 6. We begin with the convex hull.

Definition 31 *The convex hull of a function $f(\cdot)$ is the greatest convex function that is pointwise smaller than f. That is, if $f : [0,1] \to \mathbb{R}$ then $g : [0,1] \to \mathbb{R}$ is the convex hull of f if:*

1. *g is convex;*
2. *$g \leq f$, that is $g(x) \leq f(x)$, for all $x \in [0,1]$;*
3. *if h is a convex function and $h \leq f$ then $h \leq g$.*

The convex hull of a function exists and has an explicit expression (see Rockafellar: 36). We do not consider here the more general case.

Proposition 11 *If $h : [0,1] \to \mathbb{R}$ is continuous then the function g defined below is the convex hull of h:*

$$g(q) = \min \left\{ \sum_{l=1}^{n} \lambda_l h(r_l); \lambda_l, r_l \in [0,1], \sum_{l=1}^{n} \lambda_l = 1, \sum_{l=1}^{n} \lambda_l r_l = q \right\} \qquad \text{(D.1)}$$

Proof: The minimum is attained since h is continuous. It is immediate that $g(q) \leq h(q)$ for every q. Now if $f \leq h$ is a convex function then for any convex combination $q = \sum_{l=1}^{n} \lambda_l r_l$ we have that

$$f(q) = f \left(\sum_{l=1}^{n} \lambda_l r_l \right) \leq \sum_{l} \lambda_l f(r_l) \leq \sum_{l} \lambda_l h(r_l).$$

Hence $f(q) \leq g(q)$. It remains to prove that g is convex. Suppose $\lambda \in (0,1)$ and $q_1, q_2 \in [0,1]$. Then there exists $\omega_l, r_l, \omega_l', r_l'$ such that

$$q_1 = \sum_{l=1}^{n} \omega_l r_l; \omega_l \geq 0, r_l \in [0,1], \sum_{l=1}^{n} \omega_l = 1;$$

$$q_2 = \sum_{l=1}^{n} \omega_l' r_l'; \omega_l' \geq 0, r_l' \in [0,1], \sum_{l=1}^{n} \omega_l' = 1;$$

$$g(q_1) = \sum_{l=1}^{n} \omega_l g(r_l), g(q_2) = \sum_{l=1}^{n} \omega_l' h(r_l').$$

We have that

$$\lambda g(q_1) + (1-\lambda)g(q_2) = \lambda \sum_{l=1}^{n} \omega_l h(r_l) + (1-\lambda) \sum_{l=1}^{n} \omega_l' h(r_l')$$

$$= \sum_{l=1}^{n} \lambda \omega_l h(r_l) + \sum_{l=1}^{n} (1-\lambda)\omega_l' h(r_l')$$

$$= \sum_{i=1}^{2n} \theta_i h(s_i);$$

$$\theta_i = \begin{cases} \lambda \omega_i & \text{if } i \leq n \\ (1-\lambda)\omega_l' & \text{if } i = l+n, l \leq n \end{cases}$$

and

$$s_i = \begin{cases} r_i & \text{if } i \leq n \\ r_l' & \text{if } i = l+n, l \leq n. \end{cases}$$

Thus,

$$g(\lambda q_1 + (1-\lambda)q_2) \leq \sum_{i=1}^{2n} \theta_i h(s_i) = \lambda g(q_1) + (1-\lambda)g(q_2). \qquad \square$$

Lemma 14   *If $g(x) < f(x)$ then $g'(y) = g'(x)$ in a neighborhood of x.*

Proof: Suppose $g(x) < f(x)$. There are $\lambda_l \geq 0, \sum_l \lambda_l = 1, x_l \in [0,1]$, $x = \sum_l \lambda_l x_l$ such that $g(x) = \sum_l \lambda_l f(x_l)$. Since

$$g(x) \leq \sum_l \lambda_l g(x_l) \leq \sum_l \lambda_l f(x_l) = g(x),$$

we conclude that $g(x_l) = f(x_l)$ for every l. We first show that there is a $\theta \in [0,1]$ such that $g(x) = \theta f(a_k) + (1-\theta)f(a_l)$ and $\theta a_k + (1-\theta)a_l = x$. To see this note that if λ^* is a solution of

$$\min \sum_{l=1}^{n} \lambda_l b_l,$$

$$\lambda_l > 0, \quad \sum_{l=1}^{n} \lambda_l < 1, \quad \sum_{l=1}^{n} \lambda_l a_l = x$$

then for some μ real

$$b_l = \mu a_l, \quad 1 \le l \le n$$

and in this case $\sum_l \lambda_l b_l = \mu x$ for every λ and therefore for some λ with $\lambda_l = 0$ as well. Now consider the problem

$$\min \sum_{l=1}^{n} \lambda_l b_l,$$

$$\lambda_l \ge 0, \quad \sum_{l=1}^{n} \lambda_l = 1, \quad \sum_{l=1}^{n} \lambda_l a_l = x,$$

and consider the solution λ^* with the greatest number of zero coefficients λ_l^*. From the previous case we see that $n = 2$. Define $\alpha = a_k$ and $\beta = a_l$, we may write

$$g(\theta \alpha + (1 - \theta)\beta) = \theta f(\alpha) + (1 - \theta) f(\beta),$$

$$\theta \alpha + (1 - \theta)\beta = x.$$

Without loss of generality $\alpha < x < \beta$. Now consider y, y' such that $\alpha < y < x < y' < \beta$. There are $a, b \in (0, 1)$ such that $a\alpha + (1-a)x = y$ and $bx + (1-b)\beta = y'$. Namely $a = (x - y)/(x - \alpha)$ and $b = (\beta - y')/(\beta - x)$. Then

$$g(y) \le ag(\alpha) + (1 - a)g(x),$$

$$g(y') \le bg(x) + (1 - b)g(\beta).$$

Moreover, $r := \frac{y' - x}{y' - y} \in (0, 1)$ is such that $ry + (1 - r)y' = x$. Then

$$g(x) \le rg(y) + (1 - r)g(y')$$
$$\le rag(\alpha) + (r(1 - a) + (1 - r)b)g(x) + (1 - r)(1 - b)g(\beta), \qquad \text{(D.2)}$$

and thus,

$$g(x) \le \frac{ra}{ra + (1 - r)(1 - b)} f(\alpha) + \frac{(1 - r)(1 - b)}{ra + (1 - r)(1 - b)} f(\beta)$$

$$= \frac{-\beta + x}{-\beta + \alpha} f(\alpha) + -\frac{x - \alpha}{-\beta + \alpha} f(\beta)$$

$$= \theta f(\alpha) + (1 - \theta) f(\beta) = g(x).$$

Thus the inequalities in (D.2) are equalities and this ends the proof. $\qquad\square$

We now consider the one-sided derivative of a convex function.

Proposition 12 *If $g : [0, 1) \to \mathbb{R}$ is convex then for every $x \in [0, 1)$ there exists*

$$g'_+(x) = \lim_{r \downarrow 0} \frac{g(x + r) - g(x)}{r}. \qquad (D.3)$$

Moreover, the function $x \to g'_+(x)$ is increasing.

Proof: First note that if $a < b$ and $c < d, a \le c, b \le d$ then

$$\frac{g(b) - g(a)}{b - a} \le \frac{g(d) - g(c)}{d - c}.$$

To see this consider first $a = c$. That is $a = c < b \le d$. Then if $r = (d-b)/(d-a)$ we have that

$$g(b) = g(ra + (1 - r)d) \le \frac{d - b}{d - a} g(a) + \frac{b - a}{d - a} g(d).$$

The case $b = d$ is analogous. Thus we have that

$$\frac{g(b) - g(a)}{b - a} \le \frac{g(d) - g(a)}{d - a}, a < b < d.$$

Therefore, the ratio $(g(b) - g(a))/(b - a)$ decreases with $b > a$ for every a. The same is therefore true of $(g(d) - g(c))/(d - c)$. We see from (D.3) that $(g(d) - g(c))/(d - c)$ has a lower bound (namely $(g(b)-g(a))/(b-a)$). Therefore there exists

$$g'_+(c) = \lim_{d \downarrow c} \frac{g(d) - g(c)}{d - c}.$$

We see also from (D.3) that $g'_+(a) \le g'_+(c)$ whenever $a < c$. $\qquad \square$

References

Ashenfelter, O. and Graddy, K. (2003), 'Auctions and the price of art', *Journal of Economic Literature*, 41(3): 763–787.

Athey, S. and Haile, P. (2005), *Non-Parametric Approaches to Auctions*, Mimeo: Yale University. Available at http://www.econ.yale.edu/~pah29/hbk.pdf.

Baron, D. and Myerson, R. (1982), 'Regulating a monopolist with unknown costs', *Econometrica* 50: 911–930.

Bulow, J. and Roberts, J. (1989), 'The simple economics of optimal auctions', *The Journal of Political Economy* 97: 1060–1090.

Capen, E. C., Clapp, R. V., and Campbell, W. M. (1971), 'Competitive bidding in high-risk situations', *Journal of Petroleum Technology* 23: 641–653.

Cassady, R. Jr. (1967), *Auctions and Auctioneering*, Berkeley and Los Angeles: University of California Press.

Chung, K. L. (1974), *A Course in Probability Theory*, Academic Press.

Cremer, J. and MacLean, R. P. (1988), 'Full extraction of the surplus in Bayesian and dominant strategy auctions', *Econometrica* 56: 1247–1257.

Engelbrecht-Wiggans (1980), 'Auctions and bidding models: A survey', *Management Science* 26(2): 119–142.

Evans and Peck (2007), *Possible Design for a Greenhouse Gas Emissions Trading System*, Mimeo. Available at http://www.emissionstrading.nsw.gov.au/_data/assets/pdf_file/0015.

Fudenberg, D. and Tirole, J. (1991), *Game Theory*, MIT Press.

Grant, S., Kaiji, A., Menezes, F. M., and Ryan, M. J. (2006), 'Auctions with options for reauction', *International Journal of Economic Theory*, 2: 17–39.

Harsanyi, J. (1967–68), 'Games with incomplete information played by Bayesian players'. *Management Science*, 14: 159–182, 320–334, 486–502.

Holt, C., Shobe, W., Burtraw, D., Palmer, K., and Goeree, J. (2007), *Auction Design for Selling CO_2 Emission Allowances Under the Regional Greenhouse Gas Initiative*. Mimeo. Available at http://www.coopercenter.org/sitefiles/documents/rggi_final_repor.

Jones, C., Menezes, F. M., and Vella, F. (2004), 'Auction price anomalies: Evidence from wool auctions in Australia', *The Economic Record*, 80(250): 271–288.

Kagel, J. (1995), 'Auctions: A survey of experimental research,' in Kagel, J. and Roth, A. (eds.), *The Handbook of Experimental Economics*, Princeton University Press.

Karlin, S. (1957), 'Polya type distributions II', *Annals of Mathematical Statistics*, 28, 281–308.

Karlin, S. and Rinott, Y. (1980), 'Classes of orderings of measures and related correlation inequalities, I and II', *Journal of Multivariate Analysis*, 10: 467–516.

Karlin, S. and Rubin, H. (1956), 'Distributions possessing a monotone likelihood ratio', *Journal of the American Statistical Association*, 51: 637–643.

Klemperer, P. (1999), 'Auction theory: A guide to the literature', *Journal of Economic Surveys*, 13(3): 227–286.

Klemperer, P. (2004), *Auctions: Theory and Practice*, Princeton University Press.

Krishna, V. (2002), *Auction Theory*, Academic Press.

Laffont, J. J. and Tirole, J. (1993), *A Theory of Incentives in Procurement and Regulation*, Cambridge and London: MIT Press.

Lebrun, B. and Tremblay, M. C. (2003), 'Multiunit pay your bid auctions with one dimensional multi-unit demands', *International Economic Review*, 44: 1135–1172.

Mas-Colell, A., Whinston, M., and Green, J. (1995), *Microeconomic Theory*, Oxford University Press.

Maskin, E. S. and Riley, J. G. (1985), 'Auction theory with private values', *American Economic Review*, 75: 150–155.

McAfee, R. P. and McMillan, J. (1987), 'Auctions and bidding', *Journal of Economic Literature*, 25(2): 699–738.

McAfee, R. P. and Reny, P. J. (1992), 'Correlated information and mechanism design', *Econometrica*, 60: 395–421.

Milgrom, P. R. (1985), 'The economics of competitive bidding: A selective survey', In L. Hurwicz, D. Schmeidler, and H. Sonnenschein (eds.), *Social Goals and Social Organization: Essays in Memory of Elisha Pazner*, Cambridge: Cambridge University Press.

Milgrom, P. R. (1987), 'Auction theory', in Truman F. Bewley (ed.), *Advances in Economic Theory: Fifth World Congress*, Cambridge University Press.

Milgrom, P. R. (1989), 'Auctions and bidding: A primer', *Journal of Economic Perspectives*, 3: 3–22.

Milgrom, P. (2004). *Putting Auction Theory to Work*, Cambridge University Press.

Milgrom, P. (2007), 'Package auctions and exchanges', *Econometrica*, 75(4): 935–965.

Milgrom, P. R. and Weber, R. J. (1982), 'A theory of auctions and competitive bidding', *Econometrica*, 50(5): 1089–1122.

Monteiro, P. (2007), 'First-price auction symmetric equilibria with a general distribution', to appear in *Games and Economic Behavior*.

Monteiro, P. and B. fux Svaiter (2007), *Optimal Auction with a General Distribution: Virtual Valuation without a Density*, Mimeo.

Myerson, R. B. (1981), 'Optimal auction design', *Mathematics of Operations Research*, 6: 58–73.

Riley, J. G. (1989), 'Expected revenue from open and sealed bid auctions', *Journal of Economic Perspectives*, 3(3): 41–50.

Riley, J. G. and Samuelson, W. F. (1981), 'Optimal auctions', *American Economic Review*, 71(3): 381–392.

Rockafellar, R. T. (1966), *Convex Analysis*. Princeton University Press.

Roth, A. (2002), 'The economist as engineer: Game theory, experimentation, and computation as tools for design economics', *Econometrica*, 70(4): 1341–1378.

Vickrey, William (1961), 'Counterspeculation, auctions and competitive sealed tenders', *Journal of Finance*, 16(1): 8–37.

Wilson, R. (1992), 'Strategic analysis of auctions.' In Aumann, R. and Hart, S. (eds.) *Handbook of Game Theory* vol. 1, 227–280, Elsevier Science.

Wilson, R. (2002), 'Architecture of power markets', *Econometrica*, 70(4): 1299–1340.

Wolfstetter (1996), 'Auctions: An introduction', *Journal of Economic Surveys*, 10: 367–421.

Wolfstetter (1999), *Topics in Microeconomics: Industrial Organization, Auctions, and Incentives*, Cambridge University Press.

Index of Notations

Index of Proper Names

Index